YESTERDAY

Yesterday, all my troubles seemed so far aw
now it looks as though they're here to sta
oh I believe in yesterda

Suddenly, I'm not half the man I used to b
There's a shadow hanging over me
Yesterday came suddenly.

middle↗
— Why she had to go, I don't know
she wouldn't say,
I said something wrong, now I long
for yesterday.....

Yesterday, love was such an easy ga
F
Now I need a place to hide away
oh I believe in yesterda

Paul McCartney's handwritten words for 'Yesterday', the world's
most recorded song.

YE
ay

1296

Also by Ray Coleman

LENNON
The Definitive Biography

THE CARPENTERS
The Authorized Biography

CLAPTON
The Authorized Biography of Eric Clapton

FRANK SINATRA
A Celebration

STONE ALONE
The Definitive Story of the Rolling Stones
Co-written with Bill Wyman

ROD STEWART
The Biography

BRIAN EPSTEIN
The Man Who Made the Beatles

I'LL NEVER WALK ALONE
Co-written with Gerry Marsden

McCARTNEY
YESTERDAY
. . . and today

by Ray Coleman

DOVE
BOOKS

For Pamela
with love

First published in Great Britain in 1995 by Boxtree Limited, Broadwall House, 21 Broadwall, London SE1 9PL. This edition published by arrangement with Boxtree Limited.

ISBN 0-7871-1038-8

Printed in the United States of America

Dove Books
8955 Beverly Boulevard
Los Angeles, CA 90048

Distributed by Penguin USA

Text designed and typeset by SX Composing, Rayleigh, Essex
Cover design by Bradbury and Williams

First Dove Printing: September 1996

10 9 8 7 6 5 4 3 2 1

Contents

Acknowledgements

The author wishes to thank Paul McCartney for permission to reproduce his handwritten lyrics for 'Yesterday' in this book.

Formal permission for the publication of the lyrics and sheet music is acknowledged in the following terms:

YESTERDAY: Words and Music by John Lennon and Paul McCartney. © 1965 NORTHERN SONGS LTD. Copyright renewed. All rights controlled and administered by EMI BLACKWOOD MUSIC INC. under license from SONY/ATV SONGS LLC.

All Rights Reserved. International Copyright Secured. Used by Permission.

Author's Note

'Yesterday' is much more than a song. A mere two minutes of plaintive, romantic sentimentality and mournfulness, it is one of the most exceptional and triumphant moments in the history of popular music. It is either beautiful or mawkish, depending on your view. What is beyond debate is its power to touch the spirit, as with the greatest songs. 'Yesterday's deceptively simple words and music are the perfect example of music's strengths . . . as art, as therapy, as entertainment.

The song has defined and divided the life and work of its composer, Paul McCartney. Since he is a writer who aims to reach people with memorable songs rather than deal in the obscure, 'Yesterday' must be considered his greatest songwriting achievement. He considers it his 'most complete song' and, in view of his output during four decades, that is a remarkable statement.

Its statistics are unparalleled. Nearly 2,500 artists have recorded it. It has been played on American radio six and a half million times; if broadcast continuously that would take nearly thirty years. As the most recorded song in history, 'Yesterday' has versions by artists with styles as diverse as Ray Charles, Frank Sinatra, Placido Domingo, Liberace, Benny Goodman, Dr John, Howard Keel, José Feliciano, Erroll Garner, Elvis Presley, Tito Rodriguez and Billie Jo Spears, plus many internationally celebrated orchestras. Only a really special piece of music could reach such a wide span of performers, and be interpreted so innovatively.

Music, like other art forms, brings highly subjective responses, and to touch a nerve with artists and audiences to the degree that

'Yesterday' has done requires some rare ingredients. Where did it come from? What motivated its writer, who sang it first? What was his frame of reference, his muse, for creating both the lyric and the melody?

Paul McCartney was twenty-one years old when he began writing the song. It was the first time a Beatle had ventured into solo recording and, in the context of their story in the mid-1960s, it was considered a pretty ballad. In Britain it was not released as a single until 1976 – eleven years after it was recorded and six years after the Beatles had split. In America, where it was released as a single in 1965, the year it was recorded, it went to the top of the chart and stayed there for four weeks.

Though it featured McCartney singing alone and playing acoustic guitar with a string quartet, the recording was credited 'The Beatles', and the song bore the songwriting partnership 'Lennon–McCartney'. As a Beatles single, it sold more than 3 million copies internationally. As a feature on records by other artists, its total sales figure is beyond calculation.

As a song, it utterly bisects the entire phenomenon of the Beatles as well as presenting a microcosm of Paul McCartney the man, the songwriter, the performer. It also points to the bedrock of his musical background, and thus provides an insight into the chemistry of the Beatles. This book is therefore part documentary, part celebration of 'Yesterday' and, by extension, a portrait of its creator drawn largely by himself.

Paul McCartney, while justly proud of the song, its impact and its achievements, was not the only person to appear slightly bemused by the idea of a book dedicated to the story of his song 'Yesterday'. Others, bewildered, suggested that there were better songs, more interesting and unusual compositions. And could the theme of one song really stand up to such scrutiny?

Any such argument subsides against the sheer weight of 'Yesterday''s influence, as a song and as an event – creatively, statistically and individually in relation to its composer. From what vantage point did he write a song that was to attract 2,500 other versions? How, where and why did he write it? Since it sounds partly autobiographical, why did he appear so introspective at a time of excitement, with the Beatles story at a peak? Did this first Beatle solo bring any resentment within the group? How on earth did a guitar-toting pop star get involved with a string quartet, unheard of for an erstwhile rock 'n' roller at that time? Vital to this exploration of the song, what kind of pedigree in music did Paul take into the recording studio when he went in to commit it to vinyl?

And, in the unbelievable-but-true category, how did the ownership of 'Yesterday' pass in 1985 into the hands of Michael Jackson, where it remains, to the annoyance of Paul McCartney, and to the indignation of Beatles lovers around the world?

This book is called *Yesterday and Today* because that is precisely what Paul's song, allied to the Beatles story, is and will always be: a synthesis of nostalgia and current impact on a world that will continually recognize their legacy as the best group in popular music. Other fine groups came and went, making their impact; but the Beatles were something else. It is thirty-two years since they came blazing out of Liverpool to set an individualistic benchmark for music and provide an eight-year-long soundtrack for the 1960s. In the 1990s they continue to be relevant, frozen in their time and yet timeless; vigorous, endlessly creative, prolific and absolutely unrepeatable.

'Yesterday' is very much what the Beatles were all about. It broke barriers, both for them and for popular music generally, and it played a large part in stretching the Beatles' appeal beyond the young.

Yesterday and Today, besides being the title of the American album on which the song appeared in 1966, was also the cover story title of an article which I wrote for *Radio Times* in 1992 to mark Paul McCartney's fiftieth birthday. That profile aimed to capture McCartney the person, beyond Paul the Beatle, and part of it might have gone some way to explaining why he could have written a song like 'Yesterday' some twenty-seven years earlier:

> McCartney was always outside the general scrum of rock 'n' roll. He had a vision of his music beyond its function as a totem of youth ... with the Beatles, McCartney always had more sense of destiny than the others. While some 1960s figures saw rock 'n' roll itself as their stepping stone to fame and fortune, the ambitious McCartney was more scientific. His musical palette had a broader range.
>
> He remains a man of extraordinary paradoxes and elusive

spirit. Gregarious, amusing and charming in company, he tends to distrust people outside his family, perhaps understandable after his battles inside and outside the Beatles. He likes control, although there is still something of the old hippy in his fundamental outlook. He cherishes his position in the hierarchy of entertainment but prefers to present himself as one of the lads. He wants to be viewed as equally acceptable to high society and to a shop assistant. He can be alternately bombastic and insecure, thoughtful and mercurial; compassionate and unforgiving; open and impenetrable.

His public image as a cheery, thumbs-up, lightweight man-of-the-people pop star has irritated him as much as his critics, I wrote, and they taunted him for his alleged superficiality. Friends who have known him since his earliest Liverpool and Beatles years observed a new sophistication and self-assuredness about him as he approached fifty. A sharp-eyed, youthful enthusiasm remains, now joined by the personality of an elder statesman, a diplomat who knows his responsibilities.

George Martin, Paul's friend and producer of the Beatles and of McCartney as a soloist, considers him 'a genius of twentieth-century music'. Unequivocally, I believe that Paul's genius and creative muse stretches beyond the categories of music and art.

Linda, his wife, a Libran who believes she balances his Gemini spirit, is insightful on the man and his complexities: 'He's an artist, and artists are moody . . . sometimes he's very huggy and sometimes not. But how many songs has this guy written? Do you know what I mean? How much pressure has he had and how many lives has he lived? So he might come on like he's normal, but there's a lot of turmoil in there.'

To all these facts and observations of Paul McCartney, it must be added that he is a master of communication. During our conversations for this book, one of his most telling remarks concerned his admiration for the work of other artists. He always wanted to hear their most popular work, he said. If he went to a concert by, say, Simon and Garfunkel, or Bob Dylan, or the Rolling Stones, he would be waiting to hear their biggest hits. He had less time or patience for the esoteric indulgences which some artists often inflict on an audience. He has never subscribed to the indifferent attitude of some artists towards record sales. 'I think that's what *does* matter,' he says. 'The people out there with their pennies, going to spend them. That's a big move, to spend your money on someone.'

That ingredient in Paul's make-up, a desire to reach people with his art, sounds simplistic. But achieving it is difficult, as any song-writer will testify. Paul's wish to be a populist is the key to understanding one aspect of his genius, and of how he could write the most recorded song in history. I thank him for his spirited co-operation in interviews for this book, and also thank Linda McCartney for her helpful observations and for the use of her outstanding photographs.

My gratitude is due to many friends who helped this project with encouragement, research and advice.

In New York, Sue Weiner grasped the scope and spirit of this subject before anyone, and her support has been an inspirational tower of strength as well as a great practical help from the book's inception. Jim O'Donnell's assistance has been invaluable, and my thanks also to Marisa Sabounghi for her unflagging research in Manhattan.

In Britain, my appreciation goes to George Martin for his inter-view, and to his assistant, Shirley Burns. My valued friend Mark Lewisohn, the world's foremost Beatles historian, helped enor-mously by sharing his unrivalled knowledge, particularly in the maze that led to the sale of the Beatles compositions to Michael Jackson.

Thank you to Shelagh Jones and Alan Crowder at MPL in London for facilitating this book during my researches.

For interviews and interest in the subject, I wish to thank Peter Asher, Elizabeth Robbins, Richard Carpenter, Paul Cooper, Lori Citero, Richard Clayderman, Nathan East, Dennis Elsas, Kenneth Essex, Keith Emerson, Louisa Fuller, Roger Greenaway, Laura Gross, Nigel Hunter, Shelagh Johnston, Denis Knowles, Phyllis Lattner, Zoe Metcalf, Mickie Monro, Steve Phillips, Olivier Tous-saint, Bruce Welch and Dr Glenn Wilson.

My thanks also to Michael Alcock and Vicky Monk at the publishers, Boxtree, in London, to Annie Lee, my exceptional manuscript editor, Dave Read of EMI Music, London, and Phil Graham at Broadcast Music Incorporated; and to Andy Linehan at the National Sound Archive, London, and Mark Rigby at the Mechanical Copyright Protection Society.

Above all, of course, thanks to Paul McCartney for checking my manuscript so meticulously and for writing that rarity – an extraordinary song that richly deserved a book.

Ray Coleman
Cornwall, England

1

Birth of a Classic

'It was the only song I ever dreamed'

London, the 1960s: Wimpole Street, that elegant, bustling artery slightly north-west of Oxford Circus, would seem an unlikely birthplace for high artistic creativity. Hallowed ground for the highest echelons of the British medical profession, the thoroughfare had an aura of spruce residential comfort, too. Society's sea change during that decade could not, surely, have penetrated those houses. This was Old England at its most noble; the architect Thomas Leverton laid out Wimpole Street and its blood brother, Harley Street, in 1804, when anyone living in central London was only a couple of miles from open countryside. Now it was part of a city which Paul McCartney loved.

Wimpole Street's narrow-fronted houses, five storeys high, with round-headed front doors topped by fanlights of lead, were white-painted, deceptively spacious, and described famously by John Betjeman as 'those regular, weary rows where the doctors wait to foretell death as politely as possible'.

In the 1990s, dental surgeons soothe their patients with lush orchestral versions of songs (like 'Yesterday') from the 1960s and beyond. Thirty years ago, any music from 'those beat groups' would have been considered by most to have been unseemly. Wimpole Street and Harley Street were bastions of the Establishment, populated by eminent figures from the 'professions'. In distance, it was a mile or so from the hip basement clubs that helped shape the spirit of Swinging London, teeming as they were with pop musicians, actors, models. Psychologically the medical zone was light years away.

Number 57 Wimpole Street, two houses in from the intersection with New Cavendish Street, seemed to blend, outwardly at least, with the somewhat haughty atmosphere of the area. Inside, it was very much a family home. The residents, Dr Richard Asher and his wife, Margaret, were at a peak in their spheres of work. A respected doctor who also wrote prolifically on all aspects of medicine including psychiatry, Dr Asher, with his wife and their three young children, had moved to Wimpole Street from their flat in nearby Great Portland Street in 1957. It was not merely a prestigious address for Dr Asher; it also offered space for Margaret, a professor at London's Royal Academy of Music, to give private tuition on the oboe in the basement music-room. There, too, Dr Asher would often relax at the grand piano, demonstrating considerable talent as an amateur player of the classics. Music of all styles shaped their children's early years, and it was a family destined to be linked closely with the arts.

By 1963 the Asher children were teenagers. Peter, aged nineteen, had met a fellow student at Westminster School named Gordon Waller, with whom he was to forge a creditable career as a singing duo akin to the Everly Brothers. Flame-haired Jane Asher was, at seventeen, an aspiring actress whose distinguished career had begun at the age of six with an acclaimed performance as a deaf mute in the movie *Mandy* (it was entitled *A Crash of Silence* in the US). And fifteen-year-old Clare Asher was at school.

A splendid home-maker and cook, Margaret Asher attached name-plates to each room in her house. She established an atmosphere exuding warmth and a love of culture at the onset of a decade that was to prove eventful for the Asher family. She could not have guessed, at the start of 1963, that by the year's end the nameplates such as Peter's Room, Jane's Room, and Clare's Room would need to be augmented by one which read: Paul's Room.

The Sixties, that extraordinary pageant now both cherished and scorned, began in effect in 1963. The year in which Paul McCartney would reach the age of twenty-one, it was the time when the Beatles provoked a seismic shift in the consciousness of Britain through the medium of popular music.

In November of that year, Paul, by then the boyfriend of Jane Asher, moved into the small room at the very top of 57 Wimpole Street – 'a bit of an artist's garret', as he recalls it affectionately, 'right next to Peter Asher's room. It was one of those huge Wimpole Street houses and Jane lived a couple of floors down, next to her mum and dad.' Paul's room, with its bed, easy chair, record player and small piano, overlooked the rear of the house while his neighbour Peter's had a view of Wimpole Street.

A Beatle's route to this desirable, stable environment in 1963 had been circuitous, and reflected the aspiration of the inner man, during the tumult of new stardom, for real values. At the start of the year, the Beatles had been living in their native Liverpool. On their visits to London for recording sessions they stayed in hotels, also meeting writers and photographers. Their first base, the traditional Royal Court in Sloane Square, was succeeded as Beatles headquarters by the modish President in Russell Square. Here, Paul and John Lennon, George Harrison and Ringo Starr would usually share rooms in those partnerships. As 1963 progressed, they scored four chart-topping singles ('Please Please Me', 'From Me to You', 'I Want to Hold Your Hand' and 'She Loves You') and toured Britain four times. They felt as though they were 'in transit', and they knew the future would bring even more travelling.

Hotel life quickly lost its allure for them. It was essential when they were in London, the Beatles told their manager, Brian Epstein, that they had a 'group flat'. In the autumn of that year, all four Beatles moved into 57 Green Street, off Park Lane, Mayfair, where each had a separate bedroom.

Comfortable though it was, it was rented accommodation devoid of charm and they had neither the time nor inclination to decorate it. Paul remembers that he hated it and described it as 'austere'. The others went through a phase of thinking they would decorate it, but Paul, unusually for such a fastidious young man, could not be bothered. He knew that for him, anyway, it was going to be temporary. 'The whole atmosphere of my upbringing in Liverpool had been very homey. Even though my mum had died and it was just me and my brother and my dad, there were always aunties around cooking nice meals.' He missed that.

Fate decreed that the Green Street home would be a short-lived address for all the Beatles, more so than any of them expected. On 8 April 1963, John Lennon had become a father when his son Julian had been born to his wife Cynthia in Liverpool. By November, John was ready to set up a new home in the Kensington area of London with his wife and child. George and Ringo were happy to stay on in Green Street for a time, but Paul felt restless and with John's imminent departure he started to look around for a new home.

On 18 April 1963, after a Beatles concert at London's Royal Albert Hall, Paul had met, backstage, Jane Asher, who had earlier posed, assuming the role of a screaming Beatles fan, for a photographer from the *Radio Times*.

As Paul's romance with Jane began, he often visited her Wimpole Street home and immediately sensed the family camaraderie that he had left behind in Liverpool. When he casually mentioned to Jane's mother that he disliked the cheerlessness of his Green Street 'Beatles flat' and was looking for an alternative, she responded: 'Why don't you stay here for a little while?' It could, Margaret Asher suggested, be a temporary home during his search for something more permanent; Paul was keen on staying in central London. 'It was such a nice household instead of a cold flat in Mayfair,' Paul recalls. 'Margaret Asher cooked, I liked the family . . . and I hadn't been happy with Green Street because I was used to a family situation.' The Ashers were just that.

His outlook might, he agrees, have been a little chauvinistic, but he had been raised in a house where his mother or his aunts cooked and were a powerful presence. An extended family of aunts, uncles and cousins were always in and out of the McCartney Liverpool home, and Margaret Asher's offer was accepted instantly with gratitude.

Dr Asher diplomatically checked with all his neighbours to ensure that they had no objection to the arrival of a young, long-haired pop star in their midst. He was able to assure them of the young man's impeccable behaviour and manners. He would not reduce the tone of the area; a few autograph-hunting fans might be noticed but they were to be dealt with discreetly.

As Paul McCartney moved into Wimpole Street in November 1963, the Beatles story was gathering speed. One year earlier, their tentative beginning with 'Love Me Do' had promised little. But on 13 October 1963, their appearance on the major British TV show *Sunday Night at the London Palladium* caused uproar. Watched by 15 million, they sang four songs before meeting wild scenes of fan fever outside the theatre. The word Beatlemania was born that night. And as their hit records sold by the million, they released their second album, *With the Beatles*, in November.

A key to the success story of the Beatles was evident on that album, just as it was as they stepped on to stages around Britain. Raw energy and the exuberance of rock 'n' roll merged with Paul McCartney's penchant for melodic romanticism. Alongside the upbeat album tracks 'Roll Over Beethoven' and 'Please Mister Postman', Paul McCartney stepped forward, just as he did in concerts, to sing two powerful love songs, 'All My Loving' (which he wrote) and 'Till There Was You'.

The roles and personalities of the individual Beatles were delineated quickly, and glibly, by a British media eager to pigeonhole them as just another group of four lads hitting the pop big-time. John Lennon was the dangerous, abrasive, opinionated one. Paul McCartney was the cherubic-faced charmer and soothsayer, whom every mother in the land felt was handsome, intelligent, caring, a perfect potential son-in-law. George Harrison was a secure musical foundation, laconic with his humour, happy to be the foil to the eminent hit-writing leadership of Lennon and McCartney. Ringo Starr was the moptop-shaking, grinning drummer whose quick wit helped the quartet's neat blend of cynicism and enthusiasm.

It was not as simple as that. But stereotype descriptions were needed quickly, as the Beatles were overthrowing a jaded scene and building the bridges of a fresh youth culture. In 1963, nobody was very concerned about the complexities of the characters of the 'Fab Four', the 'moptops'.

The rise of the Beatles also coincided with the arrival of a new form of night-club populated exclusively by the young, and the coining of the word discothèque. Over his favourite drink, then as now, of Scotch and Coke, a socially mobile McCartney enjoyed mingling with the entire cast of 1960s London, celebrities from the spheres of art and cinema, the theatre and books. 'I vaguely resent people knowing something that I don't,' declared the inquisitive Beatle at that time.

Paul enjoyed London by night, and among his regular places to visit were the Saddle Room in Hamilton Place, the Ad Lib in Leicester Place (where all the Beatles held court regularly) and, later, the Bag o' Nails in Kingly Street, the Cromwellian in Kensington, and the Pickwick Club in Great Newport Street. Often, Paul and Jane would dine at a restaurant called Tiddy Dols in Shepherd Market; and they would watch mainstream show-

business cabaret at the Talk of the Town off Leicester Square.*
Because he loved nocturnal London, Paul would visit a club most
nights when he was not working and, notoriously fond of sleep,
he would rise at about midday unless there was an earlier appointment.

Late in 1963, he awoke one such late morning at Wimpole
Street realizing that he had actually dreamed a tune. 'I awoke with
this tune in my head. [He hums the tune: "Da da da . . ."] I
thought: what is *that*? I know *that*. I know *that*.

His first thought was that it was one of those standard tunes his
father, a pianist, had played back home in Liverpool. Paul had
been raised on an eclectic musical diet, since his father revelled in
standards like 'Lullaby of the Leaves', 'Stairway to Paradise', 'and
"Chicago"; all that old jazz stuff', as Paul recalls.

'I first thought: oh, it must be one of those old songs. . . I've
just forgotten which one. But I had this piano by the bed . . .'
And, with a melody in his head, the next move was natural. 'I just
fell out of bed, found out what key I had dreamed it in, and it
seemed near G, and I played it. I said to myself: I wonder what it
is, you know. I just couldn't figure it out all, because I'd just
woken up. And I got a couple of chords to it. I got the G, then I
got the nice F sharp minor seventh, that was the big waaaahhhh.
That led very naturally to the B which led very naturally to the E
minor. It just kept sort of tumbling out with those chords. I
thought: well, this is very nice, but it's a nick, it's a nick [from another song]. I don't know what it is.'

Intrigued with the sound whirling around his head, Paul
decided to canvass opinions. 'We were always very careful,' he
says of his songwriting partnership with John Lennon. 'The great
danger with writing is that you write someone else's song without
realizing. You spend three hours . . . and you've written a Bob
Dylan classic. This one, I was convinced, was just something I'd
heard before. I said to people: well, it can't be mine; I just woke
up *dreaming* it!

---

* Paul was the only Beatle to remain a London resident throughout the Beatles
years. John and his wife Cynthia, with their young son, eventually moved to
Weybridge, Surrey, with Ringo and his wife Maureen settling on the same
estate soon after their wedding in 1965. George Harrison, who married Pattie
Boyd in 1966, moved to Esher, Surrey.

'There was no logic to it at all. And I'd never had that. And I've never had it since. This was the crazy thing about this song. It was fairly mystical when I think about it, because of the circumstances. It was the only song I ever dreamed.'

The Beatles were a pop group. The generic description of 'rock' had not arrived in the mid-1960s, and the term 'band' was at that time reserved for brassy dance orchestras or jazz line-ups. Quaint though 'pop group' now sounds, it perfectly mirrored what the Beatles and thousands of others who followed them were all about. For while they loved rock 'n' roll, inspired by the giants like Elvis Presley and Chuck Berry, the Beatles cross-fertilized the best of popular music to produce a hybrid, and the reason that was possible can be traced to Paul McCartney's musical education. He loved the surge of rock, but never wanted to lose his love of other influences. The aim was to make pop *and* rock 'n' roll hit singles. In the 1970s, the evolution of pop into rock, and the ascendance of albums as creative works of art, dwarfed the old-fashioned pop single and, to a large degree, the philosophy of 1960s pop.

The Beatles, as Paul points out, sat astride show business and new pop-rock, which they had largely invented, in the early 1960s. Unashamedly ambitious for success, with hit singles and TV and radio shows to boost their chances at every opportunity, the Beatles rubbed shoulders with the glitterati of an entertainment world they were actually dominating, if not overturning.

'It wasn't the rock industry at all,' Paul says of those years. There was no hardcore rock 'n' roll movement and the young pop acts like Cliff Richard and Adam Faith performed in tandem with such adult ballad singers as Shirley Bassey and Frankie Vaughan. That was the entertainment world into which the Beatles were baptized when they arrived in London with their early hits. 'We'd be doing concert bills and Dave Allen would be introducing us, and we'd be second on the bill to [ballad singer] Frank Ifield, comedian Ken Dodd, people like that.'

This integration meant that they had none of the divisive 'them-and-us' attitude that infected the polarizing rock bands of the 1970s and beyond. Darlings of the young, the Beatles were equally comfortable with troupers, entertainers from the old school. The Beatles simply wanted to make hits, not speak for a disaffected part of the nation. They were, notes Paul, quite simply, 'crossover showbiz'. They were so keen to achieve success in all areas that when they toured Britain in 1963 they asked Roger Greenaway, a singer with a group on their bill called the Kestrels, to teach them how to bow in unison at the end of their songs.

One of the epicentres for the show-business fraternity that attracted the Beatles was the home of the ebullient singer Alma Cogan. Her first-floor flat at Stafford Court, on Kensington High Street, was shared by Alma, her sister Sandra Caron, an actress, and their mother, Fay.

The clique there, including Beatles manager Brian Epstein and composer Lionel Bart, loved her parties, which began around midnight when concerts had ended. Alma Cogan attracted a VIP guest-list: Sammy Davis Junior, Michael Caine, Stanley Baker, Bruce Forsyth, Tommy Steele and Terence Stamp were just a few of the celebrities who mingled with Paul McCartney and John Lennon. 'It was the sort of place,' says Lionel Bart, 'that you could go to at three in the morning, throw coins up at the window, and eventually a face would look out and throw the keys down.'

At one such party in late 1963, Paul said to Alma that he had a new tune that he wanted her to hear. He added that he was intrigued by it himself and would like her opinion. This was not unusual; it was part of the interaction that existed in London show business in 1963. Paul said he would go round and play it for Alma on her piano one day soon.

Paul had already tried out his haunting melody on John Lennon, who believed it sounded original. But so high was John and Paul's productivity that if a song was lying around unfinished for long, or did not cry out for immediate help from the other partner, it went to the back of their 'queue'. This tune therefore assumed no priority in their hectic lives. Paul decided to play the tune informally to people older than himself or John, writers who had good ears for popular music that pre-dated the Beatles.

At the Fulham Road home of Lionel Bart, Paul courted the view of the respected composer who, like him, could not read or write music. Bart had written hits including 'Living Doll' for Cliff Richard, 'As Long as He Needs Me' (which Shirley Bassey sang into the charts) and had scored enormous successes with his shows *Oliver!* in 1960 and *Blitz* in 1962. In 1964 and 1965 he would create *Maggie May* and *Twang!!* When Paul hummed him the melody, Bart recalls that he told him he could not categorize it but, to his ears, it was worth pursuing.

Late one evening in the autumn of 1963, Paul went to the home of Alma Cogan with his new melody very much on his mind. Ten years older than Paul, she represented a generation of show business which preceded the Beatles and Elvis Presley, yet she had broad tastes and a good instinct for commercial sounds. Known by her public as 'the girl with a laugh in her voice', Alma had enjoyed a string of seventeen hit singles including 'Bell Bottom Blues', 'Sugartime' and the chart-topping 'Dreamboat' in May 1955.

If Paul's melody had been conceived by him a few years later, he would have carried around a cassette of himself playing piano and humming it, perhaps. But in 1963, there was no such invention. And so when they were not writing in the studio, he and John Lennon *had* to carry their melodies in their heads. 'We had a rule which was: if *we* can't remember it, how are *they* going to, it's no good. That was a rule and we lost, probably, one or two average songs that way.' As Paul says, the ones that got away 'couldn't have been good enough, because if he couldn't remember the tune, I would, and vice versa'.

His new melody idea was different. It was a tune that stayed inside Paul's psyche and refused to budge. 'I couldn't help it,' he recalls. Because it seemed so unusual in scope, different from the material he and John collaborated on, he had to press ahead with it independently. Arriving at Alma Cogan's home, Paul remembers: 'I played the melody for her and she said: "It's lovely." It was a little bit embarrassing because I think she thought I'd written it for her. Maybe I didn't make it very clear by saying: here's a song I've written; what do you think of it? I probably said: "This is something I've written; does this remind you of anything?"' McCartney was still concerned that he might have sub-consciously been playing a derivative of someone else's melody.

Alma's sister, Sandra, taking up the story, declares that her mother, Fay, walked into the lounge as Paul sat at their piano, and said to him, Alma and Sandra: 'Anyone like some scrambled eggs?' That, Sandra says, prompted Paul to give it a bizarre working title. Sitting at the piano, he began to sing: 'Scrambled eggs

. . . Oh my baby how I love your legs . . . oh . . . scrambled eggs.' Still wanting affirmation that he had developed something new, he asked Alma if she, with her considerable knowledge of mainstream popular songs, recognized the tune.

'She said: "No. It's original. Nice song." Later, I did hear that Alma *had* thought I was pitching her a song.' That would have been quite feasible in Alma's view. McCartney and Lennon were happy to spread their songwriting skills around, offering demonstrations to other artists in the Brian Epstein management stable, such as Cilla Black and Billy J. Kramer.

'Pitching songs was part of the thrill of it,' Paul says of the period. 'We were learning all the stuff we'd seen in films. It had always been my great dream to be a songwriter. I'd seen films like *101 Dalmatians*, and the idea of a guy with a piano in a garret was very romantic for me. I often thought: Jeez, if I could earn my *living* by doing that, it would be great. It was always a great image . . . the wife coming in with a cup of tea or something, and the writer saying: "Thank you, dear; I'm just working on something . . ."'

His self-image, even in those heady days when he was a huge star, was of a creative soul whose boundaries exceeded the public perception of the Beatles. To some, Paul, John, George and Ringo represented long hair, Yeah Yeah Yeah, sharp repartee and a few catchy songs. McCartney, much more than any of his colleagues, was going to be a songwriter in the grand tradition.

'It's *yours!*' all his friends, in and out of the Beatles, insisted. 'We've never heard it before!' Finally, Paul accepted that it was something that he had dreamed, that had come to him. 'I thought: wow, that's really good. I've never had this happen.' It was, he smiles, rather like finding an item and handing it in to the police; 'If no one claims it, I'll have it! So . . . then I didn't have any words.'

Next, working on the piano in his bedroom at Wimpole Street, he remembers 'putting the middle in, what we used to call middle-eights, even if they were middle-sixteen bars or middle-thirty-twos. They were always, to us, middle eights, because we had heard some musicians call that part of a song the middle-eight.'

'Scrambled Eggs (Oh my baby how I love your legs)' was still its whimsical title. 'But I knew I wasn't going to be able to get away with that.' Paul was pleased with the additional work he had put in to finish the melody. 'The turnaround [in the middle] worked, balanced it up. It picked up from the melody, then followed it to earth. There is a beginning, a middle and an end as we were always taught in school about our essays. That was very satisfying about it. It felt complete.' (As an eleven-year-old schoolboy, Paul had been a prize essayist on the subject of the Coronation in 1953, winning a contest from 200 entries. He won two books, one being the obligatory prize about the Queen, plus his own choice, a book on modern art.)

The sounds in the Asher house, with the oboe coming from the basement and classical piano from Dr Asher, could be seen as conducive to the creation of such a song. But as Paul points out, it was not conceived as a piece of classical music. 'The environment in which I created it was not unconducive. But the only connection with Margaret [Asher] was that she later used it as a test piece to teach people the oboe, of which I was very proud. She thought it was good as a melody. But I dreamed it more as just a nice ballad.'

By then, 'Scrambled Eggs' was familiar to all the Beatles. Doodling with it in the studio and at each other's homes, Paul was acutely aware that a fine tune had been conceived by him but that it remained unhatched. He talked about the tune as an unfinished project, and he was a young man in a hurry to get things done. He confessed to the other Beatles that he had not hit the right theme for the lyrics. 'Blimey!' George Harrison said once with his characteristically droll humour. 'He's always talking about that song. You'd think he was Beethoven or somebody . . .'

The work schedule of the Beatles in 1963 and 1964 would give any modern rock band, and perhaps anyone in show business, apoplexy. It was a measure of their drive and ambition, which increased unremittingly from the start of 1964, that their songwriting and recording operations blossomed so richly; they fulfilled a packed schedule of engagements while their inventiveness continued to flourish. While 1963, when Paul's big song was conceived in his head, was their big year in Britain, the start of 1964 was to establish them around the world. On

14 January 1964, after ten nights appearing in their own Christmas show at the Astoria, Finsbury Park, London, the Beatles set off for France for concerts in Versailles and in Paris at the Olympia.

Rapid stardom had not diminished the Beatles' enthusiasm for individual growth in their music, and 1964 was the year that found them blooming in that direction. George Harrison, submerged as a songwriter by the titanic partnership of Lennon and McCartney, gave the group a fresh sound by adopting, sometimes, the twelve-string guitar, quite a revolution at that time. And while Paul was *en route* to creating his *magnum opus*, John would that year write such contrasting beauties as 'If I Fell' and 'A Hard Day's Night'.

In Paris, Paul asked for a grand piano to be moved into their suite at the Hôtel George V, partly so that he could develop his song a little. It was still 'Scrambled Eggs' set to a melody, and it did not feel right. The song came and went during the hubbub of the Beatles' first visit to France. George Martin, the Beatles' producer, visiting the hotel, heard Paul play the melody again and remembers being 'really impressed' by its originality. He was already used to startling originality from the Beatles, but this was something new. However, George told Paul, he would have to come up with an interesting lyric . . . and it was such an un-Beatle-like song, defying categorization, that it presented him, as the producer of the Beatles, with a slight dilemma.

Martin added that, strong though the melody appeared for 'Scrambled Eggs', he wondered how John, George and Ringo's contribution could fit into the performance of the melody and/or vocal. Subconsciously, that remark caused Paul to give the song less attention than other surefire hits such as 'Can't Buy Me Love'.

There were other matters to preoccupy the Beatles during that visit to Paris. Their live shows failed to ignite much excitement among the cynical French, but from America to the Hôtel George V came the news that they and their manager had hungered for. Their single 'I Want to Hold Your Hand', which Paul and John had written in the basement at Wimpole Street, had soared from number 43 to the top of the US Hot Hundred published by *Billboard* magazine. It was the breakthrough to US success that the Beatles had awaited (and which their manager had always predicted) and it had come true with astonishing force. British acts had never triumphed in the States on anything like this scale. The euphoria in the Beatles' suite was contagious, long before they could properly grasp the scale of their achievement.

By 7 February 1964 the Beatles were on Pan American flight number 101 from London to New York, a flight that would be immortalized and travelled on by Beatles fans for many years. The Beatles were excited but apprehensive. At Kennedy airport, 3,000 American teenagers gave them a rapturous reception, and two days later they gave their first performance on *The Ed Sullivan Show*.

Seventy-three million people saw them perform five songs, which included the two McCartney stage hits 'All My Loving' and 'Till There Was You'. Such songs had by then firmly established Paul as the Beatle who sang the prettiest songs. It would be nine-teen months before the song now referred to as 'Scrambled Eggs', lying metaphorically in Paul's back pocket, would be premièred on this same *Ed Sullivan Show* to significantly recast the Beatles' popularity. That 1964 appearance was to mesmerize teenagers. Neither Paul nor anyone else knew that his unfinished song was to wield a different power in 1965.

This American trip, which included concerts in Washington DC and New York, plus a trip to Miami to perform again on *The Ed Sullivan Show*, was followed by a frenetic schedule through 1964 – recording sessions, trips to Hong Kong, the Netherlands, Denmark and Australia and New Zealand, a twenty-five-concert, first full American and Canadian tour, a long British concert tour and then a Christmas season at the Odeon, Hammersmith.

Throughout that year there were signs that Paul was becoming increasingly entrenched in his commitment to rich melodicism in his songwriting. Two songs in particular bore the feelings of wist-fulness that were to pour from McCartney's pen to establish his central role in the Beatles. 'And I Love Her', a gorgeous ballad that would be sung by scores of other artists, featured Paul writing and singing at his most poetically attractive. 'Things We Said Today' was another melody and lyric with an unhackneyed theme and an unusually structured melody. And, as a clincher, he turned in 'Can't Buy Me Love'. Released on 20 March 1964, this single attracted advance orders of more than a million and it sold more than 2 million copies within a week of its release. Rocky without

being wild, and interpreted famously in a jazz style by Ella Fitz-
gerald, to Paul's delight, 'Can't Buy Me Love' was another
example of his versatility.

During the pandemonium of the first US visits in 1964, and
long beyond them, Paul's song-in-waiting went on the back bur-
ner. It was not even on record. Paul would mention it to the
other Beatles and George Martin occasionally . . . but, not surprisingly, it was not considered to be an urgent project. Its texture
was weirdly outside the accessibility of the style that had swept
the Beatles to fame.

Incredibly, the song that would become a classic was going to
wait another year, making a total of approximately twenty months
from the moment he dreamed it until its arrival in the recording
studio.

'We were on the cusp,' says Paul McCartney, pinpointing the
Beatles' crossover from traditional show-business values into the
more dangerous realm of rock 'n' roll – or, in 1960s parlance, beat
groups. Their sounds and looks mirrored a new voice of youth,
but they carried no youthful snobbery towards the old guard.
Lennon, playing his role of angry young man to the hilt, sneered
about established stars, but he and the Beatles delighted in mingling with the show-business fraternity which their parents held
in such high esteem. A phoney war, whipped up by the media,
pitched them as bidding to revolutionize the scene, aiming to
overthrow such balladeers as Shirley Bassey, Val Doonican,
Frankie Vaughan and Petula Clark. That happened, to a degree,
but more by accident than design.

Manager Brian Epstein, however, viewed the Beatles as firmly
in show business proper. He encouraged them to learn from the
past. Indeed, in putting them in suits and ties he had placed them
in his early ambitions, alongside the Shadows, Cliff Richard's
famous backing band who enjoyed success in their own right. It
was a fair analogy; the Shadows had pioneered the three-guitars-
and-drums line-up in Britain, and since 1959 they had scored a

raft of hits including 'Apache', 'FBI', 'Wonderful Land', 'Dance On' and 'Foot Tapper'.*

The first 'summit' meeting of Cliff Richard, Britain's leading pop star, the Shadows, and the fast-rising Beatles occurred on 13 April 1963. Bruce Welch, the Shadows' rhythm guitarist, threw a party at his home at 157 Headstone Lane, North Harrow, Middlesex, and invited all four Beatles. Later that summer, Welch continued his friendship with Paul McCartney, attending his twenty-first birthday party in Liverpool. The Shadows were appearing in a summer season at Blackpool at the time.

'Paul and Jane Asher met me in the doorway of the Liverpool Empire to guide us to his home,' Welch remembers. 'At the party, he said they were facing what we had experienced, in the Shadows, for a few years. Being recognized by fans all the time, there was just no privacy.'

With his income from those Shadows hits, twenty-two-year-old Welch had recently bought a home in southern Portugal. He told Paul that he was welcome to free use of his holiday villa at any time. Through the rest of 1963 and the next year, McCartney's schedule was so hectic that he forgot the kind offer. But they would meet occasionally, at various London clubs. Sharing the same record company (the Shadows recorded for Columbia, the Beatles for Parlophone), they would also bump into each other at EMI headquarters in Manchester Square, London.

At one such meeting early in 1965, as the Beatles prepared to start the schedule for their second film, Bruce Welch said he was going to his home in Portugal for a break, 'and don't forget, Paul, it's there if you want it'. This time Paul was attracted by the offer, but no date for the trip could be fixed as the Beatles' activities were so demanding. After their Christmas season at the Odeon, Hammersmith, they plunged into recording sessions for the soundtrack of their second film, which would be entitled *Help!* In February and March they went on location in the Bahamas and to

---

* When he was battling to get interest in the Beatles from reluctant record companies, Epstein wrote to EMI on 8 December 1961: 'These four boys, who are superb instrumentalists, also produce some exciting and pulsating vocals. They play mostly their own compositions and one of the boys has written a song which I really believe to be the hottest material since [the Cliff Richard–Shadows hit] "Living Doll".'

Austria, before moving to Britain to complete filming at the film studio at Twickenham, Middlesex.

There was a piano on one of the stages at the Twickenham studio, and during the shooting of the *Help!* movie, in the interminable waits between camera shoots, Paul would wander over and start tinkling the melody to the song which he told producer Dick Lester, and film workers who listened, was without a title. Finally, after days of hearing Paul repeatedly playing the same tune, Lester's fuse blew. 'It got to the point where I said to him: "If you play that bloody song any longer, I'll have the piano taken off stage. Either finish it, or give it up!"'

Dick James, the Beatles' music publisher, who greatly admired their work, recalled to me how Paul McCartney had first unveiled to him his masterpiece: 'They were doing the filming of *Help!* and I went to Twickenham Studios. They had that enormous set of all the different doorways they went in and out of. In the Paul McCartney bedroom section, so to speak, there was a Hammond organ which came up from a hole in the ground in one very short scene. The director and the crew were up the other end, lighting the set, and there was obviously going to be a twenty-minute or half-hour break while they were getting the lights and the camera lined up.

'And Paul said to me, "Come and listen to this. It's my latest tune, we'll be recording it soon, I've got an idea but I haven't worked out the lyric yet." And he switched on the Hammond organ and very quietly just held the keys and used the bass part. Paul, in his construction of the song, always seemed to feature the bass before almost any other part of the melody. He played the left hand on the bass of the organ, and used the words "Scrambled Eggs" as the title. Funny words, but you really didn't have to be a great musician or even a music man to know that it was one of the greatest melodies that your ears had ever heard,' James added.

'It was an amazing song even then, as great as any of the Cole Porters or any of the Noël Cowards. Just a magnificent melody. If our industry could find half a dozen to ten songs like that a year, then nobody would be able to say they can't write songs like they used to do.'

Still, with dotty lyrics, even a strong tune was inadequate for a Beatles track and it was clear that Paul would need either iron discipline, or a changed environment, to get the words right.

At this time, Paul and Jane Asher often visited a club called Downstairs at the Pickwick in Great Newport Street. Meeting Bruce Welch there one evening, they finally arranged a date when they could accept his offer to visit Portugal for the first time in their lives and on 27 May 1965, Paul and Jane flew from London to the villa of the Shadows' rhythm guitarist. In those years before the Algarve became a fashionable resort for Europeans, Albufeira was a peaceful fishing village where pop stars like Cliff Richard and Frank Ifield had homes close to the one owned by Bruce Welch. Above anything else, they could revel in the anonymity. 'It was a joy of a spot for us,' Welch says. 'The locals would not know a Shadow or a Beatle, and though that sounds nothing now, in those years that was something so important for us. Paul had been working very hard, as we had done, and he told me he was looking forward to a couple of weeks of peacefulness in the villa.'

The journey to Albufeira was a long one in 1965. A ninety-minute flight took Paul and Jane to Lisbon (this was in the years before nearby Faro airport was opened), and from Lisbon a five-hour journey by road was necessary. It was on that warm, rather dusty journey, as he sat next to Jane, in the back of a chauffeured car, that Paul remembers scribbling the theme to the song that had been hanging around for some nineteen months. 'I hate the idea of "time to kill",' Paul says, explaining why the car journey seemed an opportunity to write. 'It seems such a waste of life, to kill precious moments. Linda says it's "time to fill".' The words came, he says, quickly and naturally:

> Yesterday
> All my troubles seemed so far away
> Now it looks as though they're here to stay
> Oh I believe in yesterday

The rhythm of the lyric seemed OK. Paul was always an intuitive writer rather than one who would 'construct' a song to a theme. He relied on his natural instincts to provide the subjects. Usually, these were about love and relationships. 'Yesterday' emerged as something strangely different. It tumbled out, rather as the melody had done so long ago, from the sky. The reason for this would become apparent later, but for the moment, as the perfectionist in the songwriter anxiously penned the words to that melody, the most important objective was to structure the words as they came through, and to marry them to a demanding tune.

The spacious house of Bruce Welch in Albufeira comprised four bedrooms, two bathrooms, lounge, dining room and kitchen. With its sea view, it was an idyllic spot at which to arrive, confidently feeling that an interesting song was nearing completion. As Paul stepped from the car, Bruce Welch remembers, 'He said straight away: 'Have you got a guitar? I could see he had been writing lyrics on the way down; he had the paper in his hand as he arrived.'

Walking into the lounge, Welch handed McCartney the only guitar he had in his holiday home, a 1959 Martin model 0018. 'Being a left-handed player, he had to play it upside down. He said: "What do you think of this?" almost immediately, and started singing the song. I didn't know those passing chords he had put into the composition. I was a three-chords merchant. I guess I was the first to hear it with the words. I knew it was magic, with those beautiful chord progressions, but only later, when it was recorded, did I realize just what a song he had begun in Portugal. I did say it sounded lovely, and he said something about wanting to polish it up while he was there.'

Bruce Welch and his wife – who had been packing their luggage while hearing the song – left for London as Paul and Jane settled in for their holiday. Very little work was necessary to complete the song, but the stark nature of the words was like nothing heard from a Beatle. It seemed to come from somewhere within him . . .

> Suddenly
> I'm not half the man I used to be
> There's a shadow hanging over me
> Oh yesterday came suddenly.

Such simplicity was the song's strength, yet there was something ambiguous about the third verse:

> Why she had to go, I don't know
> She wouldn't say
> I said something wrong
> Now I long for yesterday

Whom was Paul addressing? A lost lover, it would appear. There was, though, something curiously autobiographical which did not sit quite so simply. Paul and Jane Asher were entrenched together at this time, the epitome of vibrant Young London. If it were a straightforward lament for a romantic split, it did not add up, for Paul was outwardly a very happy fellow.

> Yesterday
> Love was such an easy game to play
> Now I need a place to hide away
> Oh I believe in yesterday.

It was inconceivable that a leading Beatle would want to hide away from anyone or anything in 1965.

After two weeks in Portugal, Paul was forced to return to London a day earlier than scheduled. The reason was another of the dramatic events which made the Beatles hot news almost every day. Brian Epstein decreed that Paul should be back in Britain by midnight on 11 June when a news embargo was lifted to announce that the Queen had awarded the MBE to Paul, John, George and Ringo. On 12 June, as news of their forthcoming investiture at Buckingham Palace swept around an astonished world, the Beatles gave an impromptu press conference at Twickenham Film studios. They had gone to see an early cut of their film *Help!*. Asked what he thought of the MBE award, Paul quipped that he thought the initials stood for Mister Brian Epstein.

When he told his Beatles colleagues that he had re-named 'Scrambled Eggs' as 'Yesterday' and completed the lyric, there was little response. He phoned George Martin and said he was ready to record it. The producer was a little sceptical about the title. 'It was unoriginal,' George Martin remembers as his first reaction. 'And I said to Paul: "There is a song, admittedly in the plural, called Yesterdays, which is a big standard." Paul replied: "I haven't heard of that and there can't be many people who have. And anyway, mine's called Yesterday . . ."'*

---

* 'Yesterdays', written by Jerome Kern and Otto Harbach, has been recorded extensively, mostly by jazz-based artists. Peggy Lee, a McCartney favourite, recorded it, as well as Count Basie, John Coltrane, Dave Brubeck, Ray Conniff, Clifford Brown and Gato Barbieri.

The recording session for 'Yesterday' was set for 14 June, two days after the announcement of the MBE awards. Paul remembers the tenor of his first discussion with the Beatles about the recording. 'I said to everyone something like: "OK, now we'll get round to this song 'Yesterday'," And, as always, we'd sit around with George Martin; and I'd sit down with the guitar in the studio there and play de-da-da [Paul hums 'Yesterday''s melody]. And I looked at the guys and said: "How are we going to do this?" John said: "Well, I can't really sing anything over it. Or play rhythm guitar over it. What can we do on that, that won't spoil it?"' George and Ringo reacted similarly about their musical roles.

'So they said: "Maybe you should just do it on your own as a little solo thing. It wouldn't be unheard of." John said: "It's *yours*. It's good. Just you and an acoustic guitar would be all right." Either John, George and Ringo could not think of anything to add to it, or, as Paul says, 'They were just very sensitive to the fact that it maybe didn't *need* anything.'

Paul was more eager to press ahead with this new song than he dared admit at the time. Fired by his love of music and a natural ear, he believed that an artist knew instinctively when he had written a potential hit, and this was one of those songs. Rebutting all the rumours and stories that have percolated into Beatles mythology, he shows how possessive he was about 'Yesterday'. He states that, contrary to rumours, he never offered 'Yesterday' to another singer. 'I *knew* I wanted it for myself. I *played* it to a lot of people, and sometimes when that happens they *think* you're pitching it to them. That was never the case with "Yesterday".'

Paul, aged six and his four-year-old brother Michael with their mother Mary on holiday in Wales (© *Paul and Michael McCartney, 1981*)

Mary and Jim McCartney with their sons at their Liverpool home (© *Paul and Michael McCartney, 1981*)

Paul strums his guitar on a visit to the beach with his cousin, Bett Robbins, who was an important influence on his tastes in music (© *Paul and Michael McCartney, 1981*)

Paul photographed in Hamburg in 1960 by Astrid Kirchherr, who helped shape the Beatles' hairstyle. Her fiancé, 'fifth Beatle' Stuart Sutcliffe who died aged 21, is in the background (*Astrid Kirchherr/Star File*)

Paul duetting with George Harrison at the Odd Spot Club, Liverpool, on 29 March, 1962 (*Apple Corps*)

The late-1962 look before fame, in Liverpool (*Apple Corps*)

One of the Beatles' favourite artists, Little Richard, shared the bill with them at the Tower Ballroom, New Brighton, on 12 October 1962 (*Apple Corps*)

Paul on stage at Liverpool's Cavern, where they honed their act before mesmerised fans in 1962 (*Apple Corps*)

With producer George Martin, the Beatles record their third single, 'From Me To You', at EMI studios, Abbey Road, on 5 March 1963 (*Apple Corps*)

Touring days: Paul at Weston-Super-Mare during a seaside residency in 1963 (*Apple Corps*)

2

Roots in Music

'It was never rock 'n' roll to me'

It seemed such a pensive, melancholy song to be gestating across three key calendar years of Beatlemania, 1963 to 1965. These were heady times, in which the Beatles secured a multitude of awards, won the hearts and heads of millions around the world, and became the most influential force, musically and sociologically, since Elvis Presley. Touring America and being fêted in his homeland, Paul McCartney never forgot the melody, but now the lyrics for a song he had called 'Yesterday', while poignant, seemed at odds with the euphoria that surrounded the Beatles.

George Martin believes the words are 'the weakest part of the song' and represent a yearning by Paul for less frenzied times. 'Even though he was only twenty-two [when he finally recorded it], he had lived more than twenty-two years,' Martin says. 'It was a pretty complicated life at this time. They were in the middle of the trauma of being world heroes; this song happened two-thirds of the way through their touring years.' So Paul had already had his fill of hotel rooms, fans outside the door, and the prison of being famous. The threats, the tiresome aspect of being on the road, the noise, the hullabaloo – 'They got really sick to the teeth with it. So his lyrics are: "Yesterday, all my troubles seemed so far away."'

Paul, however, rejects George Martin's theory that 'Yesterday' was a reaction to the mayhem of Beatlemania. 'That's George's theory about a lot of stuff,' Paul laughs. 'George also analyses "When I'm 64" as a young guy's view of hell. I don't quite agree with some of his analyses on these things. On "Yesterday", I don't think it was that at all, really. To us, it didn't seem too crazy. I think that to George, to people who *looked* at our lives, it *looked*

crazy. To us, it was all we knew. It was very nice. We were earning a lot of money. It was fast and active. But so are my kids' lives
and your kids' lives. You say to yourself: "My God, how do they
do it?" Tearing about . . . but that's what you do at that age. I
think that maybe it's a little bit too easy to think that I was yearning for quieter times.'

Contrasting with any reaction to the success of the Beatles, a
darker reason for the lyrics emerges from Paul McCartney's own
reflections on his past in this song. He believes he may possibly
have written 'Yesterday' as a catharsis for the death of his mother
when he was aged fourteen.

> Suddenly, I'm not half the man I used to be
> There's a shadow hanging over me
> Yesterday came suddenly.
>
> Why she had to go, I don't know
> She wouldn't say
> I said something wrong. Now I long for yesterday . . .
>
> Yesterday
> Love was such an easy game to play
> Now I need a place to hide away
> Oh I believe in yesterday.

Anguish, regret and lost love permeate the lyrics, underpinned
by a brooding self-examination. The melody, conceived from his
spirit, arrived at Paul's hands from deep within his subconscious;
he did not sit down to work it out. To him, there remains something 'weird, awesome, spooky' in trying to explain how he woke
up feeling driven to the piano, where the tune spilled out of him.

The words, still spiritual, were rather different in their origin.
They were the product of a man in search of a theme, but still
generated from within. This was not an artist bent on delivering a
commercial three-minute song, which was the case with so many
Beatles tracks. To reach the root of 'Yesterday' and to touch the
core of much of McCartney's *oeuvre*, it is necessary to delve into
his boyhood.

He was born James Paul McCartney on 18 June 1942. His mother, Mary, qualified for the privilege of a private ward in Walton Hospital, Liverpool, because she had previously been the sister in charge of the maternity section. Formerly Mary Patricia Mohin, daughter of a coal merchant, she hailed originally from Ireland, moving at age eleven to Fazakerley, Liverpool, and on 15 April 1941 she married James McCartney, a cotton salesman, the son of a tobacco cutter from Everton. Mary was thirty-two, James thirty-nine, at the arrival of their first-born.

The couple had met when Mary was staying with her friend, James's sister, during one of Liverpool's countless air raids by Hitler's bombers. Married at St Swithen's Roman Catholic Chapel, Gill Moss, Liverpool, they moved into furnished rooms at Sunbury Road, Anfield, which was to be baby Paul's first home. Jim McCartney was 'over the moon with joy' when his first son arrived. 'Because he was a bachelor who married rather late, nobody thought he would ever marry,' says Bett Robbins, his niece, whose mother was one of four daughters and three brothers who included Jim. 'He was an absolutely doting father when Paul arrived.' Bett remembers her Aunt Mary as 'softly spoken, not gushy, very quiet . . . and I remember she had quite a nice singing voice around the house.'

After the birth, Mary suspended her work while Jim continued to work diligently at Napier's ammunition-making factory. Shortly afterwards they moved to a small, government-subsidized house on the Wirral, the quieter side of the Mersey, at 92 Broadway, Wallasey Village. But in a matter of months, Jim's work at Napier's ended and he secured a job in the war-torn city centre as an inspector in the Liverpool Corporation Cleansing Department. This meant that it was essential to live in the city centre and the family of three moved to Sir Thomas White Gardens.

Jim's work was neither pleasurable nor well-paid. A self-educated and intelligent man, he found it dispiriting that, with a second child expected, the family purse would be extremely stretched. On 7 January 1944, Paul's brother was born. He was named Peter Michael, though both sons were called by their second given names. Soon the family was on the move again, to a 'prefab' bungalow at Roach Avenue on the Knowlsley estate. Facing the family's financial pressure, Mary McCartney returned to her profession, becoming a part-time health visitor. Shortly after the birth of Michael, Mary had to return to the hospital for treatment for mastitis, a breast disease.

Mary missed her nursing career and, while health visiting provided a vocation and a small income, a return to more active service attracted her for two reasons. First, the role of the health visitor was less satisfying to her than full-time nursing; and second, the extra income would be very welcome. She became a domiciliary midwife, a job that brought with it a council house with a nominal rent, and the McCartney family thus moved again, this time to 72 Western Avenue, Speke, an estate which would later be dominated by those who worked at the Ford motor factory nearby.

'My Mum was the upwardly mobile force,' Paul remembers. 'She was always moving us to a better address; originally we had to go out to the sticks of Liverpool because of her work as a midwife. Roads were unmade but the midwife's house came free. So economically it was a good idea. She always wanted to move out of rough areas.'

Disciplined and cheerful, and running a meticulously clean and tidy house, Mary McCartney established her reputation as a first-class midwife and conscientious mother. By contrast, Jim McCartney was frustrated by the fact that his income barely equalled that of his tenacious wife. At the end of the war he had resumed his job as a salesman at the Liverpool Cotton Exchange, but his pay was poor.

They were, however, model parents in these war years and, with an extended family of aunts and uncles, the McCartney brothers enjoyed a rumbustious childhood, the economic position of the family being firmly working-class. They did not starve, the household furniture was quite adequate, but there was not much surplus money for luxuries. Paul became aware of this when his schooling began at Stockton Wood infants' school, and later when he won a scholarship to the poshest school in the city, the Liverpool Institute.

It was a music-conscious house. Mary McCartney whistled a lot, Paul says. 'That's one of my fond memories of my mum. You don't hear many women whistling. She was quite musical. My father was even more so; he was a pretty good pianist.'

When he was aged ten, Jim McCartney had burst an eardrum when he fell from a wall during childhood pranks. This meant he had avoided conscription into the armed forces during the war, though he served as a fireman and helped to extinguish incendiary bombs. For most of his childhood he had warmed to music, the sounds of jazz and the big bands, and the ballad singing of artists such as Bing Crosby and Frank Sinatra. Teaching himself piano and trumpet, he had formed a band by the time he met his wife-to-be: initially called the Masked Melody Makers, it developed into Jim Mac's Band. Jim gave up trumpet when, as Paul remembers it, 'his teeth went' and he needed false dentures.

From a furniture and music store in Allerton called North End Music Stores (NEMS), run by Harry Epstein, Jim bought a second-hand piano.* At home, he would play the songs of the era, jazzy material made famous by Fats Waller, like 'Chicago' and 'Stumbling', plus rich ballads such as 'Lullaby of the Leaves' and 'Stairway to Paradise'. Adept at these strong melodies, he could also play piano in the 'stride' style popularized by such jazz players as Meade Lux Lewis and Earl Hines.

Paul traces his formative years in music to those days, when he was about ten years old. 'It all dates back to my dad, who with his friend Freddy Rimmer used to be always playing these old tunes, jazz songs. And it was never rock 'n' roll to me when I was growing up. I grew up loving the music my dad was making and I particularly liked the singing of Peggy Lee, who was introduced to me by my cousin, Bett Robbins.'

Twelve years older than Paul, Bett Robbins remembers how her enjoyment of music augmented the influence of Jim McCartney in influencing the boy's tastes. At her home in Boaler Street, adjoining a shop where her mother ran a sewing repairs business, she often looked after Paul and Michael. There was no garden at the small terraced house, and they spent several hours at a time indoors, Bett using her love of music to keep the brothers occupied.

'I had a banjolele, a cross between a banjo and a ukulele, at that time,' she says. 'I wasn't very good at it, but I enjoyed it. Paul was a youngish twelve and he was fascinated by it. He picked it up and played it but wasn't, of course, producing any terrific sounds. I said: "Look, if you want to put your fingers so, in that triangle,

---

* Harry's son was Brian, later to become the Beatles' manager. Paul still has his father's piano.

you get a D7 on that one chord. I taught him three basic chords on two songs, "The Man from Arizona" and "Has Anybody Seen My Gal". He loved it. He never put the thing down.' He was intrigued, too, by her book of basic chord graphs, and she taught him the chords, also, to a song called 'Ragtime Cowboy Joe'.

Paul vividly recalls Bett's record collection and the impression it made on him in his pre-teenage years. 'She'd say: "Listen to this . . . a lovely song." So eventually I went out and bought a few Peggy Lee records and "Till There Was You" was among them; I had no idea until much later that it was from *The Music Man*, mixed in with songs like "76 Trombones" and all that . . . I don't think I'd have done it if I'd known that. There would have been too much of a stigma in our world. A *show* tune! Are you kidding?'

The 78rpm records that Bett Robbins played on her wind-up gramophone in that house were similar in flavour to those championed by Jim McCartney. 'I used to love a song by Peggy Lee called "Johnny Guitar",' she says, 'and I used to sing it and pretend I was Peggy Lee.'

The standard ballads of those mid-1950s years were a part of her collection which Paul enjoyed: Frank Sinatra singing 'All the Things You Are'; Al Martino singing 'Star Eyes'; Peggy Lee's 'The Folks Who Live on the Hill' and Woody Herman's Orchestra's million-selling 'Laura'. The Peggy Lee–George Shearing album *Beauty and the Beat* was a favourite in the Robbins collection.

While Jim Mac's Band, led by Jim McCartney, enjoyed only modest success playing the dance-halls in the Liverpool area, his talent had a strong effect on his family. Sing-songs were a regular feature of the McCartney household. 'That lovely music in Jim came apparently from nowhere,' reflects Bett Robbins. 'He used to sit at the piano and out came all these wonderful chords. He couldn't read music at all.' His piano had to be 'rescued' from the air-raid shelter where it had been stored, with sandbags all over it, during the war. 'It still played miraculously,' says Bett. At Christmas and New Year, the entire McCartney clan would gather to sing songs such as 'Carolina Moon' and the Al Jolson classics 'Baby Face' and 'When the Red Red Robin Comes Bob, Bob, Bobbin' Along'.

Another dimension of Bett's record collection might, she feels, have influenced Paul more than he realized. 'He never actively took an interest in any of my light classical music but I used to say to him: "You're missing some good stuff."' Despite the boy's indifference, Bett played to him pop classics such as Grieg's *Peer Gynt Suite*, *Scheherazade*, the *Holberg Suite* and *La Calinda*.

Paul would grow to cherish such childhood memories, of his abundant family of aunts, uncles and cousins, and of the genial atmosphere created in the houses around Merseyside where his diligent parents stepping-stoned their way to improving their lot. His broad tastes in music, which were to be so important a contribution to the Beatles' success, were a direct result of the sounds of his boyhood, in those years before rock 'n' roll arrived in his life. Many years later, after seeing the world through the hurricane of the Beatles, Paul positively glowed on the subject of his family and its values. After Speke, they had moved to 20 Forthlin Road in the desirable part of Allerton, south Liverpool.

Pipe-smoking, slipper-wearing, and with a keen sense of humour based on proverbs and decency, Jim McCartney was a father who keenly influenced his eldest son. Though a passive man, he was unquestionably the head of the household, administering an occasional wallop to either son when he or Mary considered they had breached the parental line of good behaviour. Conversely, Jim was demonstrative, perhaps more so than Mary. Ambitious for both sons, as Michael joined Paul at the prestigious Liverpool Institute, they hoped their eldest would enter the professions, perhaps as a doctor or accountant. A popular boy at school, Paul was usually chosen as form captain. With his special talent as a communicator, he was reckoned by several observers to be a natural for the role of schoolteacher.

Michael asserts that he identified more closely than Paul with their mother, and that she catered more for his [Michael's] neediness. His elder brother was more independent, he adds. Paul is not so sure; perhaps Michael felt closer to their mother because of the brothers' difference in age, he says now. He refutes any theory that he was aligned more with his father than his mother, despite the musical path he shared with Jim. 'I don't think that's actually true. A younger son gets a lot of attention and cuddling when he arrives. In my own mind, I identified with both of my parents: I think they were both great. We were very lucky to have them as parents. Perception is a funny thing. Mike, being the younger brother, might have spent a little more time with Mum, but that's all there was to it.' Whatever the case, no sibling rivalry entered their respective relationships with their mother and father.

They were young boys when the thunderbolt of Mary's death hit them. Throughout the summer of 1955 she had complained of pains in the chest area, and as they increased, she took to using large doses of BiSodol, an antacid powder usually used for in- digestion. But the trouble was far more deep-rooted and lay in the mastitis for which she had been treated shortly after Michael's birth.

In the late summer of 1956, Michael, then twelve, heard her crying in her bedroom and when he ran in to ask her what the trouble was, he saw her with a crucifix. 'Nothing, love,' she re- plied. But the truth was that a specialist had diagnosed her pain as breast cancer. Soon, she was in Northern Hospital. Being a nurse, she knew just how serious her condition was, and confided in her relations that she would regret not seeing her sons grow up.

Paul recalls that he and Michael went with their father to see her in hospital, where she had undergone a mastectomy oper- ation. 'It was a huge shock to us, because suddenly she was very ill, and we were very young. There was a little bit of blood on the sheets and it was really creepy for us at that age. Nobody was holding out much hope for her. This was very scary.'

In the tense days after the operation, Paul and Michael went to stay with their Uncle Joe and Auntie Joan. The dreaded news came swiftly, and Joan told them as they woke to go to school one morning: 'Love, your Mum's dead.' It was 31 October 1956.

'My reaction was very strange,' Paul remembers. 'Mum was a working nurse. There wasn't a lot of money around – and she was half the family pay packet. My reaction was: "How are we going to get by without her money?" When I think back on it, I think, Oh God, *what*? Did I *really* say that? It was a terrible, logical thought which was preceded by the normal feelings of grief. It was very tough to take. And then, seeing your father cry for the first time in your life was not easy, a terrible thing for a kid. They had been quite stable, as a marriage. I don't remember seeing them argue; there might have been heated discussions, but there was never a lot of argument.'

Paul's idyllic family background had been shattered abruptly.

Mary was a mere forty-seven. Paul was fourteen, Michael twelve. Certain that his mother's death affected him deeply and that his reaction was the superficial, nervous response of a fourteen-year-old in shock, Paul continues: 'I could have changed my story by now. I don't need to tell you that. I could have said: yes, I was very saddened by my mother's death . . . ' He could, also, apply a traditional interpretation to his song 'Yesterday', that it is a nostalgic ballad about lost love. But that would be too simplistic. Paul cannot be certain that the song was a long-delayed, subconscious reading of his feelings, some eight years after the tragic loss of his mother. 'I would probably have to go into deep hypnosis to get that one out of me, lie on a couch for a few months.' But there is too much additional evidence of the man's emotional candour in his music for his instinct to be wrong. Consider his song 'Let It Be', that valediction for the break-up of the Beatles, in which he sings: 'When I find myself in times of trouble, Mother Mary comes to me, speaking words of wisdom, let it be.' Consider his spiritual song 'Lady Madonna', in which he sings of 'children at her feet, wonder how you manage to make ends meet'. Consider, too, his affectionate song 'Put It There', in which he remembered his father, who died on 18 March 1976.

Put it there, if it weighs a ton
That's what a father said to his young son.

'Put It There' was one of his father's 'mad' expressions, like: 'There's no hairs on a seagull's chest.' 'Put it there, if it weighs a ton', his father would say, stretching out his hand to end any friction. 'I hate to see things go so wrong', Paul's optimistic song adds.

These are but a few of many signals that some of Paul McCartney's most impactful work is autobiographical. As a stream-of-consciousness artist who writes as he thinks rather than sculpts his lyrics, he does not often stop long enough to apply forensic examination to what he is saying. In 'Yesterday', however, he seems to be facing up to the reality that it was not merely a piece of nostalgic poetry wedded to a plaintive melody. It was something of a *cri de coeur*, and the realization makes it an even more astonishing achievement at the age of twenty-two. Paul will probably never be able to describe satisfactorily how the melody came to him. Other songwriters believe some melodies are 'sent' to them, that they do not consciously create some of their work but that it is 'given' or channelled from a force they do not entirely control.

That is apparently what happened with 'Yesterday' one autumn morning in 1963, and some fifteen months later when the words fitted into place. A tune that had come to earth so mystically was joined by words of heartfelt, if coded, spirituality.

Psychologically, both the words and the music of 'Yesterday' target some of our most vulnerable emotions. 'The song looks backwards to a time when life seemed simpler and better,' says Dr Glenn Wilson, a psychologist at the University of London.* 'The older you get the harder it is to see more fun in the future than you had in the past. Indeed, the older we get, the less we get in positive, rewarding experiences. We acquire all this baggage of losing people, by death or desertion. Generally, life always looks a little better looking backwards.

'And it's a perfectly valid function of music to remind people that they're not alone in their feelings. Songs provide social support; that's why the greatest proportion of song lyrics are about love gone wrong, or lost, broken relationships.' People experiencing that need to be touched by a song that sympathizes with their situation.

Could Paul be writing from his subconscious, partly about his mother, eight years after her death and without realizing it at the time? Dr Wilson believes that was very likely. 'The song is very mournful. It looks back to an earlier time and he wants to undo mistakes he has made in the past. The wording could come from the subconscious; something has gone wrong in a relationship with a girlfriend, or he has regrets about saying the wrong thing. The success of the song is down to the fact that it would ring a bell in anybody's life, whether the individual receiving it connects it with a lost girlfriend, wife or parent. We must all have said things we regretted in the past. We regret them particularly when we don't have a chance to put matters right. When a person has

* Dr Wilson is Reader in Personality at the Institute of Psychiatry, University of London. A semi-professional singer, he is the author of *Psychology for Performing Artists: Butterflies and Bouquets*, published by Jessica Kingsley, London 1994.

died, there's a feeling of a lack of completion, of not having said: "Dad, I love you," before it's too late, and then spending the rest of our lives regretting that.'

That year of 1956, when Paul's mother died, was marked by profound change for British teenagers. Rock 'n' roll had made its first noises the previous year, when Bill Haley's Comets scored a hit with 'Rock Around the Clock'. This extraordinary sound challenged the balladeers who dominated the British hit parade, as it was called: Alma Cogan with 'Dreamboat', Jimmy Young with 'The Man from Laramie', Ruby Murray with 'Softly, Softly' and Dickie Valentine with 'Finger of Suspicion' – all safe and sound melodies, the sort of music Jim McCartney might enjoy, but with minimal teenage appeal.

When Bill Haley's initial record was followed by Elvis Presley's 'Heartbreak Hotel' and 'Don't be Cruel', young people had a new sound to adopt as part of their self-expression. With rock 'n' roll, too, came a curiously British uniform, that of the Teddy Boy, with very tight black trousers known as drainpipes, bootlace tie, lurid-coloured socks, and greasy hair designed like an elephant's trunk at the front and a d.a. (duck's arse) at the rear. A Teddy Boy's girlfriend had to wear a full skirt which, when she danced, displayed her suspenders holding up those black seamed stockings, a tight sweater to emphasize her assets, stiletto-heeled shoes and a waspie belt.

Though rock made a strong impact, it did not make a takeover. Doris Day gave us the lilting 'Que Sera Sera', Pat Boone crooned 'I'll Be Home', and Johnnie Ray, the emotive 'Nabob of Sob' who said he cried real tears on stage, sang 'Glad Rag Doll' and 'Just Walkin' in the Rain'. From America, Frankie Lymon and the Teenagers with 'Why Do Fools Fall in Love' pre-dated the Michael Jackson sound with infectious energy and simplicity.

The new sounds laid the foundations for a music that would stand for ever, revolutionizing the minds of teenagers like Paul McCartney. Little Richard, later to be an important influence on Paul, recorded a string of seven million-sellers including 'Long Tall Sally', 'Rip It Up' and 'Lucille'. Carl Perkins, later to become Paul's friend, wrote a rock anthem, 'Blue Suede Shoes', which Elvis Presley took to the best-sellers. Gene Vincent and Screaming

Jay Hawkins were making their impact, while in Britain Tommy Steele arrived with the tepid 'Rock with the Caveman'.

Jim McCartney had arranged for eleven-year-old Paul to be auditioned for the junior choir at Liverpool Cathedral, but he was not accepted. However, he had shown his usual practicality in encouraging his eldest son's clear interest in music. 'My dad was the big influence because he was playing piano all the time by ear,' Paul recalls. 'I used to try to get him to teach me, but he said no, you've got to get lessons.' Paul demurred on that. 'I spent a lot of time just looking at the piano and taught myself,' Paul recalls. 'I learned chords, then from knowing C and the break-up of C I could basically play things like "A Whole Lotta Shakin".' Later, he recalls, John Lennon 'used to pick up a few little things when he'd come round to our house. And if I had a few hours I'd just play around on the piano, finding chords. That was one of the great excitements: "Wow, *that* goes with *that* one." I just taught myself.'

When he had asked his father to teach him, he replied: 'I can't play, son.' Paul said: '"You play *great*" – because he did. He played lovely old-fashioned stride piano. He wrote some stuff. I actually did a song of his with Chet Atkins and Floyd Cramer called "Walking in the Park with Eloise". I said to my dad: "Do you know that song you wrote?" He said: "I didn't write it, I made it up." I said: "I know what you mean, but we call that writing these days, Dad!"'

Next came the influence of Lonnie Donegan. On 11 November 1956 fourteen-year-old Paul went to the Liverpool Empire to see a concert by the star of a new British music described as skiffle. With a simple three-chord style, Donegan sang nasally his big hits 'Rock Island Line', 'Cumberland Gap' and 'Putting on the Style', and many thousands of British teenagers were hooked into picking up a guitar to emulate his earthy simplicity. Impoverished though he was, Jim McCartney had recently managed to find £15 to buy Paul a trumpet which Paul later traded in for a Zenith guitar. And like teenagers all over Britain, Paul was listening to Radio Luxembourg, that precursor of the pirate radio stations that beamed the best-selling music into Britain from the heart of Europe.

At the Liverpool Institute, Paul was in the higher echelon of academic boys, on course, if he wished, for university in the years when such a path was not so frequent as in the decades that followed. He took his studies seriously, and applied the same seriousness to the guitar, which he played, as he wrote, left-handed. In the bathroom at Forthlin Road, he found he could achieve his desired effect of echo, and he practised relentlessly. Application was everything to him and he taught himself the guitar with passion, dedication, and the extraordinary attention to detail that would mark his life, He quickly mastered the chord changes and the lyrics of the hits he heard on record and on the radio.

To Jim McCartney and brother Michael, Paul's assiduity with his guitar was partly explained by the need to submerge his grief at the death of his mother. Despite the flow of relatives and aunts who would take time off from their own families to go to the McCartney house and cook a 'Sunday roast on Monday nights' for Jim, Paul and Michael, there was an emptiness around the house. In the aftermath of such a family death and a shock, any fourteen-year-old would feel bereft. The guitar was no substitute but it provided a comfort, an absorbing hobby, at this important juncture.

By 1957 the force of rock 'n' roll was becoming more tangible and, appealingly to Paul's ears, touched with melodicism, too. As Russia launched the first satellite, Sputnik 1, the sound on Radio Luxembourg was of Buddy Holly and the Crickets singing 'That'll Be the Day', a song later named by Paul as the most influential song and sound of his youth. The record was actually credited to the Crickets, with Holly as featured vocalist, but Buddy's popularity forced a switch later that year when they were credited as Buddy Holly and the Crickets on their second million-seller, 'Peggy Sue'. This was a sound central to Paul McCartney's evolution, fusing Holly's love of Presley with country and western, gospel and Texas-Mexican influences. To all that, Holly added a plaintively appealing voice. Paul was immediately hooked, as Holly began a two-year string of successes that would become evergreens: songs like 'Not Fade Away', 'True Love Ways', 'Words of Love' and 'Rave On'.

The Everly Brothers' vocal harmonies on 'Wake Up Little Susie', 'All I Have to Do Is Dream' and 'Cathy's Clown' impressed Paul too. Don and Phil Everly, with artists as different in style as Duane Eddy and Bobby Darin, sat outside the hard rock formula. Their music owed more to harmonic strength than to the posturing and driving beat that came from the rock pioneers like Elvis and Little Richard. Even Jim McCartney, then aged fifty-four and like most of his generation rather cynical about a new brigade of youth who seemed not to have mastered their instruments, could recognize the sweet melodies of Buddy Holly and the Everly Brothers.

Paul was drawn to both with equal interest. As a fifteen-year-old he identified with the verve of rock 'n' roll, and as a fledgeling musician he thrilled to the more melodic songs that were coming over the airwaves. It was from this pot-pourri of sounds that Paul's eclectic tastes in music were born, enabling him to straddle pop and rock. With his black and white flecked jacket and tight black trousers, he displayed a tokenism towards the rock 'n' roll culture. As a teenager growing up in the 1950s, he understood and enjoyed part of the rebelliousness that some adopted as an essential adjunct to rock 'n' roll music. As long as it carried a good song, he loved that music and determined to perfect his guitar-playing of the hits of the era. But unlike so many, he was never enslaved to rock 'n' roll. With the sounds of Peggy Lee and Fats Waller embedded in his psyche, Paul headed for his fifteenth birthday knowing, instinctively, that there were only two forms of music: good and bad. His musical base was wholly different from that of the teenager who was to become his songwriting partner.

John Lennon came from a contrasting and less secure background. Nearly two years older than Paul, he had emerged from an emotionally bruised childhood, his parents playing out a tug-of-war for his custody upon the breakdown of their marriage. When John was aged three, his mother believed that the best environment for him was in the care of her sister in the sedate Liverpool suburb of Woolton. John's Aunt Mimi and Uncle George raised him steadfastly, with values not dissimilar to those of Mary and Jim McCartney. A dairyman, George Smith was able to give John a home that was materialistically more fortunate than the McCartneys'. But several fundamental differences shaped John.

A potentially bright student at the academic Quarry Bank Grammar School, the young Lennon was the precise opposite of the young McCartney, lacking any application and failing all his examinations. A reprobate at the age of fourteen, he embraced rock 'n' roll as his saviour. However, contrasting with Paul's encouragement from his father, John met strong opposition to his love of pop music from his Aunt Mimi. (Uncle George had died in 1955 before music had completely gripped Lennon, who, like Paul, listened nightly under his bedclothes to the sounds of Radio Luxembourg.) To Lennon, rock 'n' roll was a lifeline, and unlike Paul, he grew up regarding 'old' popular music as the enemy.

And while Paul enjoyed a strong family base, John's contact with his few far-flung relatives was erratic. Consequently, he emerged as a loner, a drifter for whom art and rock 'n' roll quickly became his only vocations. An avid reader, he would later combine a waspish wit and lyrical word-play to mesmerizing effect; but as a teenager, he was a problem to his aunt, who was in despair at his talent wasting away.

At sixteen he had adopted the regalia of the Teddy Boy. On 6 July 1957, with his group The Quarry Men, formed in the wake of the skiffle craze, John was the musical attraction at the garden fête in the grounds of St Mary's Church, Woolton. His playing was crude; he busked the words to 'Come Go with Me', the Del Vikings song. But his appearance on stage had a rugged magnetism.

In the crowd, Paul, just fifteen, saw the show and met John afterwards in the church hall. An extraordinary symbiosis occurred between the two teenagers. John was already a warrior, all set to rampage through art college, which he would join two months after that garden party. A rock 'n' roll animal almost by birthright, he was a primitive guitarist who loved the urgency of the new sounds of Elvis Presley and Lonnie Donegan. His mother, Julia, a vibrant spirit, had taught him a few chords on her ukulele and his aunt had relented to his pressure to buy him a guitar on installments. But by contrast with Paul he was an undisciplined player. 'All I can play is chunk-chunk-chunk,' he would tell me during the Beatles years, when his work was underpinned by the studious lead guitar of George Harrison. Pop music, to Lennon, was the vehicle that would become his salvation. In Liverpool, in Beatles years, many observers would say that had he not been a success in pop music, his future could have been extremely dodgy.

In that church hall, Paul's musical superiority was instantly evident. Demonstrating the wizardry on the guitar that resulted from hours of practice, he could show John the dazzling solo as played by Eddie Cochran on 'Twenty Flight Rock'. Even at fifteen, he was on the way to becoming a consummate musician with a natural ear. Lennon was impressed. United, they would eventually recruit George Harrison and Ringo Starr and go on to create musical and cultural history.

The erratic, poetic, philosophical *angst* of John Lennon had found, in Paul McCartney, a genius of a very different hue. The rich tapestry of sounds in Paul's head, stretching from theatrical soundtracks through jazz to rock 'n' roll, was the foundation that would both blend and clash with John. Paul would enable the Beatles to be credited with magnificent music such as 'Here, There and Everywhere', 'Eleanor Rigby' and 'Michelle'. John's teenage stance, built on rockier foundations, brought to their partnership a sarcastic wit, sharp observation, and an artistic, autobiographical edge. To Lennon, the music was secondary to a method of expression at that stage, as well as being a career he sorely needed. As they grew together, he admired Paul's musicianship – but rarely said so.

When they first met and Paul told John that his mother had died, John was incredulous. 'I don't know how you'd cope with that,' Lennon remarked. A year after they became friends, a cruel twist of fate sealed their brotherhood. John's mother lived a short distance from where John lived with Aunt Mimi at 251 Menlove Avenue. Leaving the house on the night of 15 July 1958 after visiting her sister, Julia was hit by a car and sent spinning in the air. She died, instantly, aged forty-four.

The suddenness of that death, and the closeness of Julia's age to that of Mary McCartney when she died, struck a sombre and eerie note for the two teenagers. 'That actually became a huge link between John and me,' Paul says now. 'As kids, at a very formative age, it kind of bonded us.' Young and with a black sense of humour, they gave each other comfort when people remarked on the Beatles' achievements.

'People would say: "Does your mother like this?" and we'd say [in a matter-of-fact-style]: "Oh, she died a couple of years ago." At that point John and I would look at each other sardonically;

we'd play that one on people.' They waited for an embarrassed re-action. Putting a brave front on their emotional darkness, they developed a kinship.

It was a 'front' of bravado. 'We couldn't be seen, in Liverpool at that age, to be saying: "Mother died. It's terrible" . . . which is what we were feeling inside. We toughed it out. Even to the point when, if someone came to our houses and asked if our mother was there, we'd reply quickly: "Oh, she died a couple of months ago."' That threw the onus for a response back on the questioner, who became apologetic. Paul and John would ex-change such stories of how they dealt with their trauma.

Eventually, when the pandemonium of the Beatles had sub-sided, John articulated his own thoughts about his mother in his songs 'Julia' and 'Mother'. He was undergoing psychotherapy at the time and much of his unsettled early life, buried for so long, surfaced in his work. Neither Paul nor the McCartney family nor the Beatles could have been expected to deduce in the mid-1960s that Paul's lyric for 'Yesterday' might be *his* inner voice.

The song was an anachronism in the evolution of the Beatles. It had no special relevance to the 1960s, nor to any other decade; it could have been written at any time, not necessarily by a twenty-two-year-old pop star. It belonged, then as now, to the soul of McCartney. The sentimentalist deep inside him was the essential ingredient. With relish, Paul talks of how a song like 'Yesterday' would have come naturally to him because he always loved pour-ing emotion into his work: 'Dad loved harmony. That's where my tastes come from. People can't realize that now, because rock 'n' roll came in so big and so quickly that it ate up everything else.'

His enjoyment of the urgency of that new music became mixed with his love of ballads to inform all his future work. By the time he met John, Paul could play a little piano and guitar, drawing from a sweep of styles he admired equally, and apply a scholarly determination to any challenge that faced him, as the elder son, with his widower father.

The Beatles went to Hamburg to learn their craft the hard way and returned triumphantly to Liverpool's Cavern Club. 'In Ham-burg I played songs like "A Taste of Honey" and "Besame Mucho",' Paul remembers. 'And what interested me was the key change from minor to major instead of from major to minor. I *loved* that major in there: *"Besame . . . "* Ooh, that really thrilled me. It wasn't social climbing in a musical way. It was that these songs thrilled me somewhere deep down.'

What McCartney took into the Beatles was a frame of musical reference that belied his youth: a keen ear for the songs of George and Ira Gershwin, Jerome Kern and Cole Porter to build on the group's rock 'n' roll base. Melodious qualities, rather than raunch, were the cornerstone. And the lyrics he loved carried sentiment. The other Beatles were either reluctant to display it at that stage or had not enjoyed the advantage of a household in which such music was played.

The emotion in Paul McCartney lay partly hidden in the high tide years of the Beatles. The suave diplomat, the keen careerist trading song for song with his collaborator and competitor John Lennon, the collector of fine art and lover of the theatre showed Paul as an extrovert. But he could not have written songs like 'All My Loving', 'Michelle' and 'Here There and Everywhere' if he had not been tearful inside. These were not merely songs tailored for an audience. They came, also, from within.

Paul feels that whereas many of his contemporaries entered the music arena as rock 'n' rollers, he arrived with an entirely different ethos. 'Going right back, I came in on the wave of Billy Cotton [a popular British dance band featured on the BBC Light Programme every Sunday lunchtime] . . . I was always in favour of being a professional musician, not a rock 'n' roll player. I was trying to impress musicians, and train myself as a guy who knew his instrument, knew how to arrange, knew about songs.

'There was some rock 'n' roll in my record collection but I also loved things like Fats Waller and I used to do his song "Your Feet's Too Big", at the Cavern. And they used to come off more as comedy records, because Fats is really comedy anyway. One of my all-time favourite records is "Cheek to Cheek" by Fred Astaire. I just love the tune, the melody, I love his vocal style.

'So I had a deep love of all that. So in my own mind, yes, I think I was always trying to write something as good as that. And I think when I got "Yesterday", or really when "Yesterday" got to me because it was in a dream, I finally thought: Wow, I've actually done it, you know? I've actually written one of those tunes. And I continued to write those tunes with things like "Let It Be", "Here There and Everywhere", "The Long and Winding

Road". To me, those songs were trying to write something substantial, that would stand in their own right rather than just have the Beatles do the songs.'

Sentimentality played a very large part in Paul's art, too. 'All my life, I've been able to admit to sentimentality,' he told me. 'And perhaps in some ways it would be cooler to not admit it so readily. But I'm not going to start that now. Because I'm very proud of being able to cry. I say that if God had not meant us to cry, he wouldn't have given us tears. I think it's a most important part of nature, but people cover it up.

'I *like* to be sentimental. I don't see it as a bad word at all. Particularly now that I've got kids. I'll cry at a film. The kids will turn round and say [in an embarrassed tone]: "*Dad!*" I say: "I know I'm a man and I know I'm your father but this [scene] touches me deeply." It's nearly always a father and children situation that gets me, a father who's losing one of his children . . . and at that, I'm done in. Because I can actually relate to it. People cover it up. I don't think anyone hates sentimentality, but they try to pretend it's not right to show it. Even a murderer doesn't hate it: talk to a murderer about his mum and he'll cry. The biggest criers we knew were the gangsters in Hamburg; they'd cry at the drop of a hat. People who had been in jail.'

That sentimentality has always been part of him. 'And it's almost embarrassing to talk about because it's not cool. And I present a nice, big, fat sentimental target for people to shoot at. That's wonderful for the critics. And everybody's criticizing everything about soft old Paul – whacky, thumbs-aloft McCartney! That used to bother me for years, but then I wondered what the hell I was worrying about. Being ridiculed for putting thumbs-aloft? It means optimism, and in this world . . .'

3

A String Quartet!

'My God, we have a winner!'

On 13 April 1965 Paul McCartney bought a London house, a three-storey nineteenth-century detached Victorian property in St John's Wood. The night Paul purchased the property, which he bought for £40,000, the Beatles recorded *Help!* as the soundtrack for their new movie. Although it would be another year before he would finally settle into his new home, Paul frequently visited it to oversee the structural alterations he wanted. Visitors would eventually remark on the sedate ambience and good taste of the house and its furnishings; it was neither a rock 'n' roller's garish fun palace nor the house of someone from the *nouveau riche*. Benjamin Britten's work for the 1953 Coronation of Elizabeth II, *Gloriana*, played regularly in the drawing-room to typify Paul's interests beyond the Beatles.

A city dweller all his life, Paul told me several times in those years how much he loved 'the look of London'. He drove around the city in a black Mini Cooper, singing the praises of its skyline, its bustle, its cosmopolitan mix. The other three Beatles moved to suburbia but he was resolute that he wanted a city base during these exciting years.

Paul's new home was well positioned for its proximity to the EMI Studios, a mere five minutes walk away in Abbey Road. This was the domain of the Beatles and their producer, George Martin, who since their first single, 'Love Me Do', in 1962, had brilliantly steered their recording career, interpreting the often radical requests of Paul and John. At that time, in 1965, as Paul was establishing his new home, with George Martin an occasional visitor, the producer was to infuse Paul's unexpected song 'Yesterday' with a dramatic suggestion.

The good fortune of the Beatles in finding Martin, and vice versa, cannot be exaggerated, although when they met they certainly needed him more than he was looking for a beat group from Liverpool. At the precise time when four ambitious young men were bursting out of their chrysalis, they enjoyed an instant rapport with their producer.

Classically trained in composition, conducting, harmony and counterpoint at the Guildhall School of Music, thirty-six-year-old Martin had also, coincidentally, been taught the oboe by Margaret Asher. His broad taste would help Paul both practically and inventively to realize the best, and the most innovative, twists of sound and effects, on 'Yesterday' and many other songs.

Martin was prized by the Beatles because he was associated with the Goons, whom they loved. He produced the individual recordings of Spike Milligan, Peter Sellers and Michael Bentine. Paul was equally impressed with Martin's activities across a wide range of artists. He produced Michael Flanders and Donald Swann, Rolf Harris with 'Tie Me Kangaroo Down, Sport', jazz stars Cleo Laine and John Dankworth, Stan Getz and Humphrey Lyttelton, comedian Bernard 'Right Said Fred' Cribbins, the *Beyond the Fringe* team, and masterminded the fast-moving careers of most of Brian Epstein's Liverpool stable of acts, including Cilla Black, Billy J. Kramer and Gerry and the Pacemakers.

Paul attributes the mild-mannered Martin's former vocation in the Fleet Air Arm to his brilliant contribution to the Beatles' success. 'He was an observer in planes,' McCartney says. 'He didn't navigate or fly the things. So he had the job of a producer even in the Fleet Air Arm! In the studio, he didn't engineer, he didn't write the songs, or play an instrument. As a producer, as in the Fleet Air Arm, he sat and observed. He pulled it all together, you're ultimately responsible, you're the captain. I think that's where George got his excellent bedside manner. He'd dealt with navigators and pilots . . . so that he could deal with us when we got out of line.' Such powers of persuasion, as well as considerable expertise, were to be important in sealing the success of 'Yesterday'.

A man with such an orthodox background in music might have found the Beatles' primitive instincts abhorrent, for they challenged all traditional approaches to record-making from the start. But Martin's response was always patient, his benign style concealing a quicksilver mind. His willingness to adapt was valued by the Beatles. And as a man who tended to analyse a melody first, ahead of the lyrics, he had more affinity with Paul than with John, although he paid full tribute to Lennon's random brilliance.

'Yesterday' had been whirling in Paul's head sporadically over a twenty-month period before he finally entered number 2 studio, the Beatles' familiar and favourite place of work, within the EMI complex on Abbey Road, to record the song. In the afternoon, the Beatles recorded two McCartney compositions, the folksy 'I've Just Seen a Face' and the rocker 'I'm Down'. This belting Little-Richard-style song might almost be expected to have damaged his vocal cords, since seven 'takes' were needed before the Beatles were satisfied with the finish. After such a marathon session the singer would have been justified in adjourning for the evening.

Talking of that day as typical of the intensity with which the Beatles recorded, Paul says: 'We'd show up at 10.30 and in the first session we were expected to get a couple of songs. Everyone did. Wally Ridley [another EMI producer] did a whole album in that time. We felt if he could do a whole album, we at least had got to come up with two songs. It would be just slovenly if we didn't. So we'd sit down, run through a song for fifteen, twenty minutes. How long can you run through a song without beating it to death? You always had the song. There was no making it up on the spot until much later . . . this was lads looking for work, trying to prove themselves with their first contract. So we'd go in and they'd say: what do you want to start with? Oh, "I'm Down", or whatever it was. Maybe I didn't want to get into the ballad early. It was probably a case of "let's kick off and get rid of any nerves."'

A mere ninety minutes after the completion of those two vocally demanding songs, one of the Beatles was back in the same room . . . to record 'Yesterday'. Singing to his own acoustic guitar accompaniment, Paul recorded two 'takes alone' on that night of 14 June, in a three-and-a-half hour session that began at 7pm. When he had finished, the four-track tape was put into storage, with the second 'take' being marked 'BEST' to await Paul's planned return to the studio a few days later.

'We didn't use headphones,' George Martin recalls of the session. 'And so there was a leakage from the speaker into his microphone. That gave the impression of double tracking of the voices that you can now hear on the record.'

The balance engineer for the session was Norman Smith (later known as successful singer Hurricane Smith), and Phil McDonald (later a successful engineer in his own right) was the tape machine operator. Paul's softly sung vocal, coming after a long day's session of rock 'n' roll, was remarkably controlled. Yes, he agrees now, it was 'wild' to ponder that he sang it after punishing his voice with the heavy demands of the song 'I'm Down' earlier that day. 'But,' he smiles, 'I was only twenty-two. That's what you do at that age ... When we'd done, I thought: Oh, that sounds pretty nice. I hope nobody minds that it's just me.' As the first Beatle to step outside the group with a solo piece of music, he felt slightly apprehensive, but was comforted by the fact that the other three had said they could add nothing to it. Unity was of paramount importance to the Beatles in 1965.

At that point, his acoustic performance in the can, George Martin suggested something radical. Pleased with the session, the Beatles' producer adjourned with McCartney to look over his new home round the corner in Cavendish Avenue. 'Why don't we get some strings, a violin, a cello ... perhaps we could go for a very different sound. It sounds very nice, but perhaps it needs something.'

Paul was appalled at the thought. 'Are you *kidding*? The Beatles is a rock 'n' roll group! We can't end up sounding like Mantovani!' Wide though his tastes always were, Paul was already feeling exposed by the song's solo treatment, and he now felt defensive of the Beatles' reputation as the hippest band on the planet. He recoiled from the worry that something too syrupy might happen if strings were added.

Always the diplomat, George Martin tried another route. 'Let's try it, with, say, a string quartet. Just try it. If you hate it, we can wipe it and you can go back to playing it on your own.' He underlined his belief that it would not suit a full Beatles performance, but it sounded as if it needed some extra instrumentation.

Paul remembers: 'I said: "That sounds like a good deal." So I went round to George Martin's house and that's where we started to develop the process which was to be carried on to greater lengths as we got more and more into musical development later. He would sit at the piano and say: "OK, now what are the chords?' And then he'd say: "Normal string quartet voicing would be like this . . ." and I would ask for something different. My big inclusion was the cello bit at the seventh, in the middle. George said: "Mozart wouldn't have done that!"' McCartney retorted that if that was so, it should *definitely* be used! 'This became a joke among us. The Beatles would not take any rules; we were all about breaking rules.'

By that time, Paul had played 'Yesterday' on the grand piano at Wimpole Street. Peter Asher remembers telling him how much he admired the song. 'He said it would be the first song they'd ever done with strings,' Asher recalls. 'I thought he meant a traditional orchestra and said that would be great. He said no, a string quartet. I thought it sounded unusual, but it was right. So much hipper!'

The studio was booked for a two-hour session from 2pm on 17 June to complete 'Yesterday'. Paul recorded a new vocal overdub, but it was not used on the final record. He then met the musicians who would comprise the string quartet, though they were not named as such. Because he lacked a formal education, Paul felt slightly intimidated at the prospect of talking about serious music with such players. 'I'd like to talk more with classical players,' he said at the time, 'but they ask you how you'll want it – legato, fortissimo, or what. All I can say to them is: you just *feel* it.'

As they walked into the studio to play their scored parts for 'Yesterday', Paul remembers that he was still wary of what effect they might have on a song which he felt needed simplicity above all else. The quartet had been a routine booking by George Martin and his secretary (and later wife), Judy Lockhart-Smith. Tony Gilbert was first violinist, and nominal leader; the second violinist was Sidney Sax; Spanish-born Francisco Gabarro played cello; and Kenneth Essex viola. All were session musicians prominent in British popular music in the 1960s, notably as regular members of the orchestra featured on BBC television's Thursday night chart programme *Top of the Pops*. Freelancers, in demand, they were hired regularly for string-laden albums supervised by George Martin and other record producers.

When Paul first heard the violins strike up, he frowned and quickly expressed his concern.

'George, what's going on? What's that shaking sound?'

'It's vibrato, Paul.'

'Do they have to play it like that?'

'Well,' said George, 'not all string players do.'

Paul's instant dislike of vibrato playing, whereby the fingers 'wobble' the note to add a certain richness, depth and resonance, was traceable to his dislike of 'anything schmaltzy', as he says now. 'I'd never worked with string players before this. I later found out that it was a trick fiddle players use, to cover up if they might go a little out of tune. They go both sides of the note. It sounded a little too gypsy-like for me; I said: excuse me, what's going on here? Have they got palsy or something? I asked George if they could play without vibrato. George said they could, but they'd have to play the notes more accurately.'

Martin, recalling the episode and Paul's 'definite bee in his bonnet' about vibrato violin sounds, asked Paul what he had against the technique. McCartney answered that it reminded him of Mantovani's lush strings, of the Victor Sylvester Orchestra which he'd heard on the radio as a child and which used that effect from the violin. Wide though his interests were in music, there was a line, never to be crossed, between rich, fine music and over-the-top cornball. Vibrato represented that to him.

Martin asked Tony Gilbert, the first violinist and spokesman for the quartet, if the players could drop the vibrato effect. 'So then they played it straight, note for note, without vibrato. It sounded, to my ears and to everyone's but Paul's, really harsh, staid. Paul said he liked it better. So his wish was met. But of course the musicians found it very hard to drop their usual style of playing, so a little vibrato, but not much, crept back.'

Paul sums up his view: 'When they dropped the vibrato, it sounded stronger. Before, it had sounded quite classical enough. Now it was no longer like the old gypsy violinist playing round a camp fire! It was ... on the money!' Francisco Gabarro, whose 'blue' cello sound helped to stamp the atmospheric instrumental accompaniment, remembered meeting Paul in the EMI canteen after the string quartet session. 'Paul said: "Well, my God, we have a winner there!" I said: "Well, congratulations to you."'

George Martin had written out the score, Paul adding considerably to it with some original ideas. For a twenty-two-year-old international pop idol to be immersing himself in violin and cello sounds in mid-1965 was unheard of, but 'He got very enthusiastic about the whole thing,' Martin remembers. 'It was Paul's idea, for example, to feature that cello line at the end of the second middle-eight, where there is a "blue" cello note. It's a minor against a major. Paul thought of that, and I wished it had been me. John Lennon fell in love with that particular sound when he first heard it.' McCartney also advanced the idea of the first violin holding the high note in the final section.

'We were writing the score as we went along,' says Paul. 'He said sevenths wouldn't fit in with a baroque sound. I said: "Put it in!" That was a good thing about working with George. He would say: "You can't double a third [note]." I would say: "You wanna bet?" George was very good at breaking the rules of music. He couldn't have produced the Beatles if he hadn't been willing to do those things.'

Kenneth Essex remembers the actual time spent by him and the other three string players on dubbing their strings as short. 'We were actually booked for two hours, but were there for less than that. As far as we were concerned, we were just turning up for a normal session and the fact that it was Paul McCartney was not something that would have made a big difference to us in those years. We played for everybody. George Martin put the parts in front of us and we played them. We didn't realize it was going to be a smash hit.'

They were paid by the Musicians' Union scale: Tony Gilbert, as leader, received £6.15s., while Essex, Gabarro and Sax were paid five guineas (£5.5s.). Laurie Gold was paid £1.10s. for copying the parts and there was a £2 secretarial fee.

The string session for 'Yesterday' therefore cost EMI a grand total of £26. George Martin was paid the fixed fee of £15 for all rights to his arrangement, and the Beatles, as a matter of course in all their recording work, received £7 each from EMI for performing on each session; since it was considered a Beatles session, Lennon, Harrison and Starr would have qualified for this payment, which was always paid in addition to their royalty.

'The string players didn't recall anything about the song to me,' George Martin says. 'It was just another job for them. In those days, people thought the Beatles were going to be a nine-day wonder. Even then, in 1965, people were saying: "It's bound to

peter out soon."' After the session, Paul autographed his producer's musical annotation with the words: 'YESTERDAY', written by
Paul McCartney, Mozart and George Martin.'

The tonality of Paul's voice delivery was remarkable. Though
the lyrics were somewhat sentimental, he stopped short of sounding lachrymose. There was a commanding authority about his
singing, laced with a frailty that was destined to touch many
millions of hearts. He had displayed no diffidence whatsoever. 'It
was goose pimple time,' Paul admits today. 'When I heard the
strings working on it, I thought: oh, gosh, this *is* going to work.
I'd not heard strings on my kind of pop record before. "Save the
Last Dance for Me" [the Drifters hit] was the first strings I'd
heard on a pop record. That was great, innovative. But this was
not strings on "Yesterday". It was a little baroque string quartet. I
then realized George had been spot-on with his decision. When
we'd finished, one of the blokes in the studio came up to me and
said: "Very nice song." He didn't have to do that. It swelled the
ego.'

That night, quietly euphoric, Paul adjourned to a favourite
Beatles hang-out, the Ad Lib Club in Leicester Place. 'I saw Terry
Doran, a mate of ours, and I said: "I just recorded this *great* song.
It's *so good*!" Later Terry told me he thought I was such an arro-
gant bastard, saying that.'

Next day, Paul telephoned Dick James, the Beatles' music
publisher. Excitedly, Paul told him: 'I've just recorded a new song
. . . and I want you to make it song of the year.' Paul went on to
describe it as very different from anything Dick would have heard
from the Beatles. James immediately rang George Martin to
arrange to hear 'Yesterday'. He remembered it as 'Scrambled
Eggs', but now, with potent lyrics, it was something special. To
the ears of James, whose own music was rooted in the era of
crooning ballads, it was a revelation. The Beatles had, for two
years, triumphed mostly as a young, lively beat group. But here
was a fully matured sound.

James rang Paul back. 'That's wonderful,' he said, confirming
that it would be 'easy' to promote such a sound into a hit. Paul
McCartney and a string quartet! The sound was stupendous, the
novelty value amazing.

Brian Epstein's wildest dreams had come true. By 1965 the Beatles, whom he had vowed would be 'bigger than Elvis', were a worldwide phenomenon. He had helped to turn four leather-clad teenagers from the Liverpool Cavern into adored Establishment figures. Royalty's nod of approval with the MBE was augmented by sixteen-year-old Prince Charles's enthusiasm for the new sound of British pop. He shaped his hair Beatle-style, but when the press said he was aligning himself with Paul, John, George and Ringo, he said defensively that he had looked that way since he was two years old. At Windsor Castle, he played Beatles and Rolling Stones records at his teenage parties.

Epstein's master plan was complete. On 15 August, at New York's Shea Stadium, the crowning moment in their touring days came when 55,600 fans, the record for any pop concert at that time, saw the Beatles perform. The glamour of touring, however, had long passed for the Beatles. It had become a gruelling charade in which they could not hear their own music above the screams, and the exhaustion caused by life on the road had lost its appeal. Epstein sensed during that USA trek that their days on the road were numbered; and when that happened, his role as a manager would inevitably diminish.

The Beatles were now serious studio musicians whose 1965 albums, *Help!* and *Rubber Soul*, magnified their reputation. As Epstein watched their growth with palpable pride, he also saw himself as the unifier who would paper over any cracks when the Beatles were threatened with internal friction. In awe of the song-writing axis of John and Paul, he considered them 'very fine, extraordinary young men . . . I don't believe anything like them will happen again and I believe that happen is the word, since no one could have *created* anything in show business with such appeal and magnetism.'

'Yesterday', however, posed a problem for Epstein. A classical music enthusiast, he considered it 'exquisite'.* But as the first

---

* Brian Epstein had wide tastes in music, originally preferring the classics. Broadcasting on BBC's *Desert Island Discs* on 18 November 1964, he named two Paul McCartney compositions among his eight records to be taken on his imaginary desert island: 'She's a Woman', performed by the Beatles, and 'All My Loving', performed by the George Martin Orchestra. Classical music, including his favourites, Sibelius and Bach, dominated his other choices.

record made by a solo Beatle, it was political dynamite. George Martin knew it could be a hit but felt it should probably be released as a McCartney single.

'I actually went to Brian and said: "What are you going to call this? Is it Paul McCartney?" And he looked at me very sternly and said: "No. It is the Beatles." He did not want to divide his holy quartet. Though it wasn't the Beatles at all, it had to remain so, as part of their recordings. I don't think it irritated Paul at the time, because he considered himself to be a Beatle above all other things.'

Epstein might have resisted Martin's lobbying for a solo credit because, as Beatles manager, he was wary of McCartney, an odd fact since Paul had a far more ambitious and pragmatic outlook than John in defining the Beatles' goal of world success. And Paul's musical tastes paralleled Epstein's.

Writing in his autobiography, *A Cellarful of Noise*, published in 1964, Brian summarized the caution with which he approached Paul:

> Paul can be temperamental and moody and difficult to deal with but I know him very well and he me. This means that we compromise on our clash of personalities. He is a great one for not wishing to hear about things and if he doesn't want to know he switches himself off, settles down in a chair, puts one booted foot across his knee and pretends to read a newspaper, having consciously made his face an impassive mask.
>
> But he has enormous talent and inside he has a great tenderness and great feeling which are sometimes concealed by an angry exterior. I believe that he is the most obviously charming Beatle with strangers, autograph hunters, fans and other artists. He has a magnificent smile and an eagerness both of which he uses, not for effect, but because he knows they are assets which will bring happiness to those around him.
>
> Paul is very much a world star, very musical with a voice more melodic than John's, and therefore more commercially acceptable. Also, and this is vital to me, he has great loyalty to the other Beatles and to the organization around him. Therefore, I ignore his moods

and hold him in high esteem. I would not care to lose
him as a friend.

Not only did Epstein veto any suggestion that Paul should be
named as a soloist on the record; he decreed that since it was not
typical of the Beatles' sound, it should not even be released as a
single. George Martin, carrying a torch for the song, knew better
than to press for what he believed would have been democratic: a
single released under Paul's name. But McCartney had no illu-
sions. Considering himself part of a unit, he did not even bother
to mention 'Yesterday' as a potential single. It was, he says now,
too different from the Beatles' image in 1965 to be viewed as a
bestselling British release.

It would have caused far too many ripples, and, in Paul's view,
it was regarded by many 'insiders' to be too radical a departure
from the Beatles' image to be considered. The Beatles were not
yet ready to step outside their gilded musical cage; coming a year
before their pathfinding album *Revolver* and two years before *Sgt
Pepper's Lonely Hearts Club Band*, 'Yesterday' was far too McCartney, far too much of a break with their tradition, and perhaps
even too close to traditional popular music to be a blockbuster
Beatles single for the masses. A more muscular sound was expected. And so, in Britain, 'Yesterday' was scheduled to join,
illogically, the thirteen songs that formed the soundtrack album
from the Beatles' film *Help!* Released in August 1965, this
featured such future winning songs as 'You're Going to Lose That
Girl' and 'You've Got to Hide Your Love Away'.

'We had a stupid policy, which seemed to make sense at the
time,' says George Martin, 'that any track we put on an album was
not to be issued as a single. And vice versa; a single made for that
purpose did not go on an album.'

Because Beatles lyrics were scarcely scrutinized in the 1960s, the
pathos of the song bypassed the critics. It was considered merely
nostalgic, or even 'mawkish', Paul running amok with the treacle.
Its deeper possibilities as a piece of writing from within Paul's
psyche were lost, as they were on the Lennon film title track
'Help!'. Analysing that song later, after the Beatles years, John
admitted that it was a cry from within himself during the wild experiences of Beatlemania. This marked a contrasting response by
the two men to their success and how to deal with it. Paul says

'Yesterday' was not a commentary on his life in the Beatles, while John said 'Help!' was just that. Midway through the euphoria of the Beatles years, marching forward creatively, the two architects of the world's greatest pop group were exploring their inner selves in two of their most significant pieces of work. 'Yesterday' and 'Help!' were signposts, invisible at the time, that the Fab Four moptops were slowly emerging as individuals.

'Paul's song showed that there was life within the Beatles as well as the group identity,' George Martin says. 'What kept the Beatles head and shoulders above everyone else is that they were prepared to change, do different things. No one record was a carbon copy of another. We never fell into the *Star Wars Two* syndrome, remaking something under a new title.'

With 'Yesterday' lying virtually dormant on the *Help!* album, neither McCartney nor Martin had any vision of the golden future life of this maverick of a song. 'Paul had absolutely no idea of its potential and neither had I,' George Martin admits. 'I knew it was a good song and that making a record of it would be worthwhile, but I never could have predicted that it would eventually become such a classic.'

Flanked by its neighbouring tracks on the album, 'I've Just Seen a Face' and 'Dizzy Miss Lizzy', 'Yesterday' did not even attract much radio airplay in Britain. In a vintage year for pop records, it was considered by some to be a pleasing novelty sound, and some called it Paul's soppy indulgence. In later years, Beatles fans would carp at the running order on the *Help!* album which caused 'Yesterday' to precede the raucous 'Dizzy Miss Lizzy'. 'But we did that kind of thing for a reason,' Paul says, adding that sequencing was a co-operative decision which also involved George Martin. 'It was as if to say: "Ah, that was a nice soft ballad. But this is what we're like as well: *rock 'n' roll!*"'

'Yesterday' generated more querulousness than serious analysis by the critics. A few gossips and national newspaper columnists, always hungry for a Beatles scandal, pointed out that McCartney had been in the studio alone and that this was the result: shock, horror, a solo Beatles performance with strings instead of Lennon, Harrison and Starr!

Were they splitting up? So soon? Was this the first chink of trouble in the ranks? The Beatles story had now been running successfully for two-and-a-half years, and that was reckoned to be quite enough for a pop act. The Beatles were special, but new heroes were needed: from America came the urgent sounds of Bob Dylan, praised to the hilt by McCartney and Lennon, and a profound influence on articulate writers like them.

The innovation of using a string quartet received very few merit points, either. 'Yesterday' was glossed over as an oddball, a gimmicky, tangential 'make-weight' for the soundtrack album of a film that attracted considerable attention.

A slice of deadpan humour marked the world live première of 'Yesterday' in Britain. John Lennon would later describe 1965 as his 'fat Elvis' period, in which he lived smugly in the stockbroker belt, twenty miles from London, 'like standing at a bus stop, waiting for something to happen'. Paul, gripped more by the northern ethic of aspiration and perspiration, worked harder than John. And they were still treading the boards of traditional British show business.

In retrospect, the idea of an act the size of the Beatles, who bestrode the world of show business like a colossus, playing a seaside theatre in England three years after their breakthrough seems incredible. But Epstein clung to his basic policy of covering all fronts, exploiting every record to the limit. And so the first of August 1965 found the Beatles at the ABC Theatre, Blackpool, for a live performance of an ITV all-round entertainment show called *Blackpool Night Out*. Joining them on the bill were such bastions of show-business orthodoxy as husband-and-wife singers Teddy Johnson and Pearl Carr, the Lionel Blair Dancers and compères/comedians Mike and Bernie Winters. At rehearsal, sitting over the edge of the stage with his legs dangling over the pit, Paul strummed his song and told the show's orchestra: 'I've got a new song I'd like to try'. They applauded when he stopped playing. Leader Bob Sharples quickly wrote parts for the string section. 'That sounds great, Bob', Paul said. And 'Yesterday' went into the programme.

'Thank you,' said George Harrison's flat-vowelled voice on that TV show as the group finished 'Ticket to Ride' to loud applause. 'We'd like to do something now that we've never, ever done before. And it's a track off our new LP. And this song's called "Yesterday" . . . and so, *for Paul McCartney of Liverpool, opportunity knocks*.' (George's words were a satirical dig at a well-established TV show of that title which was televised weekly in those years;

its compère, Hughie Green, used seven such words to introduce the contestants.)

With backing tapes of strings, Paul, dressed neatly in the dark Beatles suit with black tie, performed his début with considerable aplomb. The screams that followed caused John, as often, to murmur 'Shurrup' to the audience before wryly introducing their next number. In what could be seen as a gentle jibe at Paul's acoustic success, Lennon introduced 'Help!' as ' . . . our latest record, or our latest electronic noise, depending on whose side you're on.'

It was extremely hip to be English in 1965, the year Swinging London was born. Ablaze in a kaleidoscope of multicoloured fresh fashions, Mary Quant's new creation the miniskirt and boutiques with names like Granny Takes a Trip and Hung on You, London was powered by a new optimism.

The year in which 'Yesterday' arrived in the recording studio was also the most fertile in popular music. The notion that 1967, the Summer of Love, with its headline-hitting flower power, kaftans and 'Hey, man' affability was as creative as 1965 is misplaced. A milestone though it was, the Beatles' *Sgt Pepper's Lonely Hearts Club Band* in 1967, together with the hippy dream of Haight-Ashbury, San Francisco, and George Harrison's persuasive forays into Indian music, did not compare with the eventfulness of the year of 1965. That year yielded an intensity, a synergy and a body of pop music classics unequalled.

Restlessness and creativity were all round us in 1965. It was not all good news, but the backdrop of events for the year formed the most perfect snapshot to define a remarkable decade. Sir Winston Churchill died, aged ninety-one. President Lyndon Johnson sent US warplanes to North Vietnam in January. Six months later, at precisely the time Paul was in the studio recording 'Yesterday', America's first ground troops went to fight Vietcong bases.

In London, a very hip photographer named David Bailey astonished the media by wearing not a suit but a crewneck sweater at his marriage to actress Catherine Deneuve. Today such a casual look sounds like a non-event. In 1965 it was a significant news item, reflecting the New Liberation. Liverpool won the FA Cup for the first time. Edward Heath succeeded Sir Alec Douglas-Home as leader of the Conservative Party, while the Labour

Government of Beatle-admiring Premier Harold Wilson announced an 'experimental' 70mph speed limit.

Three months before McCartney was in the studio recording 'Yesterday', 'Mods' and 'Rockers' had been rampaging along the seafront at Brighton, chucking deckchairs at each other. Lunch for two at one of Paul's favoured restaurants, the tile-floored Trattoria Terrazza in Romilly Street, Soho ('The chic-est, despite Swinging London's fickleness,' said *Queen* magazine), cost under £4 for two, including wine. At the Savoy Grill, also with a glass or two, lunch was £6.

The Savoy Hotel was where Bob Dylan held court that year. With his songs 'Blowin' in the Wind' and 'The Times They Are a-Changin'' already established as anthems, he renounced his role as exclusively a folk singer, adopting rock 'n' roll in 1965 with the electric ignition of a sensational new single, 'Subterranean Homesick Blues', and the landmark album *Bringing It All Back Home*.

Sounds as vital as that, as evolutionary as 'Yesterday', were all over the airwaves in 1965 and made Friday night viewing of *Ready Steady Go!* (the ITV programme hosted by Cathy McGowan and Keith Fordyce) mandatory. Here were the Righteous Brothers with the majestic beauty of the orchestral sound produced by Phil Spector on 'You've Lost That Lovin' Feelin''. McCartney's early favourites the Everly Brothers, returning with the beauty of 'Love Is Strange'. Sonny and Cher gave us the catchy 'I Got You Babe', and the magic of Tamla Motown was never more forceful, with the Supremes offering 'Stop! In the Name of Love' and 'Back in My Arms Again', plus Junior Walker's 'Shotgun', the Temptations 'My Girl', and the Miracles singing the Smokey Robinson jewel, 'Tracks of My Tears'.

The Walker Brothers made their impact with Scott Walker's resonant vocal on 'Make It Easy on Yourself' and 'My Ship Is Coming In'. There was the Lovin' Spoonful with 'Do You Believe in Magic?', the Byrds' 'Turn, Turn, Turn', Dusty Springfield's 'Some of Your Lovin'' and Stevie Wonder's 'Uptight (Everything's Alright)'.

Georgie Fame's splendidly upbeat 'Yeh Yeh' contrasted with the Rolling Stones' earliest compositions by Mick Jagger and Keith Richards, their anthems 'The Last Time' and '(I Can't Get No) Satisfaction'. The Yardbirds began a string of hits with 'For Your Love' – their guitarist, Eric Clapton, thought it was too brazenly commercial, so he quit in order to join an authentic blues band. From America came more masterpieces such as Martha and the Vandellas' 'Nowhere to Run' and the Drifters' 'At the Club'.

The year of 1965 had begun with the Who, whom Paul McCartney nominated at that time his favourite group, launching their stuttering, barrier-breaking sound on 'I Can't Explain', followed by 'Anyway Anyhow Anywhere' and, by the year's end, the sound of 'My Generation', with Pete Townshend's visionary line, 'Hope I die before I get old.' In America, three British acts reached the top with unlikely songs: Herman's Hermits with 'I'm Henry VIII I Am'; the Dave Clark Five with 'Over and Over'; and Wayne Fontana and the Mindbenders with 'Game of Love'.

Thirty years later, such acts would reunite for concerts with names like the Solid Gold Sixties Tour, attracting packed concert halls around Britain. It was that kind of year. If the Beatles had begun pop's revolution in 1963, they were still at its cutting edge two years on, for they completed 1965 with *Rubber Soul*. Featured here were such inventive perennials as 'Michelle', 'In My Life', 'Girl', 'I'm Looking Through You', 'Norwegian Wood.' and 'Run for Your Life'. The birth certificate of 'Yesterday' was set amid pop's halcyon days.

In middle-of-the-road music, which the battalions of Beatles and Rolling Stones fans were alarmed to see had not been ejected by the revolution, well-crafted songs abounded. And a huge audience proved that straight popular music had an endless shelf life. Tom Jones made his first big impact with 'It's Not Unusual'. The Seekers scored with 'The Carnival Is Over', Val Doonican with 'Walk Tall'. And the surprise biggest-selling British single of 1965 was a ballad, 'Tears', sung by Liverpool-born comedian Ken Dodd. Originally recorded by Rudy Vallee in 1929, Dodd's version sold a million, stayed at the top of the chart for six weeks, and polarized adults and teenagers.

And it was another British male singer, Matt Monro, who was first to make 'Yesterday' a hit single. This highly respected ballad-singer, who had enjoyed a substantial hit with 'Portrait of My Love' to begin his illustrious career, was managed by Don Black, who would later join the executive staff of Brian Epstein's organization. Monro, a big admirer of the Beatles and especially of Paul's melodic strengths, was also produced on the Parlophone label by George Martin.

Sitting at his home in Wembley, north London, watching the

Beatles on *Blackpool Night Out*, Monro was captivated by 'Yesterday' and by Paul's singing. Next day he phoned George Martin to ask when the song was to be released as a single. Puzzled at being told there were no plans to do so, Monro jumped in: 'Can I do it, then?' He did not, however, intend it to be his new single.

Going into the studio, Monro asked Martin if he would write the score. 'That was most difficult,' Martin recalls, 'because I had already scored it for Paul and I didn't want to do it any other way. I did re-score it for Matt, and produced his record with a string orchestra. We had French horn and I changed the harmonies. All the things Paul would hate were there, but it worked for Matt Monro.'

The singer's widow, Mickie, remembers that he planned its inclusion on his next album. She attended his session and clearly recalls his elation when he had sung the song for the first time. 'Immediately he realized how beautiful it was and he thought it would make a very good single.' There was no opposition from Paul or anyone in the Beatles camp; a strong ballad had been 'covered' appropriately by the country's foremost male solo singer.

'Yesterday' achieved its first British chart entry with the mellow-voiced Matt Monro. Entering the Top 50 of the *Record Retailer*, then Britain's music trade weekly, on 21 October 1965, his single peaked at number eight, staying in the chart for twelve weeks.

The whole feeling of the ballad, robust yet sensitive, was perfectly tailored for the pure baritone voice of Monro, who loved to enunciate every vowel and consonant with a precision he had learned from studying Frank Sinatra albums. Paul McCartney does not have a favourite version of the song but he certainly greatly admires this, a remarkable testimony to Monro given the huge diversity of styles that were to follow in the interpretation of the song.

'There were certain songs Matt would never leave out of his stage show and from that moment, "Yesterday" was sung whenever he gave a performance,' Mickie Monro says. He went on to record four other McCartney compositions, 'Michelle', 'All My Loving', 'Here, There and Everywhere' and 'The Long and Winding Road', 'but "Yesterday" remained very special to him.'

Monro adopted the song as part of a short theatrical routine in his concerts. He carried a special stool with him, and over the piano introduction to 'Yesterday' he pulled the stool towards him, looking apprehensively towards it. The stool was too high for his short frame. He tipped it towards him to hit the height of his bottom and then slid up to it. Then he would start 'Yesterday' on an artificially high note: 'all my troubles seemed so far away . . . ' and then, looking down to the floor, 'Now it looks as though they're here to stay.'

While Matt Monro's single was being prepared for release, the second cover version, the first by a female, was recorded. At nineteen, Marianne Faithfull had achieved a meteoric rise in pop music. Discovered by Rolling Stones co-manager Andrew Oldham, she enjoyed a British and American hit with 'As Tears Go By', a ballad which, like 'Yesterday', was hardly typical of the work of its composers, Rolling Stones Mick Jagger and Keith Richards. It featured a full orchestral sound to accompany Faithfull's wavering, little-girl vocal.

With her husband, art gallery owner John Dunbar, Marianne Faithful was part of Paul McCartney's coterie and at her invitation he attended her recording session on 11 October 1965.* Featuring a 100-voice choir and sweeping strings, Marianne Faithfull gave the song a hymnal quality and, like many female singers to follow her, rephrased the lyric to indicate her belief that it was purely a love song: 'Why *he* had to go, I don't know, *he* didn't say . . .'

But while Marianne Faithfull was recording, Matt Monro's version was already climbing the British chart. Her version was rush-released and entered the Top 50 on 4 November 1965, peaking at thirty-six and remaining in the chart for four weeks.

Still the Beatles' version remained consigned to the *Help!* album. But America saw it differently, more commercially. Its route to a very different status in the US came about through a situation which the Beatles, George Martin and Brian Epstein abhorred –

---

* Marianne Faithfull's recording session took place at Decca Records' studios in West Hampstead, London, where on New Year's Day 1962 the Beatles had failed an audition for the label. It was at Marianne's session that Paul met the producer-arranger Mike Leander, whom Paul invited eighteen months later to score his new song 'She's Leaving Home' when George Martin was busy at a Cilla Black recording session.

the assumed autonomy of the Capitol record label, which released their music in the US and Canada.

Since their earliest successes, the Beatles had proudly and astutely charted their own destiny, particularly in deciding what went on to their albums, what singles would be released and at what time; and what cover art would grace their work. They liked to set their own pace, tone, and timing of what came from the studio. In America, Capitol, which had initially been reluctant to accept the Beatles, had adopted a far more aggressive policy of marketing, and, as George Martin recalls: 'Having refused to take the Beatles three times in their early days, once they did sign them they assumed power of life and death over their work. They acted as though they alone had produced and created them. They re-arranged all the songs on the albums I did with the Beatles, took titles off and put together extra albums.' Such unilateralism infuriated the Beatles and everyone around them but they were powerless to stop it; the contract gave Capitol complete freedom.

For 'Yesterday', however, that assertive American policy was about to work with a fine strategy. The Beatles had triumphed in the US a year later than in their homeland, so by 1965, enormously popular though they were, Americans still regarded them as a teen-appeal rock 'n' roll group. The USA certainly did not expect a quiet ballad like 'Yesterday' to come from the Beatles.

But Capitol decided to issue it as a single. As its partnered B-side, they chose the Ringo Starr vocal on 'Act Naturally', which was a stage favourite. Recorded on the same day as the 'Yesterday' string and vocal overdub, and featuring Paul harmonizing and George Harrison playing guitar, this had been a number one country and western hit for singer Buck Owens. A lively song about show-business success, it was a buoyant contrast with the introspection of 'Yesterday'.

There was a precedent for the American decision. A record called 'A Lover's Concerto', sung by a female trio called the Toys, was getting a lot of radio play. Based on Bach's Minuet in G, the song was one of the first mergers of pop with the classics. It would eventually become a million-seller and reach number two in the American charts, causing eyebrows to be raised by classical music buffs.

'Yesterday' was released in the US on 13 September 1965, two weeks after the Beatles' twenty-five-city tour of the USA and

Canada. *Billboard*, the leading US music trade magazine, reviewed the single on 11 September 1965 in its 'Top Twenty Spotlights' section, which featured records expected to reach the top division of the publication's Hot Hundred best-sellers. 'Paul goes it alone,' *Billboard* said, 'on a Dylan-styled piece of material. Backed by strings, he displays a rich, warm ballad style. Good sound.' Paul's ground-breaker was reviewed alongside future hits by Herman's Hermits ('Just a Little Bit Better') and Dino, Desi and Billy ('Not the Lovin' Kind').

Not surprisingly, 'Yesterday' found no place in the twelve songs chosen by the Beatles to perform during their American concerts. No one would have known the song. Indeed, it would not be performed by the Beatles in concert anywhere in 1965. But Paul, particularly, was pleased when Capitol told him it was going to be released as a single. Would he, they asked politely, consider singing it on *The Ed Sullivan Show*? The power of that television programme was huge, as the Beatles knew from the previous year, when 73 million had watched their US début and Beatlemania had begun in the US as a direct result.

Recorded on 14 August and televized to the US by CBS–TV on the night of 12 September, by which time the Beatles had returned to Britain, Paul's first performance of the song on US soil was received rapturously. After the familiar 'Ticket to Ride', George Harrison stepped up to the microphone and, in the dull choice of words that marked all their comments to their audiences, he intoned: 'Thank you very much ... we'd like to carry on now with a song from our new album in England and it will be out in America shortly. And it's a song featuring just Paul, and it's called "Yesterday".'

When the screaming from the studio audience subsided, Paul's voice sounded light and confident against his acoustic guitar and a taped background of strings. When John Lennon stepped up to the microphone after Paul's performance he sounded a mite envious, or determined to prick Paul's pride. 'Thank you, Paul,' Lennon said. 'That was just like him.'

The timing of that television screening was perfect. 'Yesterday' as a single was released across America the very next day. For millions of Americans watching, it was an extraordinary moment in the escalating Beatles story. Here was an adult piece of popular music from those cute moptops who had seized the hearts of the young. 'Hey,' said parents of Beatles people and other observers. 'Maybe those noisy Beatles can actually play real music!'

'When I look at the footage,' Paul says now, 'I wonder how I ever got the nerve to step out front and sing that on *The Ed Sullivan Show*.' It must have been the swagger of youth, he believes, that carried him through. Reviewing that Sullivan show appearance, the *New York Times* noted that the song 'had the haunting quality of a folk lament that left the girls in the studio a little uncertain as to how they were supposed to react.'

It was, also, the most significant solo moment for any Beatle, since hitherto they had all been careful not to instigate anything that might cause rivalry. 'It was slightly strange for me. It might have looked as if I was trying to be Cliff Richard. In the band, nobody had ever been the front man. We used to kind-of fight about it in Hamburg, in those late-night bars. "Who's gonna be the leader? We've got to have a leader for the group."'

They would all demur, Paul remembers. 'Some people, like Bert Kaempfert in Hamburg, would want to pull me out. And Allan Williams – I remember one drunken evening saying to him: "No way, man. Get outta here! It's a band. You take us all or nothing." They thought: he could be the front guy, the Cliff Richard. He's cute. He could have the girls screaming at him. I was inside that shell, living a completely different life, but one or two people said can we make it Paul and the Beatles? I said: "No, way, it was a *verboten* thing. No no no no no. No question of that." Then people asked if John could be called the leader. Larry Parnes had wanted to pull John out. It was Long John and the Silver Beatles. No, we said, it's all or nothing. We were a foursome.*

Recording 'Yesterday' as a single track for an album – 'I think we all regarded it as a filler on the *Help!* album,' says Paul – 'was one thing. But stepping out front with it on television in the USA was different.' It wasn't even the Beatles featuring Paul McCartney, though the record label said, absurdly: The Beatles. Unmistakably, this was McCartney alone.

---

* The popular German bandleader Bert Kaempfert, who wrote Frank Sinatra's world hit 'Strangers in the Night', signed the Beatles to their first record contract, with Deutsche Grammophon, during their Hamburg years. Allan Williams was the Beatles' first manager, in Liverpool. Larry Parnes promoted their first tour anywhere (of Scotland).

'The old bugbear had come back,' Paul says. 'I felt: I hope they don't think I'm stepping out, because there was always that danger in taking a solo. There was an unwritten law that you didn't do it.'

Fuelled by the massive boost of the coast-to-coast *Ed Sullivan Show* performance, 'Yesterday' was an instant, colossal hit. Soaring into the *Billboard* magazine Hot Hundred, the record entered at number forty-five on 25 September 1965. The next week it had leapt to number three, sandwiched between Barry McGuire's anti-war song 'Eve of Destruction' (at number two) and Britain's Dave Clark Five with the vapid 'Catch Us if You Can' (at number four).

The next week, 9 October, 'Yesterday' sat proudly atop the American singles chart, having ousted the tramping beat song 'Hang On Sloopy' by the McCoys. After occupying the top position for four weeks, 'Yesterday' was displaced by the Rolling Stones' 'Get off of My Cloud'. 'Yesterday' dropped back to number three, then eleven, twelve, thirteen and twenty-six, ending up where it had entered, at number forty-five, before disappearing from the chart after a creditable run of eleven weeks. In its first ten days of American release it had sold a million copies and its final sales totalled more than double that figure in the US alone.

Such was the spectacular impact of the Beatles by 1965 that Paul says he does not recall being especially surprised when 'Yesterday' hit the top in the US. 'We'd had so much practice at being good and succeeding. I call it a staircase. We started off in Liverpool, where it went wild at the Cavern. We went to Hamburg, nothing happened to start with, then we were IT. We went to Peterborough and places like that. From nothing at those places, we were IT. In dance-halls, suddenly we were *the* act. On television and radio shows, suddenly we were the act they were asking back. So I think surprise isn't quite the right word.

'People always say to me: do you think you and John were great? I say: "We were fantastic"; and people used to think we were conceited. You have to have a certain amount of conceit if you've done that well. It would be kind of stupid, goofy, to say we're no good. It was embarrassing, though, because we were supposed to say [adopts proper English accent]: "Oh yes, I was very surprised."

'But I don't think we were. I don't think I was. We had a hell of a lot of confidence in ourselves. And it was difficult not to have confidence if you look at that staircase, the track record. Everywhere we'd gone had gone on fire. So we got used to being The Ones. The group out of Liverpool, the group out of England, the group in America, the group in every country in the whole world. Once you've conquered the whole world, nothing surprises you. Even your solo zooming to the top.'

'Yesterday''s life on albums, however, continued to be bizarre. While the British album *Help!* sold a quarter of a million very quickly, a future even stranger than its British destiny awaited the song on an American album. Capitol, having excised it from the US soundtrack album for the *Help!* movie, waited until June 1966 to schedule its release within the most controversially packaged album in Beatles history.

The title was accurate enough: using the hit single as a promotional thrust, Capitol called it *Yesterday ... And Today*. The packaging of the LP was radical, confronting the Beatles' safe image in the rapidly changing psychedelic era. The album cover, which was to pass into Beatles folklore, was both weird and shocking, and became known as the 'butcher cover'.

In a photographic studio at 1 The Vale, Chelsea on 25 March 1966, one of their regular photographers, Robert Whitaker, decided to experiment by dressing the Beatles in butcher's smocks and draping them with lumps of bloody meat. Plastic dolls, torn limb from limb and smeared with blood from the oozing flesh, completed the props for the smiling Beatles. Though he had not thought of the idea, John Lennon was the happiest of the four about the plan, believing it would help debunk their cuddly mop-top image. His sick sense of humour delighted in the unfolding drama.

The gory pictures that Whitaker took were a clumsy attempt to redefine the Beatles, conceptualizing their appearance. John Lennon told me he considered the hideous picture 'as relevant as Vietnam', and Paul, in a remark which would probably embarrass him today, commented: 'Very tasty meat'.

George Harrison described the picture session as 'sick', but John added that the Beatles did not mind doing anything that was interesting. A colour picture from the session, front-paged by *Disc* and *Music Echo*, drew a mixed response from British fans. Complaints that it was disgusting contrasted with a description of the picture as showing 'harmony, loyalty and a perfect understanding of each other'. Some readers wrote that they were becoming vegetarians immediately as a result, and that the Beatles should be ashamed of such 'hideous gimmickry'.

It was hardly high art, more a poke at the established Beatles imagery. But in America, when the albums went from Capitol Records' printers to disc jockeys, Beatles regional fan club presidents, and record reviewers in the media, phone calls expressing fury poured into the Los Angeles and New York offices of Capitol.

Quickly withdrawing the album, the record company spent a weekend extricating 750,000 records from their 'butcher covers', replacing the sleeves with a new, anodyne picture of the Beatles standing around a trunk in the office of Brian Epstein, who was livid at the furore. But before all the offending covers could be dumped, some got through the net with the new picture simply stuck over the controversial shot. Some of the butcher covers therefore arrived in the shops in disguise and fans who bought these acquired what became a prized collectors' item among Beatles students. It continues to be so.

In Hollywood, Capitol Records boss Alan Livingston made a statement: 'The original cover, created in England, was intended as pop art satire. A sampling of public opinion in the United States indicates that the design is open to misinterpretation.' Photographer Whitaker explained that in instigating the photo session he had 'wanted to do a real experiment . . . the use of a camera as a means of creating situations'.

Although *Yesterday . . . And Today* was at the top of the US charts for most of the summer of 1966, featuring Paul's anthemic title, it was the first and only Beatles album to lose money for Capitol. The cover-art operation had cost an estimated $250,000 in labour pay for the factory workers, together with printing and transport costs.

At the time, Paul described critics of the butcher cover as 'soft'. It was the fate of his special song to be caught up in that album controversy, alongside its arrival on the music landscape as a watershed in Beatles music. Its impact on the psyche of America in 1965, and on the rest of the world beyond that year, was to be overwhelming.

4

Widening the Audience

'The song captured a yearning deep inside'

'Yesterday' was not merely a rare gem of a song; its journey from Wimpole Street, London, and Albufeira, Portugal, via EMI's London studios to its position as the world's most recorded song made a lot of waves. It changed the Beatles' reputation. And the song was the springboard for their own future and that of popular music in the 1960s and beyond. 'Yesterday' provided an artistic stepping stone between the teen idol stance of rock 'n' rollers and the dramatic musical innovators of the latter half of that decade, and those who lifted it to new levels in the 1970s. 'Yesterday' was evidence that the high energy of 'I Saw Her Standing There' and the raw appeal of rockers like 'I'm Down' were but a tiny fraction of the Beatles story.

The sound of 'Yesterday' with its stark lyrics, plus the persona of Paul McCartney out front, alone, with an acoustic guitar, together produced a definitive moment. Suddenly, *everyone* had to take the Beatles seriously as musicians. They were not simply rock 'n' rollers. Parents who had hitherto maintained that the Beatles were a scruffy pop group who got lucky now faced a surprising truth: they could actually write and sing a beautiful melodic ballad. To the sceptical minority who still considered the Beatles the preserve of the young, 'Yesterday' spoke a new, adult language.

It formed the base from which Paul, with John, would help to chart popular music's new horizons. And the effect of 'Yesterday' on a generation of people of all ages, particularly in America, was enormous.

When Paul scored a number one hit in the USA with 'Yesterday', the only serious attention it got was from the radio. Disc jockeys spoke of it superficially: 'Another great track from the Fab Four.' Teenagers walked around with tiny transistor radios pinned to their ears, and were to be seen sitting silently as if in prayer, waiting for Paul's dulcet-toned smash. *Rolling Stone* magazine had not yet been born; every city had a disc jockey claiming to have a special knowledge and relationship with the guys from Liverpool. The magazines aimed at girls were jammed with breathless prose about the Beatles' personalities. 16 magazine, *Teen Set*, *Teen Screen* and *Datebook* were the literary diet of the Beatles generation. In later years, *Crawdaddy*, *Circus* and *Creem* came as the emphasis of pop and singles switched to a more contemplative world of rock and albums.

While some cynics in Britain reckoned the Beatles had 'gone soft' with 'Yesterday', the mood in the USA was different. There, the public was able to celebrate a number one hit. Americans, delineating the difference in the characteristics of the two nations, took a positive, optimistic approach. 'Initially,' says Dennis Elsas, one of New York's most articulate disc jockeys on station WNEW, 'our parents considered the Beatles another part of rock 'n' roll that they couldn't understand. By the time "A Hard Day's Night" came, adults could see them as cute, not quite so dangerous. Hipper adults were mildly amused, and took an interest. But clearly, when they heard a song like "Yesterday" on the radio, they would not be turned off by the sound. The American view would be: Look, this group don't *just* write silly little rock songs! "Yesterday" was slow. There were strings, always a grabber for that audience, strings will always get you. When you watch a motion picture and the big swell comes, the strings come through and out comes your hankie; you shed a tear.'

'"Yesterday" was hugely popular on top forty stations which repeated their songs over and over. The song was so simple in its sadness. It touched us immediately in that part that responds to heartache; we all love to wallow a little bit and, as Elton John sings, sad songs say so much.'

'It's ambiguous, too. *Why she had to go/I don't know/she didn't say*. We all know that at some point we screwed up on something. But here we don't know if he's lost her for ever. I think we think he has. And that's sad. We can identify with that. The two Beatles songs prior to "Yesterday" that were closest to love songs were "And I Love Her" and "If I Fell". Those were not so powerful.

"And I Love Her" is just a declaration. "If I Fell" is anticipation. But "Yesterday" is about lost love.'

Rock 'n' roll, as Dennis Elsas says, is usually thought of as being loud and raunchy. 'But some of the most memorable rock 'n' roll artists are best known for their ballads. "Love Me Tender" is still probably one of Elvis Presley's most popular songs. Great rockers seem to have the ability to write one of those soul-stirring ballads which touches us deeply.'

And yet, as Elsas points out: 'The Paul bashing probably began with "Yesterday". People could then say: See, he was always a softie!' The song marked the moment, for many listeners, when Paul and John began to express themselves differently as well as in unison.

'I felt we did become more accessible to more people from "Yesterday",' Paul says. 'And that widening of our audience was my role within the group. People did think of me in terms of being the public relations man. I know John told Yoko I was the best PR person ever. I'm not sure he meant it altogether as a compliment at the time: But "Yesterday" helped. Even musicians like Buddy Rich had to say when they heard it: "Hey, wait a minute. I can't deny that . . ."'

While Paul McCartney was redirecting the course of the Beatles, eventually influencing his contemporaries, Bob Dylan was busy re-defining folk music. At the Newport Festival in July 1965, Dylan played electric guitar as he swung into 'Maggie's Farm' and stunned an audience who expected only acoustic guitar accompaniment from him. As he launched next into the song that would become one of his signatures, 'Like a Rolling Stone', the crowd booed, shouting: 'Play folk music: this is a sell-out! This is a folk festival! Get rid of that band!'

Dylan had entered the rock 'n' roll arena controversially, and he was to have a strong effect on the Beatles and on their music. But while *Time* magazine noted his impact, the unexpected sound of 'Yesterday' from the pen and voice of Paul McCartney went unobserved. New York's *Village Voice* did not even deign to mention the Beatles in 1965, except to denigrate *Help!*, the Beatles' new movie.

'Yesterday' was simply born too early, in the evolution of media criticism, to receive its proper due. Axiomatically, critical appraisal for the Beatles and the shifts in popular music and culture in the

1960s and 1970s came when the era had gone. In one sense, the passage of time lent perspective; in another, it meant that the focus on the Beatles' music around 1965 was cursory, even naïve, compared with the articulacy of rock criticism that has developed since the start of the 1970s and into the 1980s and 1990s. Nothing whatsoever, at the time of 'Yesterday''s arrival, pinpointed the significance and the potential of the song, commercially or artistically or even in the context of the Beatles' trajectory.

Britain fared better than the US in music coverage. *Melody Maker*, a weekly which originally leaned towards jazz, applauding singers of the calibre of Frank Sinatra and Peggy Lee and the kind of music Jim McCartney enjoyed, had started publication in 1926. Cynical about pop, the paper heralded the Beatles as too important to ignore; its coverage was intensive and measured, but it did campaign for the Beatles to be honoured by their own country before they received the MBE.

Paul took a particular interest in the *Melody Maker* Mailbag column, which was seething with lively invective from old-timers who insisted that the new rockers could neither play nor write music.

Yet *Melody Maker* and its rival, the bigger-selling *New Musical Express*, paid scant attention to 'Yesterday' and did not see either its commercial future or its pivotal significance. 'How long before "Yesterday" becomes a standard?' asked the *New Musical Express* on 5 November 1965, nearly two months after its American release. That was the only note of prescience about the song struck by the British music press. Other pop weekly papers in Britain, *Record Mirror* and *Disc*, centered on the personalities of the Beatles, the Rolling Stones and the latest hit-makers. The country had, like America, breathless magazines for the teen-girl market, with deliciously evocative names like *Fabulous*, *Petticoat*, *Mirabelle*, *Romeo*, *Roxy*, *Valentine*, *Boyfriend* and *Rave*. All focused on the Beatles as heart-throbs but scarcely mentioned their music, still less their perceptible switch of gear with 'Yesterday'. More serious attention lay ahead in 1967, the 'summer of love', when the Beatles released *Sgt Pepper's Lonely Hearts Club Band*.

Among artists and observers, there are profound reflections on the relevance of 'Yesterday' to the Beatles and the music scene and on the impact the song had on them personally. Little Richard, the rock 'n' roll giant whose falsetto style and delivery was a seminal influence on the raunchier side of McCartney's work, speaks eloquently of the song. Describing it as a 'masterpiece', Richard says: 'That made you see something; that changed them from their rock 'n' roll thing. I think "Yesterday" brought respect to the Beatles. They weren't just a bunch of rock 'n' roll kids screaming, imitating and impersonating. They showed that they had a definition of themselves: singing in their own rights. They showed they had the ingredients, too, and that the ingredients were for the whole world and for every race, creed and culture. And it's still lasting today.'

A year after he performed 'Yesterday', Paul, like the entire pop scene, was mesmerized by the outstanding album by the Beach Boys called *Pet Sounds*. Brian Wilson, the composing genius in that band, says that while he was not bowled over by the Beatles' early hit 'I Want to Hold Your Hand', their album *Rubber Soul* was the catalyst to his response. 'I tried *Pet Sounds* as an answer to *Rubber Soul* and I understood that Paul McCartney really liked that sound. And then they went in the studio and did *Sgt Pepper*! Damn! They exploded into creativity. It was a competitive thing but they were in a world of their own.'

Wilson admires many of the Beatles ballads and says of 'Yesterday': 'It's a very sad song. It makes you cry. In a sense, it's like looking back into the past which I do a lot myself, and I see what he means because sometimes when things get all messed up you start looking for other things that make you feel better. So I'm sure that's what he had in mind when he did that. Musically I thought it was very well done.'

Christopher Reeve, of *Superman* fame, remembers the division between adults and the young that existed before 'Yesterday' forced a rethink by the cynics. He recalls how as kids, many Americans were 'stunned' by the Beatles' hairstyles when they were first seen on *The Ed Sullivan Show* ' . . . and our parents were always saying they were not talented and they didn't have any musical ability. I remember how we used to defend them. I was studying piano at the time. The harmonies they got into, and the chord progressions – this was not just standard stuff, not just rock 'n' roll. But the song that really put it over the top, so that you could go to your parents and say: "These people are musicians", was "Yesterday". It was so unexpected from rock stars. And I think that's where parents, or at least my parents, were convinced that the Beatles were real musicians.'

One American parent whom the song certainly hooked was the mother of movie star Timothy Hutton, who was nominated for an Academy Award for his first film performance, in *Ordinary People*. 'We were living in Boston and my mother was a big Beatles fan, and she loved that song. The house was filled with Beatles songs and I have a real memory about that song.' As he heard the 'lovely beginning' to 'Yesterday' over and over from his upstairs room, Hutton remembers hearing his mother replaying the single and his thought as she did so: 'There she goes again! The two hundredth time today!'

An unforgettable memory of 'Yesterday''s impact comes from Chazz Palminteri, who played the intelligent gangster in Woody Allen's *Bullets Over Broadway*: 'I remember that song because I was making love to a girl in a motel and that song came on and I said: "what a great song this is!" And I leaned over and sat on the edge of the bed and I listened to the rest of the song. And she looked at me and she got really upset about it. And then we went back to doing what we were doing. So it's one of those things I never forgot. It's absolutely true.'

The adventurousness of 'Yesterday' was a compass for the executives in the recording studio. When the Beatles began their assault on America, 'every engineer, every musician, did everything they could to imitate,' says Phil Ramone, the top-pedigree producer who has worked with Frank Sinatra, Paul Simon, Billy Joel and many others, and who co-produced McCartney's single 'Once Upon a Long Ago' in 1987. 'The brilliance of these guys was about the way they opened up the doors to something else, musically. They did not want to stop. In those days, it was hard to put bass on the vinyl like they did. We copied.'

Guitarist Craig Chaquico of Starship describes 'Yesterday' as 'one of the first songs where I realized that the lyrics were just as important as the guitar part'. Until he heard that song, he went to concerts 'where the acoustics were so bad you couldn't understand the words anyway. And I just fell in love with melodies and how the music made you feel. But I remember hearing "Yesterday", even as a little kid. I didn't have that many yesterdays as a little boy but it still reminded me of the girl I fell in love with last summer. That's the key to real good music: if it reminds you of a personal experience, really touches you in a personal way. And that song did.'

The actor-writer John Patrick Shanley, who wrote *Moonstruck*, recalls that he used the Ray Charles version of 'Yesterday' in his play *Beggars in the House of Plenty*, in New York. 'I used it to evoke a tremendous feeling of sadness about one era of my life in the Bronx, to close the second act in that play. So it means a lot to me.' The underlying yearning and sadness of the song covers many situations, Shanley considers. 'You remember all things with a certain emotional passion that was powerful in your life, even if they were unhappy. And you want to return there to revel in that feeling, on occasion. When you do, and you listen to a song like "Yesterday", it can be a very powerful combination.'

Typical of the many millions of Beatles fans, Sue Weiner hung on their every record and every nuance of their spoken words. Today she is a magazine editorial director in New York City; at sixteen, she was growing up in Levittown, in Long Island. And she fell in love with Paul McCartney – primarily through 'Yesterday'.

What Paul offered to millions was the antidote of sensitivity and affection to contrast to the Beatles' rock 'n' roll drive. Citing Paul's singing of 'Till There Was You' as 'the unforgettable moment when America met its next romantic hero', Sue Weiner says: 'There were other incredible songs. Great songs, sad songs, soft songs, hard songs. Wonderful and beautiful songs. But they were only songs . . . until "Yesterday". Nothing rang as true. From the very first instant, the song captured a yearning deep inside and then, when that pure voice, ripe with emotion, rang out the very first word "Yesterday", we all knew this was a song that would last.'

Thirty years later, Sue Weiner remembers with clarity what she loved about 'Yesterday' on first hearing. 'It shattered the myth that rock 'n' roll had to be hard to decipher. I didn't have to play the song twenty times before I knew what Paul was saying. I didn't even have to write the lyrics down to memorize them. They were as clear as song lyrics can get. And "Yesterday" hit me at a time when I was not yet ready to leave my childhood behind.'

Still a serious Beatles student and non-fanatical McCartney devotee, she says, unashamedly misty-eyed: 'I didn't know how quickly this excitement would pass and I'd long to be back to this time . . . but even though my mind didn't know, my heart heard what Paul was trying to tell us all: treasure these joyous times. They are so rare and so precious. So even in my happy hysteria (and that's the state I was in most days during the height of Beatlemania) I knew that it wouldn't last for ever. And that's what made it all the more special, and incredibly poignant. That's what "Yesterday" is all about.'

For Sue Weiner and for millions, 'No other Beatle was harmonizing over Paul's voice, no other instrument was drowning him out, and it seemed as if he was singing direct to me.' As for the lyrics: 'For the first time as a Beatles fan I caught a glimpse into Paul's soul and saw a darker place. It's only years later that I realize it's a place where the past and the future merge. As fans, we looked to the Beatles to show us the way – and Paul was giving all of his fans one of the most important life lessons. We took it deep inside our souls. We knew that one day that song would take on an entirely different meaning. And because we had learned so early, we'd be able to accept it.'

Two major British artists who studied the revolutionary music of the Beatles were transfixed by 'Yesterday' upon its release. 'The moment I heard it, I knew it was a classic,' says Justin Hayward of the Moody Blues, who wrote 'Nights in White Satin' which has sold 5 million singles and has been recorded by 100 artists. He had just left his first band job, with Marty Wilde's Wildcats, when 'Yesterday' was released. Pointing out that nobody in pop music had tried the marriage of a pop song with a string quartet, Hayward suggests 'there was some influence, particularly in the opening, of Bob Dylan; there's an inversion that Paul uses on the open chord that reminds me of "The Times They Are a-Changin"'.

Immediately a Beatles song was released in those years, Hayward recollects, 'I would learn everything they did. I had to look at everything they did from a musician's point of view, not for stage work. First, with "Yesterday", I had to work out the right chord inversions on the second bar. So many people play that wrongly.

'The song became part of every musician's life,' he adds, 'because it has a perfection of simplicity, of sentiment, and of feel.

And that's what every songwriter hopes for. The choice of instruments is exactly right on the record; the McCartney and
George Martin arrangement was just ideal. I think I knew in my
heart that McCartney and Lennon were no longer writing all their
material together. That was Paul's expression completely. I don't
think it needed to be a single. Everything from their albums got
played anyway. If Paul had never written another song, before or
afterwards, "Yesterday" would put him among the greatest songwriters of all time.'

Cliff Richard, echoing that view, shares Justin Hayward's
thought about the guitar work. 'One of "Yesterday"'s secrets is
that it's deceptively simple, and yet, though I've never played it on
the guitar, I bet it's not that simple. If you break down the chord
sequences, I imagine it's got some twist in the tail. The minute I
heard the song in 1965 I knew it was a classic,' Cliff Richard said
to me, independently of the same remark by Justin Hayward. 'I'm
not really surprised it's the most recorded song. "White Christmas" has been around much longer, but in terms of quality,
there's no doubt "Yesterday" ranges along with the best of
standards. The sign of a really good song is that it can take all
sorts of interpretations. "Yesterday" was a simple emotion to deal
with. It wasn't typical of the Beatles, but neither was "Michelle".
We all thought: Hello, what's this about? Suddenly, a middle-of-
the-road, pretty ballad.'

The Beatles had a knack, Cliff observed, of writing songs that
instantly touched the soul. 'Even if their meaning was obscure;
you just had to dig around to find what it was.' He has never
actually sung "Yesterday": 'Only in the bath, without a guitar; but
there's still time, of course.'

The song will always have a special place in the hearts and souls of
all McCartney fans, even those who were not particularly followers of Paul's work. Lori Citero, for example, was a 'Lennon girl'
as she describes herself, but 'Yesterday' reached her with extraordinary power. Three years old when it was released, she can
remember hearing it as if it were yesterday. 'It was on the radio; I
didn't know it was a Beatles song but it got through to me even
at that age. Through the years I grew to love the Beatles and that
song did something to me. Paul proved himself a different kind of

genius.' Now a nurse in New Jersey, she says: 'I thought it was a love song until I got older. Then you listen to the words and realize it could be about anyone; a relative, a sister, a lover. It affects everybody because everybody can choose who it identifies with for them.'

Until that song, Lori Citero avers, what people in America expected was 'more of the Yeah yeah yeah stuff'. What she cannot comprehend is the sight of people at his concerts 'kissing, clutching, or even making out while he's singing songs like "Yesterday". I went to a concert at Giants Stadium, New Jersey and saw that happening during "Yesterday". Unbelievable! It's the moment in a Paul McCartney concert I wait for, when he sings "Yesterday" or my other favourite "My Love". How can these people think of *that* when listening to such music?' No other song will last like 'Yesterday', she believes. 'A song will win the Grammy award and be forgotten, but 'Yesterday' should be put in a time capsule in sodium. It definitely won't come again.'

Of his live performance of the song, Paul says he values 'Yesterday' for two reasons. 'It's a candle-holding moment for the audience, and for me it's a nice change of pace. I have a pretty definite feeling that the audience will go for it. It is something they want from me.' And he responds to that expectation: 'When I play to an audience, I'm a punter. If I go to hear the Rolling Stones, I want to hear "Satisfaction". I don't want to hear too much of their new material. If I go to see Bob Dylan, I want to hear him do "Mister Tambourine Man". When people come to hear Paul McCartney a lot of them want to hear "Let It Be", "The Long and Winding Road", "Fool on the Hill" and "Yesterday".

'When I sing it now, I think back, Now I'm fifty-two, I've seen friends come and go, I've seen loved ones die, I've been in life-threatening situations with the kids; somebody's in danger; somebody's in hospital. So when I sing "I'm not half the man I used to be", I can think: well, I know what I *mean* now. Then, I was some kid. I was twenty-two. And I hadn't become a man yet, barely. And I was doing these world-worn lyrics. So it's quite funny, thinking back on it.'

While he can understand nostalgic adults needing to hear 'Yesterday', he is bemused by 'little kids welling up tears for "Yesterday" ... WOW! I think: my God, what's going on here? When I was twenty-two that same age group was doing that.

Now I'm fifty-two. Excuse me, are you sure you *ought* to be crying at this? I'm your grandad! But it does have an effect. People like sad songs. That is something that has always stuck with me.'

In a small Ohio town in 1965, Terri Hemmert was a sixteen-year-old rhythm and blues fan who suspected the Beatles were 'just another white-boys cover group', trying but failing to achieve the black sound. She was converted by their appearance on the *Ed Sullivan Show*. Now, thirty years later, as Chicago's leading disc jockey on station WXRT, Terri Hemmert reflects on how 'Yesterday' made its enormous impact on her.

'Adults at that point were not taking the Beatles seriously, but this was a really well-crafted song. Suddenly, they were contenders. They had done ballads before, but this was not typical. Songs like "And I Love Her" did not have the sophistication of "Yesterday".'

Much credit must go to George Martin, Terri Hemmert emphasizes, 'because in the wrong production hands, "Yesterday" could have sounded like a schlock ballad. It could easily have been lost. The fact that Martin put a string quartet on it, instead of a hundred and one living strings, gave the song an edge that rock fans had never heard before. I loved classical music but never thought that classics and rock would ever come together. But that song was the beginning of the whole art-rock movement, the precursor to other Paul McCartney work such as the piccolo trumpet touch in "Penny Lane", the sounds of the Moody Blues, the Beatles' *Sgt Pepper*, Procol Harum's "Whiter Shade of Pale". It all began with "Yesterday".'

The pathos of the lyrics struck Terri Hemmert and others as enigmatic: 'You aren't sure exactly what his thoughts are; he doesn't just throw it out like a typical ballad. Other versions of the song are drippy because the delivery is predictable, but Paul and that string quartet made it a masterpiece.'

Richard Carpenter, who with his sister Karen successfully recorded two Beatles songs early in a glittering career which earned them the respect of many artists, including Paul McCartney, has profound thoughts on 'Yesterday'.

'I heard it first in my car. By 1965 they were the most popular group on the planet. "Yesterday" was played on radio stations like

KHJ immediately on its arrival. It was quite a departure from anything that had been on modern pop radio. A pop song with a string quartet and acoustic guitar was really different, not just for 1965. And the studio engineer [Norman Smith] did a superb job. The song climbed out of the radio: it was right there in the room with you. Between the song itself and the treatment, it really caught my ear. It was brilliantly and simply approached as an arrangement. By this time, being a Beatles follower, I had presumed that John pretty much did his stuff and Paul did his, though the credits said Lennon–McCartney. I thought this was probably Paul's melody with lyrics by John.'

Typical of the adult generation, Harold Carpenter, Karen and Richard's father, 'just flipped when he heard it'. Keen on the music of the big bands and singers like Bing Crosby and Perry Como, rather like Jim McCartney, Harold suddenly accepted that the Beatles offered something special as well as rock. 'People say *Sgt Pepper* finally made the Beatles acceptable with the older generation,' Richard Carpenter observes, 'but I really think "Yesterday" is what set it up.'

Visiting his record store in Downey, California, to buy the single, Richard found it had quickly sold out. 'But by the time it was re-ordered and I subsequently purchased it, I'd heard it so much on the radio that I didn't even bother to put it on the turntable. My copy is as new, to this day. I knew the tune and all the lyrics. I was turning nineteen, Karen was fifteen and it was right around the time her voice was coming through. She loved the song and we recorded it on our home tape recorder and Karen sang it at the few engagements we had at that time.'

Richard Carpenter, who arranged and produced all his work with Karen, says he did not think a great deal abut the lyrics of 'Yesterday', though as a singer he admired the 'nice vowel sounds, the concentration on the A's instead of the E's. I thought far more about the construction of the song and its arrangement. It was a vindication for me, as a very early Beatles follower, that they proved the sceptics wrong and were indeed capable of producing timeless music.'

'There is only one thing to be said about a song like "Yesterday",' says Nathan East, the eminent bass guitarist who tours with Phil Collins and Eric Clapton. 'It was sent down from heaven where it was born, as one of the top five greatest songs ever written. I feel that strongly about it. Not only musically but with its lyrical content, it goes through changes and progressions that have been borrowed and stolen by so many writers after it, just as bass players have copied Paul. I don't mind admitting that I have mugged him! The first time I heard "Yesterday", when I was about ten and miming to the Beatles with a broomstick as my guitar, while I watched them on the television, I knew it was a timeless piece of work from one of those guys who invented the wheel of music.'

To a lifelong, ardent McCartney fan named Phyllis Lattner, 'Yesterday' has an especially powerful memory. Now a legal secretary in Manhattan, she was a thirteen-year-old living in Washington DC when the record was released. 'I was a carefree teenager and my biggest problem was saving up enough money for the next Beatles album which I did by saving my lunch money every day. That's how I lost my baby fat. They were the biggest influences on my life, especially Paul.'

It is people's ability to identify with the lyrics, applying whatever interpretation they wish, that makes 'Yesterday' so special, Phyllis Lattner believes. 'Everyone has a time in their lives which they wish they could go back to, whether it's for the company of someone who has died, or a pet who has gone, or an old boyfriend. It is so poignant, it almost makes you cry.' Adulthood has not diminished her appetite for following Paul's career; she has seen him perform the song thirteen times, including two successive nights at New York's Ed Sullivan Theatre in 1993. 'I long not just for any "Yesterday",' she adds, 'but for the time when the song was first released.'

To Paul McCartney, 'Yesterday' literally means Liverpool. The character of the great city that shaped him is forever embedded in Paul's soul. In 1982 I interviewed the outstanding American rock singer-writer Carl Perkins, whose rockabilly work was among the Beatles' inspiration. He had spent some time with Paul and told me an intriguing anecdote which spoke volumes. Perkins, relaxing at his home in Jackson, Tennessee, said how much the town meant to him, adding: 'And Paul told me he feels just the same about his city, Liverpool. He said: "Carl, I've tasted the jet set life, and it isn't for me. I like to get back there as often as I can, with the real people.'"

McCartney has demonstrated extraordinary attachment and loyalty to Merseyside, maintaining a house there, performing his ambitious and critically acclaimed *Oratorio* in Liverpool Cathedral; giving a majestic outdoor concert on the banks of the river at King's Dock in 1990; planning the 1995 opening of the Liverpool Institute for Performing Arts.

There is a Beatles story on every street in Liverpool, though the city was late in celebrating its heritage as the birthplace, physically and musically, of popular music's greatest group. But in 1990 'The Beatles Story', a permanent exhibition crammed with artefacts, memorabilia and replicas of the entire phenomenon of the Beatles, opened at Albert Dock. There is non-stop Beatles music and 'Yesterday' is played every day as the place teems with international tourists.

By coincidence, Shelagh Johnston, the manager of 'The Beatles Story', has a unique link to Paul's yesterdays. Her mother, Helen Carney, was a midwife, and when Shelagh was six she moved into the house at 72 Western Avenue, Speke, vacated by the McCartney family, who went to another house nearby before moving to Allerton.

When Shelagh was thirteen, her mother was surprised when the postman delivered a letter from the Royal College of Midwives addressed to her old friend Mary McCartney. Shelagh was asked to take the letter to Jim McCartney in Allerton. Visiting the McCartney home, in 1963, Shelagh found Jim McCartney welcoming; over a cup of tea he inquired about her mother and said he did not know how to cope with the fan mail that was beginning to arrive for his Beatle son. Shelagh volunteered to help, and for the next two years liaised over the fans' letters until Brian Epstein was forced to organize a fan club more formally with the appointment of a full-time secretary, Freda Kelly.

During her regular visits to Jim McCartney's home, Shelagh returned a possession of Paul's which he had left behind in the loft at Western Avenue: a Rupert Bear annual. Jim said she could keep it as a memento.

So when 'Yesterday' was released, its impression on Shelagh Johnston was touching in its evocation of her youth and that of Paul. 'Although it's a love song, I think that somewhere in there must be memories of his mother', she believes. 'For someone so young, it's a song from a person who's lived a lot. It's full of his feelings, and it's a comment on how suddenly one's life can change. The melody got to me as much as the words; the success of any song, no matter what the words are, depends on the melody. This song's story, to me, is a reflection by Paul on his childhood and how important those years were to him.'

By 1984, Shelagh Johnston was one of Liverpool's dozen official Beatles guides, having passed the rigorous test to qualify for the job. Unexpectedly, Paul phoned her one evening to ask if she still had his Rupert Bear book since he was making a film on the subject and wanted to use it. 'I said yes, I've still got it; it was in my wardrobe next to my wedding album and GCE certificates.' However, since it was a 1948 black and white edition and the film needed a coloured edition, it could not be used.

They met for a one-hour chat on the day Paul went to Liverpool in 1984 for the première of his film *Give My Regards to Broad Street*. 'We talked about our childhoods and mums and Western Avenue. I took him two roses from the garden in Western Avenue.' Paul said he would press them and keep them as a reminder of his yesterdays.

Songwriters, musicians and other artists consider 'Yesterday' important both in the story of Paul McCartney's evolution and in the story of popular music's growth.

'It was a very brave composition and a brave decision to record it,' says Keith Emerson, the keyboards player whose band Emerson, Lake and Palmer helped to implement the heavier rock sounds of the 1970s. 'Having been classically trained, my attention was drawn to it as one of the first eclectic examples of how the Beatles would progress. "Yesterday" started them in their search, whereby they would move ahead to use Indian raga forms, Salvation Army Bands, and much more.'

Pondering McCartney's early feeling that he originally believed he had subconsciously derived it from another tune, Emerson adds: 'I could have sworn I'd heard it before, that it was from a classical piece of music. But then, I *do* believe that Paul could have dreamed it. I have written songs without knowing where they came from and that's what must have happened in Paul's case with "Yesterday". Ginger Baker once said that when he played drums sometimes, it was as if someone was standing behind him, doing it.' Creativity could be scary: 'It was very untypical of what Paul McCartney had been turning out. It's as if it was beamed down to him from somewhere.'

Many songwriters believe that some of their work is sent to them by a force outside their conscious selves. This is not necessarily connected to a religious conviction, but has a bearing on a spirituality which gives birth to creativity. Since Paul has used the words 'awesome' and 'spooky' to describe its arrival in his head, this theory merits analysis. 'Even if Paul didn't want to write "Yesterday", it was going to happen,' Emerson says.

'I have a feeling he could not stop himself; he was being remotely controlled by another force that none of us can understand,' says the songwriter Roger Greenaway, composer of hits including 'I'd Like to Teach the World to Sing' and 'You've Got Your Troubles'.* 'It was coming from God knows where, rather like David Gates who woke up and wrote that song 'If' in about fifteen minutes, lyric and melody. It was a moment of inspiration, some ethereal force that determines that this will come through the writer, whether he intends it or not. There's no other reason for it. For Paul to be able to write such a classic melody on such simple chords and then put a lyric to it of that depth could probably not be done completely consciously. It wasn't contrived in any way. The Beatles plagiarized nothing and nobody, and have not been matched since. Nor will they be.'

'If you're looking for explanations,' Paul McCartney says, 'and I'm not a great one for explanations, actually . . . I'm just so lucky I'm blessed. When people say it's a God-given gift, I'm not a great religious guy but I'd go along with that. I like the word "gift" . . . it washed over me when I was younger. They used to say: "It's a gift you've got." Actually, as you get older, you think: that's a good word. Somebody gave me that. So I love all that stuff, I'm very proud of all that stuff now. Whereas when you're younger you cover it up a little bit more.' His personality was gregarious,

---

* Roger Greenaway toured Britain on Beatles concert bills in 1963 as a singer with the Kestrels. Later, as half of David and Jonathan, he made records of 'Yesterday' and 'Michelle'. A successful songwriter, he is a former chairman of the Performing Right Society and now European director of ASCAP, the songwriters' organisation.

to his advantage. 'I didn't cover it up that much because if I had, I would never even have *tried* to write a song called "Yesterday".'

'Yesterday' will not be superseded, Roger Greenaway declares. 'It's inconceivable to think of a new song being covered by more than two-and-a-half thousand artists.' This is not a negative view of future creativity, he says, but based on his theory that the saturation point in writing popular music may have been reached. Greenaway adds: 'The chromatic scale has only twelve notes. Computer experts will tell you that the combinations are almost infinite on those twelve notes. I actually believe that the combinations *that work* are not infinite.'

A more pragmatic and less euphoric view about 'Yesterday' and songwriting generally is held by Don Black, the lyricist who, coincidentally, managed Matt Monro. Black, who wrote the Grammy Award-winning song 'Born Free' as well as James Bond film themes, and has worked with Andrew Lloyd Webber on *Sunset Boulevard* among his many credits, considers 'Yesterday' truthful and honest. 'It touches a nerve and has a universal theme which every songwriter looks for. Everybody can relate to the situation where one's troubles seemed so far away. And it is unusual for such a sad song to sweep the world. Most standards carry a more optimistic air, citing love and romance. But here is a heartbreaker of a song. That's what is so rare about its success.'

But, exploding what he considers to be a myth about songwriters 'who the public sometimes think live in a pink cloud,' Don Black says: 'In reality, the job of the songwriter is to write; that's what he does. People in other walks of life get up and go to work. The songwriter gets up and goes, let's say, to the piano and stares at a blank piece of paper and fills it with words and ideas. Sometimes nothing happens, sometimes a magic happens. Paul had a great day that morning. He got up and wrote "Yesterday".'

The figures concerning 'Yesterday' are astounding, but it might be difficult to find a more impressive performance for the song than that of the French pianist Richard Clayderman. In 1978, when he was starting his career and had success in Germany, his record company there asked him to come up with songs for an album combining classical interpretations with contemporary winners. 'Yesterday' was one of his immediate popular music choices, alongside Francis Lai's 'Love Story', Paul Simon's 'Bridge Over

Troubled Water' and Henry Mancini's 'Moon River'. The instrumental album, entitled *Dreams*, has sold between 20 and 25 million copies internationally.

Describing 'Yesterday' as 'among the miraculous songs, from the gods', Richard Clayderman, who speaks little English, says he is not attuned to the words. 'I am concerned with the melody, which is just gorgeous. It brings many sensations; to any musician, "Yesterday" is perfection.' Touring the world (in 1995 he played several shows in China with the Be'jing Symphony Orchestra), Clayderman includes the song in all his concerts within a medley that includes three other songs by Paul McCartney: 'Let It Be', 'Get Back' and 'The Long and Winding Road'.

Dr Glenn Wilson notes that the inflection of the song is hymnal, and that it has a religious tone. There is almost a feeling that Paul could sing 'Amen' at any point. '"Yesterday" frequently goes to a note that is not where it actually seems to be aiming at,' he feels. 'And it has to re-settle. It always goes to a note slightly oblique to the one it is going to settle on. This tendency in song to shoot slightly astray from a key note, or a stable resting point, is one of the most emotional forms of music. It gives people a direct emotional tingle.' A song with a similar flavour, cited by the psychologist, is 'We'll Gather Lilacs (In the Spring Again)', which lyrically and musically offers a texture close to that of 'Yesterday'. With words and music by Ivor Novello, 'We'll Gather Lilacs' evoked a happier time, addressing soldiers away from home in the Second World War.

The colossal success of 'Yesterday' since the 1960s is explained thus by the psychologist: 'People are happy now to look back to what they felt was a more optimistic era: psychedelia, colourful clothes, a feeling of optimism and the new youth culture. A lot of problems we confront now had not appeared: there was not the unemployment, no AIDS, and racial problems and urban riots were not so prevalent.' 'Yesterday''s enduring popularity is locked into memories of what for millions seems to be a halcyon era.

To another observer, Liverpool-born Paul Cooper, 'Yesterday' is a very special song that has marked his life. He was four years old when the song was released by the Beatles; his thirteen-year-old sister Susan wept with joy over McCartney's 'Yesterday' as she plastered her Allerton bedroom with pictures of the Beatles and bought every record upon its release. Today, Paul Cooper sings and plays 'Yesterday' professionally, imitating McCartney as accurately as he can, for that is his role as the bass guitarist in the Bootleg Beatles, the world's most remarkable sound-alike band which has been climbing in international popularity since being formed in 1980.

Cooper has studied every nuance of McCartney's work to arrive at an almost eerie replica of his voice. In packed arenas around the world, from London's Royal Albert Hall and Palladium through to Tokyo's Budokan, all scenes of actual Beatlemania thirty years ago, Cooper and the Bootleg Beatles leave audiences transfixed. For thousands born too late to see the originals, this is the nearest they can experience to the real thing in concert and the Bootlegs deal chronologically with every phase of the Beatles story in music, aided by a backdrop of films that recall the period, from Beatlemania through to the end.

With clarity, Paul Cooper remembers how shocked his parents appeared when 'Yesterday' popped up on the *Help!* album and on television appearances. 'Until that moment they considered the Beatles long-haired louts. They didn't mind us buying the records, but suddenly with "Yesterday" it was: "Oh, OK then." The criticism suddenly stopped. They had respect. Before they knew what was happening Matt Monro had a hit with it and the game was up. I think it broke through to a whole new generation who until then had regarded them as a rock 'n' roll group.'

It has always struck Paul Cooper as odd that the twenty-two-year-old McCartney could write so introspectively about his young life: 'It's quite appealing when an older man looks back on his life, but the fascinating thing here is that he was a young man and a very successful Beatle at that.' Performing 'Yesterday' around the world, Paul Cooper says: 'I get more comments about that song than any other. At the end of every show people come up to me to say the person next to them was crying or had their head in their hands, or had goose pimples. It touches people.'

He feels 'incredible pressure' when he steps up to sing it after the group has performed 'Help!' 'It means such a lot as a song both to me and to the audience. Although I am trying to be precise with the tuning, I also want to try to sound like it's very easy. I refer back to Paul McCartney's version often, to check the tempo. He floats it; he sings it a bit faster than I do. His voice is incredibly sweet on "Yesterday". I've found I can add more pathos if I slow it down a fraction.'

As a guitarist, Paul Cooper finds McCartney's tuning arrangements for the singing and playing of 'Yesterday' to be unorthodox and 'fascinating'. 'He sings it in the key of F, but he actually plays it on the guitar in G, so the acoustic guitar has been dropped a tone. He probably did this because the open string sound of the G chord was a better sound, but he wanted his vocal to be in F. So he dropped the acoustic guitar a tone so that he could play G, but he was actually forming a G chord, which I still think is amazing, because if you do play an F, your fingers are all over the fretboard and it doesn't sound so sweet as having the open jangly bit at the end.'

The key of F, Paul Cooper points out, makes it difficult for an audience to sing along to. 'A bit high. But there's another side to performing "Yesterday". The audience wants to see me recreating it precisely like him, and you can hear a pin drop. When I first played it on stage, I thought: I'm either doing this incredibly badly, or everyone's gone home! But when the song was finished, and this still is the case, the volume of applause is unbelievable. It used to be regarded as a ballad by winsome Paul. Now it's an anthem, an even grander song than he could ever have imagined possible.'

Touring with the Bootleg Beatles, and accompanying Paul Cooper on 'Yesterday', is the classically based Duke String Quartet, whose first violinist, Louisa Fuller, observes that the sound of live strings always adds something especially personal to a song. 'If the strings were taken away from the song, it might not be such a powerful performance. The strings don't come in until the second verse and when they do, it's a really beautiful moment. People who listen to the words won't think of that. When he sings "Suddenly, I'm not half the man I used to be", the strings subconsciously move people more than they realize.

'It isn't difficult to play because it's quite slow. The only difficult part I have is in the third verse where the violin goes up to a top A, a long-held top note which everyone knows and would recognize. I have to pitch it exactly and, doing it live, I have to pluck it out of the air, coming from low down on the instrument, and then I hold the note for a long time.'

Reflecting on Paul McCartney's diktat at his recording session

that the strings should not use vibrato, Louisa Fuller explains why
there might have been resistance to Paul's wishes: 'Most people
are used to piling vibrato on to everything. Because vibrato
slightly masks any tuning problems, if it's not quite bang on, it
will still sound great. Take the vibrato away and it is laid bare. To
be asked not to do it shocks a string player because vibrato can
make a sound very sweet. You can pile on a lot of vibrato and
hope for the best. If you take vibrato away, you have to work
much, much harder with your bow to get the Beatles sound.'

The device of vibrato ('a vibration caused by wobbling very
quickly the finger that touches the string, creating a sound wave')
can make the music seem colder, says Louisa Fuller. 'In a string
quartet, where you have four people playing close harmony, as on
"Yesterday", if you are not using vibrato, the musicians have to
hit every note accurately. On the top note of the McCartney
record, vibrato is apparent . . . I don't know if it crept in and Paul
McCartney wished it hadn't, but it does sound very nice.'

If rivalry was going to enter the Beatles, then the emergence of
'Yesterday' in 1965 would have been a catalyst. 'One of the great
things about the Beatles'; Paul reflects now, 'is that we just
weren't an average rock 'n' roll act. If we were required at the
London Palladium or say on *The Ed Sullivan Show*, we could
always perform something from our cabaret days. In the earliest
days in Liverpool, I remember us asking Brian [Epstein] to get us
engagements in cabaret after we'd finished a ballroom gig; we
wanted work, any kind, for more money and experience. So we
were never just in it for rock 'n' roll. We could pull out "Till
There Was You", just as Gerry Marsden (and the Pacemakers)
could do "You'll Never Walk Alone".

'We always liked the fact that this gave us a little bit more
elbow, a little bit more status. We were able to say: well, look,
we're a strong, rocking band: "I'm Down", "Long Tall Sally",
"Twist and Shout", "Rock and Roll Music" . . . but this band's
got a lot of other things going. There's always a moment we can
turn on the ballad.'

As a group, that coalition worked perfectly. Lennon outwardly
adored the whole concept of rock 'n' roll, dismissing most other
styles of music until later in his life, when he became a self-
confessed romantic, admitting that he enjoyed ballads too. 'John

A tea break with producer George Martin at the canteen of EMI studios in the spring of 1963 (*Apple Corps*)

The house in which 'Yesterday' was born: number 57 Wimpole Street, London, where Paul lived with the family of his girlfriend Jane Asher (*Piet Schreuders*)

Alma Cogan, the ebullient singer, threw famous show business parties in the 1960s and she was one of the first people to hear Paul playing the song he initially called 'Scrambled Eggs' (*Apple Corps*)

Sightseeing on the Champs-Elysées during the Beatles' appearance at Paris Olympia, January, 1964; author Ray Coleman is to Paul's right (*Ray Coleman collection*)

The Beatles arriving in America for the first time on 7 February 1964. At a New York press conference, their press officer Brian Sommerville is at Paul's right. Paul explains his guitar style to top TV host Ed Sullivan while Beatles manager Brian Epstein looks on (*Star File/Apple Corps*)

A month after Paul had recorded 'Yesterday', the Beatles meet Princess Margaret at the première of their film *Help!* at the London Pavilion, 29 July 1965 (*Star File*)

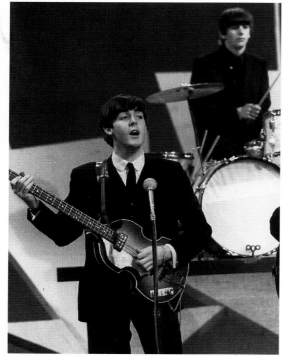

Rehearsing for the 'Ed Sullivan Show', on which Paul's song 'Yesterday' was premièred to the US audience (*Star File*)

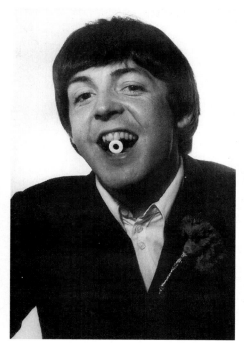

Posing with a Polo Mint during a break while recording BBC TV's 'Top Of The Pops' in 1965 (*Harry Goodwin*)

John and Paul landing in the Bahamas, about to shoot the *Help!* movie, on 22 February 1965 (*Star File*)

A serious Paul McCartney in 1965, at the time he recorded 'Yesterday' (*Apple Corps*)

Dick James, the Beatles' music publisher who controversially triggered the sale of the Lennon-McCartney songs, listens to Paul's music at EMI studios in 1967 during the making of the *Sgt Pepper* album (*Beat Publications*)

In the EMI studios recording the Beatles' *White Album*, October 1968 (*Linda McCartney*)

John and Paul in perfect harmony at a New York press conference at the Americana Hotel on 14 May 1968, where they announced the launch of their company Apple (*Linda McCartney*)

A study in concentration: Paul recording his album *Press To Play* in 1986 (*Linda McCartney*)

Paul and Linda in New York for the première of the film *Give My Regards To Broad Street* in October 1984 (*Vinnie Zuffante/Star File*)

sang the ballad "Up A Lazy River" and played the "Harry Lime" theme on guitar,' Paul remembers, as examples of John's true scope. George Harrison, whose early musical reference points were Lonnie Donegan, Carl Perkins and George Formby, was soon to lead the Beatles into exploration of Indian music forms, with his adoption and learning of the sitar. Ringo Starr admired the jazz drummer Gene Krupa and country and western music.

Paul McCartney was, though, the supreme popular music writer in the Beatles. None of the other three could, or would, have written 'Yesterday'. Whatever their organic talents, it is doubtful if Lennon or Harrison would have even marshalled the patience to nurse a song from the autumn of 1963 until reaching the recording studio in the summer of 1965. McCartney's extraordinary resolution and discipline, even at twenty-two, enabled him to see it through.

The interaction and chemistry between the four Beatles was harmonious at that stage. The roller-coaster of creative triumphs, fame and fortune was a heady mixture, and at the time 'Yesterday' was hitting the world's airwaves they still had a year before they would call a halt to their concert touring days.

But the frisson which Paul must have enjoyed as 'Yesterday' signalled his artistry must have fuelled a little envy or sideways looks, I suggested. 'There may have been resentment, but I'd have been the last to know,' he replied. 'There wasn't any open resentment of its success. I don't think there were any ripples.' American disc jockeys looking for tittle-tattle said that since 'Yesterday' represented the first solo by a Beatle, it might mean something deeper. 'Inevitably!' Paul says. 'We simply said: No, it's not that. It's just one man's solo work. There was nothing deep about it. Certainly not at that stage; the bad times came much later.

'I dunno. This was always one of the dangers, that one of us would step out . . . in a photo session once for a publicity shot. I remember showing up once in a grey suit and everyone had dark suits. And they'd take the piss out of me: "Go on, go to the front with your grey suit!" I said: "I didn't know what you were all going to wear." I wasn't consciously aware of any rifts. There were, later, when I had to sue them to save money for all of us. Then it reared again. It was three against one, me, and they said: Oh, here he is again, big-head.

'No, I'd always tried to play "Yesterday" down. That's why we didn't release it as a single in Britain. If I'd been trying to get out front, I'd have said: "Hey, this is a great song, guys. I gotta have it out; come on!" We all thought it wasn't very good for our image. We were basically a rock 'n' roll band. It seemed good for an album, a nice little filler, a slow tune: "And now for something completely different." No way did we want it out as a single, in Britain especially. America was different; Capitol could do what they liked, and they did. And what happened to "Yesterday" was very nice. But it wasn't planned that way by me.'

At the end of every year, the Beatles recorded a Christmas message to members of their fan club, sent to them on a 45rpm flexi-disc. At the end of 1965 they opened their message by satirizing 'Yesterday', singing it a capella: "Now it looks as if *we're* here to stay," they sing. It was a typical slice of Beatles buffoonery, an attempt at crossing the sound of a barbershop quartet and doo-wop. Out of tune, sounding rather like four teenagers after a drunken night out, they have a laugh in their voices as they doodle through Paul's song.

Paul McCartney's instinct that 'Yesterday' should not succumb to vaudevillian excess was confirmed by his own delivery. His soft, instantly identifiable voice gives the lyric an air of confidentiality, of being a piece of prose set to music rather than self-conscious construction as a hit song. It's beauty was, and remains, its intimacy, its unblemished innocence, and a very slight air of faltering nervousness. Listening to McCartney's voice, you could be forgiven for feeling that this was a demonstration tape, and he might want to stop the tape and re-start it. He's in your lounge, in your bedroom, in your car, and he's getting through with a rich familiarity. Like all the great standards, from 'Moonlight in Vermont' to 'Stardust', from 'Skylark' to 'Imagination', 'Yesterday' is distinctive with a simplicity and honesty that, as any songwriter will testify, is fiendishly difficult to achieve with any credibility. 'To write that three-minute hit song and come up with something lasting and memorable is what we all strive for,' says Justin Hayward. 'It's the challenge that faces us every time we go to write, and it's not often we get it right in every respect.'

The rare achievement of Paul McCartney with 'Yesterday' was that having 'heard' a melody, he marshalled his art as a brilliant communicator, marrying the tune with a message, and words, that will forever touch nerves. As the celebrated writer Alan Jay Lerner said, the best work from a songwriter usually comes when the melody arrives first; that way, he has to compress the lyric into something that already exists, and it acts as a discipline. That happened with 'Yesterday'.

Paul feels that if the string quartet had not been employed on the song, 'Yesterday' would have been 'another "This Boy", or "If I Fell" . . . the Beatles combo doing a slow song, which people were used to.' George Martin's string quartet theory was to lift the song into a different sphere.

McCartney's own performances of his song show a remarkable consistency. The two most hypnotic are on the mono album of *Help!* which projects a raw, upfront atmosphere in contrast with the more distant stereo version; and on a television documentary screened in Britain in 1973 called *James Paul McCartney*. Networked by Sir Lew Grade's ATV, this was Paul's first post-Beatles delivery of the song. The tempo is slower than usual, opening with Paul and his acoustic guitar against a taped strings. But it is the fragility of his voice through those lyrics, with an almost knowing wink in his vocals, that clinches this riveting performance. It is McCartney palpably seeking to repossess his eight-year-old song and replenish it with a warmth and an authority that only the song's writer could implant.

And by then, such a reclamation was necessary. On the road to its current status, 'Yesterday' has been caressed, orchestrated lovingly, sung raunchily, mauled, jazzed-up, over-pitched by muscular vocalists, delivered simply at the piano, and punched out conscientiously by balladeers or country singers with a ferocity it never deserved. It speaks volumes for the song that it attracts – and often survives – interpretations from every conceivable strata of artist, popular and classical.

Elvis Presley, who so feared the ascent of the Beatles, might have been expected to grip the song firmly, but he seems almost bashful with his live-on-stage-in-Las Vegas performance, captured for posterity in 1970. Marred by back-up singers who answer him back (he sings 'Yesterday', they repeat the word chorally), Presley loses the chance to give the lyric the colour and density his voice could often deliver on an emotional ballad. Tammy Wynette turns in a robust, convincing performance and Placido Domingo gives it everything, including majesty and a distant, detached dignity in a serious operatic reading. Tom Jones's unmistakable heavyweight punch is the precise opposite of Paul McCartney's gentle original, Jones grasping every ounce of the lyric firmly round the neck. It's a vintage 1968 performance, demonstrating Tom Jones's spectacular swashbuckling style.

There was a time when it would have been anathema for Frank Sinatra to cover a Beatles composition; in the early 1960s their styles of music appeared to be polarized, threatened by the thrust of Lennon and McCartney and the bombardment of British rock 'n' roll. American ballad singers over-reacted to the Beatles' long hair and youth. But here is Sinatra endorsing Paul's song with a finesse and an artistry, and that yearning and timelessness that is his hallmark. It's warming to hear a master of his style so at ease on what to him must have seemed refreshing; a newish song. Since he has spoken about the dearth of good contemporary writers, he was quick to recognize a modern gem.

Contrasting with Paul McCartney's definitive, almost pastoral reading, 'Yesterday' proves its greatness as a song by the boundaries it crosses, the unexpected genres of music it can enter with versatility. In a modern jazz setting, the trumpet of Lee Morgan and his band skips deliciously through the melody with an improvisational fire that would never have been expected to yield such a stimulating result. Erroll Garner, the master jazz pianist, flits through it politely. Sarah Vaughan converts it into a jazzy foxtrot. The Newport Male Voice Choir treat it sombrely, rather Sundayish. The Seekers sound far too pure and syrupy, reducing the words to nothing. Lou Rawls beefs it up in a near-jazz treatment. Acker Bilk's clarinet treats it to a gorgeous, limpid lower-register version.

Marianne Faithfull tries too hard to sound genteel, and the cello-laden Berlin Philharmonic Orchestra gives it predictably rich sweep. Dionne Warwick sounds utterly charmed by lyrics she can get inside, delivering an unexpectedly bewitching reading topped at the end by a church bell which sounds absolutely in keeping. Pepe Jaramillo offers a rumba treatment, and Paul's friend the late Alma Cogan, who heard the song in its true infancy, gives it a bolero treatment; her infectious stage vivacity actually comes across on record. Mary Wells, the Tamla Motown singer whom the Beatles admired so much that they invited her on one of their

British tours, performs 'Yesterday' gracefully on her album *Love Songs to the Beatles*.

The country and western contingent has indulged heavily in 'Yesterday': Merle Haggard and Willie Nelson sound comfortably together on it, but Billie Jo Spears's jerky treatment pawns the elegance of the song in favour of gimmickry. Cilla Black, a friend of the Beatles since their Liverpool years, offers a light, airy version that wins through by unaffected simplicity. There's Gladys Knight, soulful and heart-rending with her determination to rip the song apart constructively; by contrast Diana Ross and the Supremes sound strangely robotic, devoid of any emotion. Richard Clayderman's honeyed piano injects a flowery treatment that Paul was, perhaps, subconsciously fearing when he insisted that the violinists steered away from the vibrato technique. Perry Como, of course, relaxes into the song. The virtuoso jazz-based guitarist Joe Pass delivers a pristine, decorative interpretation showing how much the melody can lend itself to soulful instrumental extemporization.

Among the most astonishing versions of 'Yesterday' are those from Ray Charles and Marvin Gaye. Using his piano instead of a guitar, Charles, in his 1967 version, positively rasps the words, punctuated by telling silences: 'Suddenly . . . there's a shadow hanging over me, yeah,' he announces. ' . . . Love was such an easy game to play . . . yes it was.' Ending with block piano chords, the performance is sheer Ray Charles and it's the strength of the song that is once again proved; if it can be crunched home by Ray Charles, it has a life of its own.

Marvin Gaye, too, dramatizes the song into a mix of Motown and gospel. '*People*, now I need a place to hide away . . . now I long, long, long for yesterday . . . Talkin' 'bout yesterday,' he sings. If Ray Charles and Marvin Gaye can take hold of it, as well as disparate artists from fields a million miles apart, then 'Yesterday' has a heart and soul freely available for transplant.

There is a pleasing irony that the most convincing, unpretentious version of 'Yesterday', after McCartney's own, remains the track from the first person to cover it. Matt Monro's immaculate diction, his commanding authority and robustness, still seem perfectly tailored for this simple yet exceptional ballad. George Martin's orchestral arrangement for Monro, with neat guitar figures and light strings, sets it off comfortably and the singer offers a confident, gripping performance in the grand tradition of ballad reading.

Paul says he has heard relatively few of the cover versions but is flattered by the attention the song has merited in thirty years. 'I love it. I'm proud. The song exceeded my dreams.'

5

The Enigma of John Lennon

'He wore a suit of armour'

Paul's love of the broad tapestry of show business always transcended that of the other Beatles. To John, the entertainment world was full of posers. Rock 'n' roll was his passport to fame and fortune, from which he might become a young, contemplative philosopher. George liked rockabilly music, the sturdy guitar work of his friend Eric Clapton, and the lyrical potency of Bob Dylan. Ringo liked country and western music long before it became fashionable. None of them equalled Paul in envisioning the scope of the Beatles.

When Brian Epstein insisted that they smartened their appearance and bought them suits to replace the leathers, it was Paul who understood his motive more than Lennon, Harrison or Starr. On the borders of show business and rock 'n' roll, as he saw the Beatles, Paul was able to accept that if they were entertainers, they needed to be professionals. Lennon sometimes fought that view but usually acquiesced. The role of Beatles diplomat, as well as the one who sang romantically, was therefore established as Paul's from the beginning. And it continued throughout the decade that the Beatles lasted.

A perfect example of Paul's acceptance of the ethical boundaries of show business came when the Beatles were appearing in Rome in 1965. Epstein told them all that Noël Coward, staying in the same hotel, would like to meet them. Paul recalls that the other three sounded bored by the prospect and suggested they all pretended they were not in. But Paul thought: 'We can't snub Noël Coward! He's two flights downstairs and he's asked to meet us! He's the grand old dame of British show business and we're the new young things.' So Paul went alone to meet him.

Paul's more outward approach, and the songs he wrote such as 'Yesterday', helped the Beatles in reaching what he always believed was the goal: being admired and accepted by a wider audience. Pragmatic and persuasive, sometimes ruthless, compulsively creative, he was always able to convert, uncannily, his sentimental inner self into his work. That was how 'Yesterday', a quintessential song of yearning, came to be set amid his penchant for lyrical ambiguity. It had been so from childhood, when he was learning the ropes of popular music, linking it with the new sounds, and applying his nifty word-play to complete the picture. Once, when another songwriter told him he had hit a creative block in his search for lyrics, Paul said to him succinctly: 'Try love. It never fails'.

For Paul, the anchor of 'trouble' seems to have been, consciously or otherwise, one of his personal themes. Writing in 1973 in *Punch*, where he reviewed a book of lyrics by Paul Simon, Paul said how much he relished the challenge of such an assignment, adding that his entries as a sixth-former for the school magazine had been rejected. 'Not even a deep poem which I rather fancied, that began: "The worm chain drags slowly . . ." and ended ". . . the trouble with living is nobody dying".'

Trouble recurred as a theme for one of five poems he had published in *New Statesman and Society* in January 1995. In one, entitled 'Trouble Is', Paul wrote that 'Trouble is – shadows don't fight back.' Thirty years earlier, the lyrics of 'Yesterday' had spoken of 'a shadow hanging over me' and 'all my troubles seemed so far away'.

As a writer of poems or songs, Paul bares his sensibilities so that people can identify immediately with his recounting of everyday occurrences. The passage of time characterizes many of his songs, as in 'Yesterday'. In 'She's Leaving Home', he sang of 'Something inside that was always denied for so many years'. In 'Blackbird', he sang of 'waiting for the moment to arrive'. His song to John Lennon was entitled 'Here Today', pondering what John might say if he heard such words addressed to him.* In

---

* In the planning of 'Here Today', Paul had backed away from his initial idea of using a string quartet behind his vocal and acoustic guitar. Ever since 'Yesterday' had become a touchstone by which much of his ballad work would be measured, the idea of replicating the string quartet had worried him. But finally, discussing the idea with George Martin, who believed 'Here Today' was 'screaming out' for a string quartet, Paul agreed. He says he concluded that he

'Hold Me Tight' he sang that it 'feels so right now'. The Beatles songs included 'Things We Said Today', 'The Night Before' and 'When I'm Sixty-Four', with the reference to time being upfront in the very titles.

His songs invoking the past include 'Sgt Pepper's Lonely Hearts Club Band', in which he sings: 'It was twenty years ago today.' In 'Paperback Writer', he sings of taking 'years to write'. 'A Day in the Life' cast his mind back to getting up for school in the morning. In 'I've Just Seen a Face', he wrote: 'I can't forget the time or place where we just met.'

In 'I Saw Her Standing There', he sang that he would 'never dance with another.' In 'She's a Woman', he sang of 'love for ever and forever'. In the first Beatles hit, 'Love Me Do', he wrote that he would 'always be true'. In 'For No One', he sang of 'a love that should have lasted years'. And 'Get Back (to Where You Once Belonged)' is a powerful retrospective.

By contrast, John Lennon's nearest equivalent to baring his soul in the manner of 'Yesterday' was the beautiful 'In My Life'. Magically evocative in his autobiographical look at friends and places he had left behind, Lennon's 'In My Life' was as direct (and framed traditionally) as McCartney's 'Yesterday' was oblique (and framed in a revolutionary musical setting). Recorded exactly four months after McCartney's opus, Lennon's work differed totally in its execution, too. Paul sang an accompanying vocal on the track and, on a visit to John's house during a writing session for the lyrics, worked on a Mellotron to construct the melody's middle section.

Tender, powerful and immensely moving though 'In My Life' remains as a majestic piece of Lennon's art, it has been dwarfed by the universal popularity of 'Yesterday', and if John ever wanted to ignore Paul's commercial strength with that one song, the public would never allow him to do so. He was often confronted by the song in amusing situations. Shortly after leaving Britain for America, never to return, John was interviewed on TV's *Dick Cavett Show* on 9 September 1971. By then the Beatles had split and his relationship with Paul was at its lowest ebb. As John walked on to the television set, the resident band struck up with a McCartney composition, 'Ob-La-Di, Ob-La-Da'. John grimaced.

did not have to avoid a good idea simply because it had been done by him once before.

'Thanks for playing Paul's tune for me. It's very nice of you. Wonderful!' he cracked. 'I always get it! I sat in a restaurant in Spain and the violinist insisted on playing "Yesterday" right in my ear! Then he asked me to sign the violin! I didn't know what to say. I said: 'Well, OK.' I signed it and Yoko signed it. One day he's going to find out that Paul wrote it.'

Settled in New York, John enjoyed taking tea in the Palm Court of the Plaza Hotel. When he walked in, the violins would often strike up 'Yesterday' in his honour, oblivious of the fact that he would have preferred what was by then his own anthem, 'Imagine'. McCartney music seemed to be everywhere for John as he moved around Manhattan. When his wife was pregnant and he walked into a maternity store in Madison Avenue to buy her some clothes, he did not realize until the time came to pay with his credit card that the name of the shop was Lady Madonna. 'Another bloody Paul McCartney song!' he laughed to his friend Elliot Mintz, who accompanied him on the shopping outing.

Lennon admired the achievement of the song, and Paul's talents, too much to display any jealousy about success and creation of 'Yesterday' in Beatles years. When the song was first played to him in 1965 by Paul, he said: 'Phew, that's quite a piece of work.' And as the Beatles caravan rolled, he spoke admiringly of Paul's work. But, later, when enmity set in, he seemed less generous. 'I don't agree with the idea of loving yesterday', he said in one interview. 'I don't buy that bit about yesterday was wonderful and today's no good, even though in those days he [Paul] wouldn't have been thinking on that level. But the lyrics for "Yesterday", even though they don't make sense if you look at them as a whole – they don't resolve into any sense – they are good lines. They certainly work as lyrics to that song.'

There had been some typically waspish Lennon asides to show that the meteoric success of 'Yesterday' probably rankled occasionally. In the midst of his vindictive exchanges with Paul during the legal battle when the Beatles split, John sang in his song 'How Do You Sleep': 'The only thing you done was "Yesterday"/and since you've gone you're just another day.' In the same song, he dug at Paul: 'The sound you make is Muzak to my ears.' [John later admitted to Paul that some of the lyrics had been suggested by Allen Klein or Yoko.]

Paul was hurt by John's double-edged sword. 'He knows that's not true, that "the only thing I wrote is 'Yesterday'," Paul said shortly afterwards. 'He knows and I know that it's just not so'. Interviewed by *Playboy* magazine in 1980, John was as cryptic as ever. His old buddy had written a masterpiece which he knew had by then been recorded by about 1,500 other arists. 'Well, we know all about "Yesterday",' John said. 'I have had *so* much accolade for "Yesterday". That's Paul's song and Paul's baby. Well done. Beautiful – and I never wished I'd written it.'

While the eternal success of 'Yesterday' is a source of pride to Paul, he is faced with the reality that his most commercially successful composition bears the songwriting credit: 'Lennon–McCartney'. The name of their partnership, in that order, is as familiar to the world as Rodgers and Hammerstein, whom Paul says he originally hoped John and he would aspire to equal.

With no formal leadership of the Beatles, and with shared creativity of many of their songs, the issue of whose-name-goes-first might never have mattered. The Lennon–McCartney credit for songs, now almost a generic trademark, had its roots in a handshake during their early Liverpool years. Paul had written their first hit single, 'Love Me Do' and 'PS I Love You', but he deferred to John's name going first because, he says, both John and Brian Epstein were assertive about it.

'I said: "Whoooooah. What about McCartney–Lennon?" They said: "It just sounds better as Lennon–McCartney." I said: "McCartney–Lennon sounds pretty good."'

That argument for a switch to McCartney–Lennon won through for the pecking order on the Beatles' second single, coupling 'Please Please Me' with 'Ask Me Why', which were both Lennon compositions. Paul's name took priority, too, on the third single, which coupled the jointly written 'From Me to You' with 'Thank You Girl', a Lennon song. The wording reverted to Lennon-McCartney for the coupling of 'She Loves You' and 'I'll Get You'. Perhaps to appease Paul as the Beatles escalator to success moved so rapidly, all of their eight new songs on the Beatles' début album *Please Please Me* were credited to McCartney–Lennon.

But the plot thickened, or rather solidified, thereafter, when everything they wrote, whether alone or together, was projected as Lennon–McCartney.

'I stepped down,' Paul says. 'I have actually thought since that I should have said that some of the songs can be called Lennon–McCartney, some McCartney–Lennon.' There were clear individual levels of contribution to their works, even when they collaborated; he who had instigated the idea, or dominated a song, could have had his name first. And that would have avoided the 'slight resentment' that Paul admits has been on his mind over the years . . . 'that my greatest moment in a song [on 'Yesterday'] has got some other guy's name in front of mine. I really anticipate a possibility in the future when people might look at 'Yesterday' and say: "That's a great John Lennon song." But I have learned not to mind.'*

McCartney becomes animated, demonstrating a wide spectrum of emotions, on the subject of John Lennon. His assassination outside his New York home on 8 December 1980 came ten years after one of the most vitriolic bust-ups in the history of entertainment. In 1971, a year after McCartney had mounted an action in the High Court in London to dissolve the Beatles partnership and John and his wife Yoko had settled in New York, Paul's relationship with his former buddy plummeted. Their fights raged in public: in song, in press interviews, and through their lawyers.

Things had begun to go awry for the Beatles after the accidental death, at thirty-two, of their manager, Brian Epstein, on 27 August 1967. In conversations for this book and elsewhere, Paul has often criticized Epstein's business decisions for the Beatles. Epstein, however, had qualities as a peacemaker, and the rancour that built up after his death had no precedent within the Beatles during his tenure as their manager. Certainly he and the Beatles were growing apart in the months before his death, but he might have been able to plead successfully for unity. He had cool diplomatic skills which cured many temperamental scenes during their touring years. And the Beatles liked him.

Paul declares that a key to understanding the real Lennon, his

---

* A reversal to McCartney–Lennon was implemented by Paul on several post-Beatles records by him. All of the Beatles-era songs on the 1976 triple live album *Wings Over America*, including 'Yesterday', are credited 'McCartney–Lennon'.

own chemistry with John, and by extension the bitter scenes between them, is rooted in several factors. One is John's insecurity,
which stemmed from his childhood. Another is the suit of armour
which John wore, presenting a 'tough guy' image when he was in
fact quite sentimental. Yet another was John's political cunning.

'John shouted louder. John was a forceful guy. He was more in-
sistent on the Lennon–McCartney description,' Paul says. 'Why
did John go away with Brian on the so-called gay episode? [The
eight-day visit by Lennon with Epstein to Spain in 1963 which
provoked rumours of a homosexual liaison.] I think it was to
establish that he was the leader of the Beatles: "If you want to talk
to this group, you talk through me." I think it was a power play.'
McCartney discounts the theories that there was a homosexual encounter between Lennon and Epstein, adding that he slept in a
million hotel rooms with John and there had never been the
slightest indication that he was anything other than heterosexual.

John Lennon's wish for some sort of control stemmed from his
insecure childhood, in Paul McCartney's opinion. By the time
Paul met him, he was 'very focused, very witty, very sensitive, and
one of my theories is that he was that way because he'd come
from the school of hard knocks. If you look at his life . . . his dad
leaving him when he was two, his mum getting killed by a car
driven by an off-duty policeman who didn't get brought to book
. . . he went through some terrible things. He was brought up by
his auntie and John was always having to defend himself . . . after
all, it was Liverpool and it was the Teddy Boy era and there'd be
the odd brush with kids: "Who are *you* looking at, then?" I came
from a much more secure family, though I remember John telling
me he thought there was a jinx against the male members of his
family. His dad went away, then his Uncle George died.'*

Partly because of such traumas, John developed a battling personality and an outer shell that was difficult to penetrate, says
Paul. After flopping badly in his grammar school examinations,
John was on the verge of being expelled from Liverpool College
of Art when the Beatles came along as his lifeline. 'John read a lot,

* George Smith died two years before Paul met John. John's mother died one
year after that meeting.

you know,' Paul says. 'Lewis Carroll, the complete works of Winston Churchill; he was the only person I've ever met to this day to have read that.'

The contrast with Paul, who often did quite well at Liverpool Institute, was acute although there were examples of reprobate behaviour in the young McCartney, too. His school reports contained comments like: 'If he doesn't improve I shall punish him' (from the headmaster) and: 'He is the biggest disappointment in the class.' And so the foundation of the Beatles was an extraordinary partnership of the iconoclast and the traditionalist, both gifted but approaching their chosen art form from different perspectives. McCartney's orderly family background, 'until it went to pot when Mum died', was rooted in music and a caring, demonstrative gathering of aunts, uncles and cousins. To that, he added the natural teenage fascination with the rock 'n' roll sounds of the 1950s. Paul's was a more rounded, orderly approach to life, work and music.

Although John enjoyed debunking older music, particularly show tunes, which he told Paul he hated, buried deep in him was a sweeter person than he wanted to exhibit, particularly in the Beatles years. 'The thing about John was that he was all upfront,' Paul says. 'Most people stayed up late and got drunk with him and thought they were seeing John. You never *saw* John! Only through a few chinks in his armour did I ever see him because the armour was so tough. John was always on the surface tough, tough, tough.'

There were contradictions in Paul's partner that gave him away, however. 'He didn't like many musicals, although he enjoyed *West Side Story*. Yet one of his favourite songs was "Girl of My Dreams". And he loved "Little White Lies". He also went on to write the lullaby 'Goodnight,' which Ringo sang. That side of John he'd never dare show, except in very rare moments.*

'I remember one of my special memories. We were in Obertauern, Austria, filming for *Help!* John and I shared a room and

---

* A radio favourite in the early 1950s, the sweet ballad 'Girl of My Dreams' was recorded by Bing Crosby, Perry Como, the Four Aces and Vic Damone, all of whose music Lennon would lampoon as 'boring' during his Beatles years. 'Little White Lies' was a 1957 hit in America for Betty Johnson; it had been written twenty years earlier.

we were taking off our heavy ski boots after a day's filming, ready to have a shower and get ready for the nice bit, the evening meal and the drinks. And we were playing a cassette of our new recordings and my song 'Here, There and Everywhere' was on there. And I remember John saying: "You know, I probably like that better than any of my songs on the tape". Now, if I say that, people will say: oh great – how can we prove or disprove that? But I know it's so.' That was, Paul said, the only time John said that about 'Here, There and Everywhere' (always one of McCartney's favourites of his own work); and it was one of the rare moments when John allowed that he could enjoy a slice of sentiment in song.

'He was not the kind of guy who would say: "Hey, my mate's written 'Here, There and Everywhere'." He would never say that, so unfortunately I think the world has to have had a false impression of John. I think John was a really nice guy – covering up. He didn't dare let you see that nice side. So it was always rock 'n' roll, rock 'n' roll, rock 'n' roll . . . till you actually caught him in the right moment. When you admit to being sentimental, as I do, you set yourself up for pot shots. John could never risk making himself vulnerable like that.

'And you can see how my reputation has progressed. For some people, I'm the soppy balladeer, that's how my detractors put it. John would guard against that. It wasn't until his final album [*Double Fantasy*], with songs like 'Beautiful Boy', written for Sean [Lennon's son, five years old at the time of his father's murder], that you'd see such beautiful warmth.

'One of my other great memories of John is from when we were having some argument. I was disagreeing and we were calling each other names. We let it settle for a second and then he lowered his glasses and he said: "It's only me . . ." And then he put his glasses back on again. To me, that was John. Those were the moments when I actually saw him without the façade, the armour . . . which I loved as well, like anyone else. It was a beautiful suit of armour. But it was wonderful when he let the visor down and you'd just see the John Lennon that he was frightened to reveal to the world.'

McCartney insists that his old partner was 'no more rock 'n' roll than me. At the beginning we all bought leather jackets. You didn't have to persuade me to get the leather jackets or trousers; I was down there as fast as anyone. One of my annoyances about the film *Backbeat* is that they've actually taken my rock 'n' roll-ness off me. They give John the song 'Long Tall Sally' to sing and he never sang it in his life. But now it's set in cement. It's like the Buddy Holly and Glenn Miller stories. The Buddy Holly story doesn't even mention Norman Petty [Holly's manager and mentor] and the Glenn Miller story is apparently a sugar-coated version of his life. Now *Backbeat* has done the same thing to the story of the Beatles.'

If McCartney is keen to draw a portrait of Lennon different from John's abrasive image, he is equally prepared to admit his own flaws. Dewy-eyed though he is about people, relationships and particularly his family, he admits to handling the deaths of loved ones badly. It is another difficulty in grappling with the complexities of his personality. As one whose work centres on people's feelings, he might be expected to know how to confront the low moments as well as the many celebratory events in his life. But he's bad at it. The same fourteen-year-old who blurted out something he would later regret, upon the death of his mother, did something similarly inept when his old buddy Lennon was shot dead.

'I'm very funny when people die. I don't handle it at all well, because I'm so brought down that I try to bring myself up. So I don't show grief very well. It actually leads some people to think I don't care, and I do. I'm not good at it like some people: my brother goes to many funerals, whereas I don't, which is bad news because really, getting older, I'm just going to have to. And I hate them.

'My excuse is a conversation I once had with my Dad, who said: "I hate funerals." So when it came to the time of my Dad's funeral, in my own mind I was doing him the honour of not going. Which was very perverse, and nobody in the family appreciated it. But, knowing he hated funerals, I determined to be like him. I said to myself when it happened: "I hate funerals, too. I won't be going to this one." It's obviously a bad handling of the situation. It's so much easier just to go. If only for what people think of you.

'But I've always been kind of inward about those things. So I just deal with it myself. When John Lennon died, someone stuck a microphone in the car as I was coming out of AIR studios in London. We'd all gone to work, George Martin, me and the guys. We were all so devastated and shocked, none of us wanted to stay at home. When someone stuck that microphone in front of me and asked: "What do you think about John Lennon's death?" I said: "It's a drag," trying to come up with the most meaningful thing.'

Later, realizing how that remark appeared flippant in print, Paul regretted not saying something that reflected his real sadness. 'Of course when I got home that night I wept like a baby, calling Chapman [John's assassin] the jerk of all jerks. If my true feelings would have come out in the press, I would have looked better. But I'm actually very bad at showing my true feelings at times like that. I keep them to myself, except for showing them to my wife, my kids, and people close to me. I'm not very good in public at showing what my true feelings are.'

The assassination of John Lennon hangs over the entire story of the Beatles. The sadness of Paul McCartney at the loss of his partner has been joined by an irritation at what he sees as an inaccurate rewriting of history being applied to John's life and work, and its relationship with McCartney, Harrison and Starr. The death of John has, in McCartney's view, generated too much guesswork about their association that he finds unfair. 'There was a book of poetry in which "Blackbird", my song which John didn't have anything to do with, went down as a Lennon–McCartney poem,' he says. 'It's a pity really, because it tends to make for revisionism of the whole thing.'

The complexity of their characters has been portrayed too simplistically in Paul's view: Lennon as the tough guy, McCartney as the romantic. 'On the *surface* I think John was more rock 'n' roll, but when you scratched that surface the truth of it was that we were all very similar people who showed various sides of ourselves. And it was all to to do with how secure your upbringing was. Mine was pretty secure, until I lost my mum. But before that, it was very secure. There were always lots of babies being thrust on me, so when Linda and I finally had a baby it was no worry for me.' He vividly remembers an episode at John and Yoko's home in New York. 'Linda and I went to visit and John and Yoko wouldn't even let us touch Sean! We said: "Oh, lovely baby, come on, can we get hold of him?" They said: "No, you'd better not." We said: "Well, we've had kids, we're all right, I won't drop him." I didn't come from that syndrome where you think they're like glass when you hold them. I jiggled them and relaxed.'

That incident, and a conversation that followed which explained John's attitude, brought home to Paul their different backgrounds. 'Linda said, as American women do: "Whenever our family had company, I pretty much had to go to bed." Yoko [her father was a Japanese banker working in America] said: "When we had company, we had to go to bed, too." John said: "We didn't even *have* company." And I said: "Well, we did and we never had to go to bed. Mind you, it was always Uncle Joe, Auntie Joan, Auntie Gin and other relatives. But we never had to go to bed." And I think that meant quite a lot to John.' It underlines, to Paul, the solitariness of John's youth and the barrier he erected.

The healthy partnership and camaraderie that evolved from Paul and John's competitive streak was only one step away from sibling rivalry. It now transpires that one of John's earliest 'hurts' inflicted by Paul was McCartney's solo writing of the music for the Hayley Mills film *The Family Way* in 1966. 'I was told recently by Yoko that one of the things that hurt John over the years was me going off and doing *The Family Way*,' Paul says. The filmmaking Boulting brothers had approached him via George Martin. 'I thought this was a great opportunity. We were all free to do stuff outside the Beatles and we'd each done various little things.'

When he mentioned it to John, Paul said, 'He would have had his suit of armour on and said: "No, I don't mind." However, my reasoning would be that at exactly the same time he went off to make a film. He wrote his books [*In His Own Write* and *A Spaniard In The Works*]. It was in the spirit of all that. But what I didn't realize was that this was the first time one of us had done it on songs. John would write a book and I was supposed to not be jealous, which I wasn't. He acted in a film [*How I Won the War*]. But I didn't realize he made a distinction between all those solo things and actually writing music because this was the first time one of us had done it in film scoring. I suppose what I should have said was: "I'd like to write it with John," and then that would have been OK. It actually didn't occur to me at that time at all. So I went off, saw and liked the film, said: "Right, come on George [Martin]," and I must say it was all over very quickly.' He was especially proud of the speed with which he wrote the song 'Love in the Open Air', 'which picked up an Ivor Novello award as the best film song that year, which I was always very proud of'.

Confusion over Paul's work in the Beatles sometimes extends to the Inner Circle. Paul even had to assure George Martin that he had co-written 'Lucy in the Sky with Diamonds'. 'I remember going to John's house and him showing me Julian's drawing [from school], and John saying: "Lucy in the Sky with Diamonds. Good title, eh?" And we wrote it: it's John and me doing something like a Lewis Carroll. Now, John will have told George Martin that he had this great new song. He won't have told him: "Hey, yesterday Paul came to my house and we wrote it together." You don't. You just say: "I've got this new one." George would say: "Super, John, it's lovely." And he would assume it's John's song. In a recent book by George [Martin] it very nearly went down as one of John's solo compositions. So I find myself these days trying to fight for some of the credit, particularly because John died in such crazy circumstances.'

The prospect of 'Yesterday' being partly attributed to John in the future does concern him. 'I do resent that. So there was a little point there, way back, when I did think I should have stuck McCartney–Lennon on that one song. But you know what? These are small regrets. And it didn't happen that way. So it's fine.'

6

Publishing the Beatles

'How could you own *a song?'*

Paul McCartney does not own 'Yesterday'. Every time the song is performed (on record, on the radio or elsewhere), Paul is entitled to part of the songwriters' royalty which he shares with Yoko Ono as the executor of the Estate of John Lennon. But Paul does not control either the publishing of the song, or the destiny of this, his most successful work, in commercial decisions about its use. Along with 262 other songs written by the Beatles, most of them by Lennon and McCartney, 'Yesterday' is owned by Michael Jackson. (For the full list, see Appendix A, page 164).

The journey of 'Yesterday' out of the possession of the composer is a thirty-year odyssey which mystifies and angers students of the Beatles and followers of Paul's life and work. It is riddled with a complex web of deals and opportunities lost and won, of bruised relationships and allegations of betrayal and dishonour. While 'Yesterday' is a jewel in the crown, hundreds of other Beatles songs which he alone created are outside McCartney's control too.

Paul is saddened and frustrated that his songs are controlled by an artist whom he once considered a friend and with whom he sang on hit records. Yet for ten years, any attempt by Paul to seriously discuss a sale back to him of the works he calls 'my babies' does not even get to first base. 'Yesterday' and the vast body of Beatles songs remain firmly in the hands of Michael Jackson. And Paul says Michael will not discuss the matter with him.

Indeed, when Paul wanted to sing 'Yesterday' in his self-made film *Give My Regards to Broad Street* in 1984, he had to ask permission from the administrator of the song on behalf of Michael Jackson. Paul was originally asked to pay a nominal fee of £1 for the privilege of singing 'Yesterday'. 'And you have got to believe that was . . . *hard*,' McCartney said. Later it emerged that the fee for synchronization rights was waived.

Music publishing and song copyrights are not subjects that reach the public regularly, but what they represent – actual ownership of songs – is an immensely important aspect of the music industry. Major artists, including Elton John and Gilbert O'Sullivan, have fought famous courtroom battles over their valuable compositions, with huge sums of money being cited as their value. The mighty catalogue created by Lennon and McCartney has been a financial football for more than a quarter of a century. And it still causes Paul McCartney problems.

The Beatles' entry into the world of music publishing took place when they were aglow with the modest success of their first single, 'Love Me Do', in November 1962, and preparing to unleash 'Please Please Me', the record that would propel them to the top. 'We knew nothing about songs being *owned*,' Paul reflects of the period when he was twenty and John Lennon twenty-two. 'How could you *own* a song? It didn't seem to *exist*! It was [he snaps fingers] something in the air.'

Brian Epstein, their manager, was not much wiser in 1962. Though he ran a very successful record department in his father's Liverpool store, he was fairly naïve about the machinery of the music industry; what he knew about music, aside from a fondness for Sibelius, was restricted to sales patterns of such pop records as those by the Shadows and Anthony Newley. The actual business of the pop world was a foreign territory to the Beatles manager. He was never motivated by money, nor did he like the jungle of deal-making, for himself or the Beatles, either before or during their success. He felt passionately that their abilities, rather than tough dealing, would be their path to fame. Their fortune, he believed, would take care of itself.

Epstein did, however, fully grasp the importance of promotion for records. And he maintained correctly that a role of the music publisher was to promote aggressively fresh songs, on radio, on television, and by getting as many 'cover' versions as possible, to maximize income for the writers.

After first seeing the Beatles at Liverpool's Cavern Club on 9 November 1961, Epstein had signed them to his management two months later. For several months, he was mocked and rejected by at least five record companies before finally finding his refuge and the Beatles' future with George Martin at EMI Records.

Epstein found Martin via a music publisher named Sid Coleman, who ran the music publishing company Ardmore & Beechwood from offices above the HMV record store in Oxford Street, London. During his quest for a record deal for the Beatles, Epstein had gone to the record store to have some acetate discs cut as demonstration samples. When he casually mentioned to Coleman that he had been rebuffed by several companies, Coleman phoned George Martin, who warmed to the Beatles and to Epstein. Together, they were to help chart the evolution and revolution of popular music.

Ardmore & Beechwood was an American subsidiary of Capitol Records, which in turn was a subsidiary of EMI Records. Typically, Epstein showed his gratitude to Sid Coleman for steering him to George Martin by telling him that his company could be the publisher of the Beatles' first two songs, 'Love Me Do' and 'PS I Love You'. But Epstein was disappointed with the lack of energy, as he perceived it, of Ardmore & Beechwood in promoting the Beatles' vital début. He had vowed to everyone who would listen that the group would be 'bigger than Elvis Presley'. Inauspiciously, that first single had reached only seventeen in the British chart and Epstein felt personally humbled.

Such was the speed of the Beatles' work with George Martin that within two months they had their second self-written single ready, 'Please Please Me' and 'Ask Me Why'. Martin recalls Epstein's confidence in the record: 'He told me he was definitely not going to give the next two songs for publishing to EMI or Ardmore and Beechwood.' A habitual canvasser of opinions, Epstein asked Martin for some views on where to go. Epstein said he was considering giving the Beatles' song publishing rights to Hill & Range, Elvis Presley's publishers, who had a London office.

Martin reacted to Epstein's instinct with this advice: 'The fact that they're successful as Elvis Presley's publisher is a counter to what you should do. I think you should get somebody who's *not* successful, who *needs* to be, who would work that much harder. My second thought is that it would be much better to go to an

English publisher than to an American one, because you'll get much more response here.'

Epstein replied: 'Well, I don't know anybody in the publishing world. There are a lot of sharks there. Who would you recommend?' By then there was a strong bond between Epstein and Martin, who had recently signed the Beatles to a long-term recording contract. 'There *are* sharks there,' Martin agreed, 'but there are also some good people. I've got some very good friends I would trust with my life.'

He then named three possibilities to Epstein, as he remembers: 'Alan Holmes, an excellent man who used to run Robbins Music, very genuine, a good song man and a nice person. David Platz, whom I trusted very well. Third one was Dick James, whom I trusted extremely. And I said: "Of the three, the thing that Dick has going for him that the other two don't, is that he and his company are completely English. The others are subsidiaries of American publishers. And Dick James is very hungry. He'll bust his arse for you if you give him these songs."'

Epstein said he would arrange to meet all three men. Martin then phoned James to explain why an unknown man from Liverpool named Brian Epstein would be calling him to arrange an appointment. In those years, when show business was dominated by Tin Pan Alley, a phone call from Liverpool would be unexpected and might be rebuffed.

Explaining to James that Epstein was dissatisfied with Ardmore & Beechwood, George Martin was asked an astute question by Dick James. 'What does he think they *didn't* do for him?'

'He doesn't feel they got the Beatles any promotion,' Martin replied. 'He's looking for a publisher who can guarantee to get them on television.' Epstein, as a record retailer, knew the impact that a television appearance for the Beatles' second single would have upon the record trade. It would almost guarantee a hit.

That mention of a TV spot was one of the most important sentences ever uttered to Dick James.

Steeped in music, Dick James was a fine 'song man' and a shrewd judge of hits. He had been a professional singer since the age of eighteen, with a strong reputation as a smooth-voiced baritone in the prestigious British dance-bands of Henry Hall, Geraldo and Cyril Stapleton before going solo. In 1948 he had become the first British male singer to arrive in the US best-selling charts, reaching nineteen in *Billboard's* Hot Hundred with a ballad called 'You Can't Be True'.

Switching record labels from Decca to Parlophone in 1952, Dick met his new recording manager, the twenty-six-year-old George Martin, whose roster of artists were the balladeers of the day, singers Eve Boswell, Edna Savage and Edmund Hockridge, plus Dixieland jazz band Joe Daniels and his Hot Shots. Within a year, Martin had produced James's second big hit, his voice resounding around British homes on the radio with a powerful ballad, 'I Will Never Change'. It became his theme song.

In January 1956, James scored a colossal hit. Again produced by George Martin, James sang a song from a TV series, the novelty 'Robin Hood', which sold 500,000 copies, reaching fourteen in the charts, where it stayed for a total of eight weeks. The song's chorus, which James sang informally to his visitors in something of a self-parody of his singing style was:

> Feared by the bad
> Loved by the good
> Robin Hood, Robin Hood, Robin Hood!

An avuncular and well-liked figure in British show business, Dick James coupled traditional musicality with an astute financial grasp; yet he reflected that he had been exploited in his work as a performer. The deal under which he recorded for EMI would make business heads reel in later years. He received a derisory 2½ per cent of the retail price of all records sold.

With excellent ears for a hit song, James favoured the kind of music on which Paul McCartney had been weaned by his father, Jim: the warm, romantic ballads of Perry Como, Nat King Cole, Tony Martin and Bing Crosby. On the birth of his son Stephen, James decided to stop touring and enter the music industry. He was quite a catch for the Sidney Bron music publishing organization, because through his vocal career he had a vast list of friends and contacts in the industry, particularly at the BBC, the best outlet for 'plugging' songs.

After establishing many hits for the Bron office, James decided to launch his own publishing company. It was now 1961. With a £5,000 loan from his accountant, Charles Silver, he set up an office for Dick James Music at 132 Charing Cross Road, on the corner of Denmark Street. However, James had a tough first year as a solo publisher, despite his tenacity and solid knowledge of the music industry. The hit songs were not coming. He was worried. But his friendship with George Martin was about to reap unbelievably rich dividends for him.

James's fifteen-year-old son Stephen watched the pop scene carefully. When his father went home one night and mentioned that George Martin had signed a new group called the Beatles, the boy's ears pricked up. 'There's a chance we might be able to have them for future publishing,' Dick added.

'They're great,' Stephen remarked. He had heard their small hit 'Love Me Do'. 'Very new, very different,' he added, to his somewhat surprised dad.

On the night of 26 November 1962, the Beatles had recorded 'Please Please Me' and 'Ask Me Why'. Next day, Brian Epstein awoke in his room at the Green Park Hotel, London, with the acetate of that single in his briefcase. He had scheduled meetings with publishers at 10am and 11am.

A fastidious and punctual man, Epstein was irritated when, arriving on time for his 10am appointment, he was kept waiting because the publisher had not yet arrived in his office. By 10.15, he angrily told a secretary that if the executive could not keep to time, he could not do business with him. That said, he stomped out.

Arriving at Dick James's office twenty minutes early for his appointment, he assured James's secretary, Lee Harris, that he was happy to wait. But when she alerted James that the man from Liverpool had arrived, the jovial James bounced out of his office immediately and ushered him in, calling for coffee. 'Let's start the meeting now,' he said.

On two such contrasting treatments of the immensely proud Brian Epstein was a multi-million fortune won and lost.

'Have you heard of the Beatles?' Epstein began to Dick James. 'Yes.'

'Would you like to hear the new record?'

Taking the shellac recording of 'Please Please Me' from his briefcase, Epstein put the 45rpm acetate on the gramophone beside James's desk. When the high energy of 'Please Please Me'

stopped, James recalled later, he 'hit the ceiling', saying: 'I guarantee that will go to number one.'

How could that be achieved? Epstein asked, adding that if he
could do it, James could be the Beatles' publisher. James then instantly called upon his influential 'contacts' to again impress
Epstein, this time with a classic piece of salesmanship. With
Epstein listening, he animatedly telephoned an old friend, Philip
Jones, who had produced James as a singer when, seven years
earlier, James had hosted a weekly series for the commercial
station Radio Luxembourg. The two men had remained friends,
meeting for lunch with their wives and following each other's for-
tunes with interest. Now Philip Jones was the producer of a
highly influential pop TV series, the Saturday night networked
Thank Your Lucky Stars, launch pad for so many national hit
singles.

'Philip, have you heard of a group called the Beatles?' James
asked.

'Yes,' Jones said. 'They had a small hit with their first single.'

'Well, their next one is a smash. I've just heard it. I want you to
book them for *Thank Your Lucky Stars*,' James continued.

Even to a friend, Jones said, he could not do that without hearing the record.

'OK, I'll put it on. Wait a minute,' James said. From the
gramophone beside his desk, he played it down the telephone.

Agreeing that the performance sounded dynamic and original,
Jones booked the Beatles for their first national TV appearance,
on 19 January 1963, eight days after the single was due for release.

A glowing Epstein duly gave Dick James Music the publishing
rights to 'Please Please Me' and 'Ask Me Why'. At forty-one, the
experienced James was precisely what Epstein needed: a tenacious
foothold in the music publishing world.

'Please Please Me' rocketed to number one and the team stayed
together. James proved an energetic publisher who got on well
with the Beatles. Although he was not of their generation, they
recognized his professionalism and he really knew the ropes of the
industry. They recorded their début album on 11 February 1963,
and their third single, 'From Me to You' backed by 'Thank You
Girl', on 5 March, and all of these Lennon–McCartney copyrights
were assigned to Dick James Music, too.

Among Paul's memories from that period is a meeting arranged by Brian Epstein in Liverpool one morning. 'I think it was before we were going off to Manchester for TV or radio, when we were starting to get out of Liverpool. Brian said: "We'd better get the song publishing sorted out." We said: "Oh yes, great." We thought we were going to be the next Rodgers and Hammerstein; Lennon and McCartney! We were all excited about the idea and we didn't really know anything about it. We could understand owning a physical object, a house, a guitar, a car, which were our three ambitions at the time. But songs? We couldn't see how you could get hold of it to own it.' He describes himself and John as 'beautifully naïve'.

Remembering the early morning Liverpool meeting in a 'very dark ground floor mews flat, with no lights on', Paul recollects the lawyer present as 'presumably our representative. You have to be represented if you are going to sign for all your life like that. And Brian would have known that. We wouldn't. We learned that twenty years later, probably; I'm just beginning to learn that now, running a business of my own. I start to see what you can do and what you can't do. But of course, then we had no idea. We literally were children, in age and in mind. So we just had to trust to our great businessman. And it turned out anyway that Brian, lovely man though he was, wasn't the greatest of all businessmen. He didn't understand things quite as well as his father, for instance. Harry, I think, had a better understanding.

'So we went in there [to this mews flat] and Brian said: "We'll have to sign something to do with the songs, to make that all official." So we said: "Fine, where do we sign? You mean we're going to get published? Oh lovely, great." I'm sure neither of us ever talked about it again, really. It was just something that was done.

'My recollection is that I don't think the lawyer said: "Now, you understand, I am representing you; you must read it through for weeks and understand it all; know just what you are doing here." We actually thought he was Brian's lawyer. In retrospect I figure he must have been ours. But things were such that we wouldn't have thought we deserved our own lawyer. I don't think it was clearly explained to us.

'And that was the contract I am still under. That little murky signing in the dark mews in Liverpool is it. So it went on from there and that was the Northern Songs thing. We just didn't understand it. We didn't know what was going on at all. So we just enjoyed writing the stuff and playing it and we just hoped someone was looking after our own interests.'

As the success of the Beatles continued, Dick James had an idea without precedent in the world of music publishing. It was clear, he said to Brian Epstein, that McCartney and Lennon were very special young writers with a brilliant future. He wanted to encourage them. Rather than implement the traditional publisher-writer relationship of a percentage royalty which he would take from them in a long-term arrangement, he suggested they form a separate company which would give John and Paul better rewards, more incentive. Paul McCartney contests this statement by Dick James that he mooted the company; Paul maintains that he and John Lennon thought they were getting their own company and that what they got was neither their own company nor one weighted in their favour.

Whatever the vision behind the launch, the reality was that a company owned 50 per cent by John and Paul and Brian Epstein, and 50 per cent by Dick James, was established. The first pact between the parties was dated 11 February 1963 and the company, Northern Songs, was registered on 22 February 1963. All their existing copyrights would be vested in the company, all future compositions would be published by Northern, and all recently published material, namely the Lennon–McCartney tracks on their début album *Please Please Me* plus 'From Me to You' and 'Thank You Girl', was transferred from Dick James Music to Northern, too.* Dick James Music Ltd was appointed manager of Northern Songs Ltd for a ten-year period, expiring on 10 February 1973, at a remuneration of 10 per cent of the gross receipts of the company.

By an agreement dated 14 August 1963, Lennon and McCartney agreed to assign to Northern Songs the full copyright in all

---

* Epstein suggested to James that, as a memento of their first success together, 'Please Please Me' and 'Ask Me Why' should remain assigned to Dick James Music, where they remain to this day. However, Dick James Music was bought in 1986 by PolyGram Music, so this latter company now controls rights to those two songs.

their compositions published during the three-year period com-
mencing 28 February 1963. A total of fifty-six copyrights were
duly published under this first agreement, John and Paul's share
of the resulting royalties being paid into a private limited company they formed in May 1964. This was called Lenmac
Enterprises, owned 40 per cent each by Paul and John and 20 per
cent by Brian Epstein according to documents lodged on the official file at the Board of Trade in London. From 27 April, 1964,
NEMS Enterprises (Epstein's original company) was owned 50
per cent by Epstein, 40 per cent by his brother Clive and 2.5 per
cent by Paul, John, George and Ringo.

Although that first agreement was not due to expire until
28 February 1966, a second agreement in February 1965 varied
the original terms. Under this new agreement, Northern Songs
was assigned full copyright to all compositions written by Lennon
and McCartney (whether together or as individuals) for eight
years from 11 February 1965 to 10 February 1973, the two composers guaranteeing Northern Songs a minimum of six new
compositions per calendar year. Also under this new agreement
John and Paul nominated a new company, Maclen Music (40 per
cent owned by John, 40 per cent by Paul, 20 per cent by NEMS)
to represent their works and receive their due royalties, which
were 50 per cent in 1965, increasing to 55 per cent only for songs
written after 1969.

Although the Beatles were later to consider the rates unfair,
James had been charting new territory in publisher-songwriter relationships with the establishment of a co-owned entity like
Northern. In the years before the Beatles altered the entire fabric
of popular music by writing the vast majority of their performed
material, songwriters generally assigned their compositions to a
publisher for a return of 50 per cent. Pre-Beatles, the songwriters'
attitude was entirely different; they were grateful to see their
songs being exploited. Paul and John changed fundamentally the
status of the songwriter from 1963. They were so busy being
Beatles that they did not fully grasp that reality until much later.
Had they done so, valuable songs of the status of 'Yesterday'
might still be in the possession of Paul McCartney and the estate
of John Lennon.

In a startling move for a company whose assets were pop songwriters, Northern Songs 'went public' on 18 February 1965. The

issue of 5 million new shares was listed on the London Stock Exchange from July of that year, making part-ownership and dividends from Beatles compositions available to the public. This revolutionary flotation bewildered City businessmen, who were unaccustomed to assets like songs, which they perceived as trivial, becoming fiscal objects. But subscription at the initial price of 7s 9d (39 pence in decimal currency) was high and the share price climbed steadily, especially since the Beatles were still producing a run of hits.

Dick James was appointed managing director of the publicly quoted company, his long-time partner and accountant Emanuel (Charles) Silver, aged fifty-one, was its chairman, and together they held 1,875,000 (37.5 per cent) of the shares. Lennon and McCartney each retained 750,000 shares (15 per cent each), and George Harrison and Ringo Starr 40,000 (0.8 per cent) each.

During this period a financial decision was made which became ultimately perhaps the most disastrous in Paul and John's business set-up. In a move which can now be seen as fatally flawed, Lenmac Enterprises was sold to Northern Songs on 4 April 1966 for £365,000. At that time, Lenmac had tangible assets of some £262,000.

Then, as now, it seemed a weird move. What it did was 'free up' a nice cash lump sum for Paul and John. But the two most celebrated songwriters in the world were in effect disposing of their rights to the royalties due from their first fifty-six songs published by Northern. They were, of course, selling these rights *to* Northern, in which they owned a substantial chunk, but they were relinquishing the interest in them by their own company, which functioned solely for them. They could not have predicted the storms that lay ahead – for when, in 1969, Northern Songs was sold, Lenmac Enterprises went with it. So from that controversial day, the sale of Northern in 1969, until this time of writing in 1995, neither Paul McCartney nor John Lennon and his estate has derived any music publishing income from those first fifty-six songs. They include 'She Loves You', 'I Want to Hold Your Hand', 'All My Loving', 'Can't Buy Me Love', 'A Hard Day's Night' and all the other songs associated with the peak Beatlemania years of 1963 and 1964. (See Appendix A, page 164, for a list of the 263 copyrights in Northern Songs which are now under the control of Michael Jackson.)

In 1965, Dick James, in his active role as managing director, astutely increased the assets of Northern by acquiring the catalogue of Lawrence Wright, one of the most cherished song collections in popular music. With hundreds of golden standards, including Hoagy Carmichael's 'Stardust' and such evergreens as 'Among My Souvenirs' and 'Happy Days Are Here Again', it would yield rich dividends eternally. Paying £812,500, James beat off offers from several other companies to bring Wright into Northern. Rival bids included one from Associated TeleVision, a communications, entertainment and music publishing empire whose chairman, coincidentally, had been Dick James's former agent when he was a singer. His name was Lew Grade (now Lord Grade).

It seems ironic that the convoluted route taken by the Beatles' precious songs should have involved men who, with the experience of having been performing artists, understood the emotions of show business as well as the finances. Dick James, a former singer and prolific songwriter, was now romanced by his old friend Lew Grade, who was keen to build his song catalogue. They would meet for lunch regularly. James resisted Grade's overtures, saying that Northern was performing too well on the Stock Exchange for them to consider selling it. But if he and Charles Silver ever changed their mind, James said, Grade's ATV would get first option.

Paul and John's smouldering discontent with the royalties they earned from their music reached a peak in the summer of 1968. Brian Epstein had died a year earlier, and they wanted to explore their own business or, in Paul's words now, 'grapple with the Apple', the company they had launched as an umbrella for their work, creative and financial, and altruistically encourage other artists. In a promotional exercise, to make a film to launch the company, Paul remembers inviting Dick James to Apple's first offices in Wigmore Street, London, in June.

'It was in those days when we taped and filmed everything and we thought: that might be the thing to do, let's get Dick to come round. And we happened to have a film crew there; we thought we might just force him into doing something. On camera, he can't really say no.'

Paul recalls their approach to Dick James and the slightly reluctant response.

'Hey, Dick, I hope you don't mind this being filmed . . .' Paul
said.

'Well, all right then,' Dick replied.

Paul: 'Look, we'd really like to ask for a little bit more [percen-
tage royalty from their songs' income]. We've been more
successful now than any songwriters have been for any publisher.
And we're on a not awfully good deal, as you and we know. It's
not bad . . . but couldn't you see your way to giving us a raise?
That's really all we're doing, asking for a raise.'

Paul says now: 'We have been asking for a raise ever since to
whoever has been in charge [of Northern Songs]. And now, of
course, I am a long-serving, thirty-year employee, when even the
lowliest of people get raises. But Dick said: "No, I can't alter it.
I'm in this with Charles Silver. It would be absolutely impossible
for me to change the terms of the contract."

'We said: "Why?"'

'I now know, running a business, you can change it at a stroke
of a pen. You can say: I hereby revoke that contract. I'd like to
give these wonderful people a bit more. They should have 5 per
cent more each. It wouldn't have been difficult; Dick took on a lot
of stress which he possibly didn't need. You can only have so
many meals a day.'

'That was what we were trying to say: "Look, you've done
great. From being the guy who sang "Robin Hood" to becoming
the publisher of the Beatles.' Paul and John pointed out that Dick
had accrued a great reputation and consequently plenty of extra
business because he had the prestige that came from being the
Beatles' music publisher.

'John started to use an analogy of an acorn and an oak tree, and
it was very good, a smart thing. He almost got Dick over a barrel
on this one. He said: "Look, Dick, it was an acorn and it's grown
into an oak tree and it's even taken over the whole bloody garden
now."' Dick responded to the effect that he owned the original
acorn and he now owned the oak tree and there was 'nothing to
be done', Paul recollects.

Seen now, the filmed encounter demonstrates two generations
on a collision course: successful artists hardly camouflaging their
views that they were being exploited unreasonably, and a veteran

show-businessman appealing for reason. 'Tell me your problem,' James begins. 'Dick,' Paul responds vexatiously, 'we now think it is time we sort it [the royalties paid to Lennon–McCartney) out a bit more fairly.'

After they had made their points, Dick James implied that he could not see why Paul and John had wanted to raise the temperature in this way. 'You have got respect for each other's ability and integrity . . . I can't think of any other requirement that business associates need . . . I promise you I will try to sort it out [the request of Paul and John for a better royalty scale] as quickly as possible. I will come back and sit down with you and put it on the line.'

He added that if his professional adviser told him he was unable to do anything to meet the requests of Paul and John, 'I will still come back and honestly tell you so . . . that's the most pessimistic view I can take'.

John cut in, tetchily: 'We get advice, too, and it's up to us whether we accept it or not.'

Paul wound up the uneasy meeting: 'So, Dick, that's it. You go away and come back with something that you know won't start this argument again.'

For Dick James, who prized his integrity and fairness, such a combat was bruising. Since the death of Brian Epstein, with whom he had forged the Northern deal, James and others who had business with the Beatles considered them to be suddenly headstrong, arrogant, and, in a favourite James description, 'ingrates'. Paul says James never did return to them after that meeting with an offer.

Their head-on involvement with their own affairs was to plunge them inexorably into their personal Armageddon. 'And of course, we weren't expert in business even by then, even by the beginning of Apple,' Paul says. 'That's why Apple went wrong, because we didn't have the business sense. My basic housekeeping knowledge and my Dad's advice would always say to me: "Don't spend more than you're taking in." So I felt like I was the only one at Apple that was trying to do that.' He remembers one day trying to fire one of publicist Derek Taylor's several secretaries in the interests of economy. 'I said: "Come on, I'm trying to do a cut-back here." Everyone disagreed with me violently. George [Harrison] sort of said: "If you sack her, I'll reinstate her."

'So, I said: Whoops! And I had to back off that one. I said: "I'm only trying to save us some money." But it was taken on a more spiritual level: if you fired someone, you are not doing cutbacks, you're being a devil. Which obviously made it difficult to make any sense of it all. So we didn't know anything about business *then*. If you look at it that way, Dick only had to say to us: "Sorry lads, I can't adjust the contract . . ." Now I know that to take a pen out and make an amendment to the contract is ever so possible.

'He might have just had a sticky moment with Charles Silver, who he would have had to square; and they'd have to have had a meeting and if Charles wouldn't do it with his half, then Dick possibly could have been eminently generous and said: "Well, I'll do a bit from my half. But it's only half as much as I would have wanted to do." Some movement would have been great.'

Dick James, aggrieved by what he considered brutal treatment, loathed being pilloried and likened the session to a public trial for which he had not been given notice. The Beatles' methods of trying to sting him into action rebounded on them. In what would be an irreversible decision by Dick James, ultimately lethal to Paul and John, he decided to sell his share in their songs.

By 1969, the foundations of the Beatles had been shaken and stirred. After Epstein's death in 1967 John had stepped out with Yoko Ono and embarked on a series of public events which were ridiculed – planting acorns for peace in a cathedral precinct and posing nude on the cover of their album *Two Virgins*. Paul had met his future wife, Linda Eastman, and the Beatles were hardly united as they launched their own company. When I interviewed John in January 1969, he told me that Apple was 'losing £50,000 every week and if it carries on like this we'll be broke in six months'. My report of that went round the world's media and caught the eye of Allen Klein, a New York terrier in pop management who was then encouraged into Apple by Lennon, Harrison and Starr with a brief to sharpen its activities. Paul resisted this, and rebuked me for reporting John's loose-tongued admission of Apple's problems.

At that time, Paul was having his own difficulties with the other three Beatles. Linda's father, Lee Eastman, was a respected New York figure, a vastly experienced music industry lawyer whom Paul thought could be brought in to mastermind the Beatles' affairs. The other three said no, appointing Klein while Paul unilaterally appointed Lee Eastman his personal manager.

A saga of epic magnitude had begun. Dick James told me he felt very uneasy about the warring Beatles. Worried that the brilliant songwriting axis of McCartney and Lennon had been torn asunder by bitterness being played out in the press, he now reacted very differently to yet another wooing from Lew Grade, who was still keen to buy Northern Songs.

On 12 March 1969, Paul and Linda were married at Marylebone Register Office. This was followed by a blessing ceremony at St John's Wood parish church. That night Paul, ever the workaholic, went to work. As he had done on the eve of his wedding, he was in the recording studio producing a record by singer Jackie Lomax who was signed to the Apple label. Paul played drums on the record, an old Coasters track called 'Thumbin' A Ride'.

From mid-March until the first week in April, Paul and Linda went on honeymoon in America. On 20 March John and Yoko married in Gibraltar, and from 25 to 31 March the Lennons were in Amsterdam staging their first big 'event', their 'Bed-in' to campaign for world peace, lying in bed with the world's media present in room 902 of the Amsterdam Hilton. During their absence, on 28 March 1969, Dick James decided to accept Lew Grade's offer and sell his shares. With the predators in the City talking openly of the Beatles' apparent disharmony, James said he believed Northern Songs risked being ripped apart, with random selling of shares and eventual ownership possibly falling into the hands of industrialists who might not have any affinity with the entertainment world. Better, he told me, to keep the valuable work of the Beatles in the hands of a major British company like Lew Grade's. (This plausible explanation would later be ridiculed and attacked by the Beatles and others. Understandably, the Beatles merely wanted to know why James had not told them of his intentions.)* So James sold his own shares, and Charles Silver's, totalling 1,604,750, to ATV for shares and cash worth around £3 million. With its 137,000 shareholding already established from public purchase years earlier, ATV now owned 35 per cent of Northern Songs and announced its intention to bid for the remainder, or, at least, for another 15.1 per cent which would give it control of the company.

If Paul and John had not by then corrected their innocent youthful view that songs could not be 'owned', and felt they had vindicated their theory of a basically unfair deal, they were about to learn a harsh truth. 'Yesterday' was now beginning its journey out of McCartney's hands. Alongside many other Beatles songs which musicians and listeners the world over considered sacred, elevating pop music to an art form, Paul's historic invention was no longer a Wimpole Street dream, nor a car journey in Portugal. It was part of a collection whose future would be decreed by others.

Paul and John found out that James and Silver had sold their shares when they were informed by journalists seeking their reaction. At first Paul could not be reached, but John was confident he was speaking for them both when in Amsterdam he told the London *Financial Times*: 'I'll be sticking to my shares and I could make a pretty good guess that Paul won't sell, either.' Finally reached by the London *Daily Express*, Paul added: 'You can safely assume that my shares are not for sale to ATV.'

Asked why he had not consulted the songwriters before deciding, James declared: 'To telephone John and Paul would have been difficult. The call would have gone through a number of people and there was a need to keep it confidential.' An ebullient Lew Grade enthused: 'Northern has first-class management plus

* Lord Grade, born in Russia on 25 December 1906, is part of the greatest dynasty in the management of show business in Britain. Like his brother Bernard (later Lord) Delfont, Lew Grade began his life in entertainment as a tap dancer and later a professional ballroom dancer. He became, with his brother Leslie, a hugely successful agent to the stars. In 1962 he became managing director of ATV, succeeding the noted impresario Val Parnell, and within two years, when Lew's company took over the vast Stoll-Moss theatre group, he became chairman of that, too. A renowned and respected entrepreneur and deal-maker, he joked famously of his own astuteness: 'The trouble with this business is that the stars keep 90 per cent of my earnings.'

the talent of two brilliant musicians in Lennon and McCartney. They are brilliant, have no doubts, no matter what they may do with their private lives.' (This sentence reflected the public's new, somewhat cynical attitude towards the Beatles, and towards John particularly). When news of ATV's move hit the market place, Northern's price soared to 39s 3d.

'*Betrayal!*' The bitter feelings by Paul and John towards Dick James ran deeply in the immediate aftermath of the sale. And Paul continues to be livid to this day at the fact that neither he nor John, who provided Northern with its assets, was ever consulted before their songs began their long trail out of his control. Paul feels that the Beatles were 'not particularly well advised at that time'.

When I mentioned to Dick James the anger felt by the Beatles and their friends at his sale, he replied coolly that the decision to go with ATV was taken by Northern's board. 'The board of Northern, Clive Epstein in place of Brian, Geoffrey Ellis who had worked at Brian's company NEMS [as executive director] and their accountant Jim Isherwood at the time, backed me up in considering that that was what should be done.'

And was it a vote? I asked. 'Oh Lord, yes, it was a vote and it was a unanimous vote,' James answered. 'If there had been a vote against it, then people would have rethought it. But it was totally unanimous. Not unimportant, too, was that there were over 3,000 outside shareholders. We, the directors of a public company, had taken an oath. On becoming the director of a public company you actually do take the Bible and take the oath to act with integrity and look after the interests of the shareholders.

'Now, that wasn't only me, it wasn't only Paul, it wasn't only NEMS. It was over 3,000 independent shareholders and I don't think it would have been right or proper that they should have been dragged into a kind of potential victimization of the wrangles that would have ensued [within the Beatles] . . . well, had already started.'

And it wasn't, James continued, as if he had suddenly stood up and decided to sell to Grade. 'Lew had in fact been romancing me for months and months, since shortly after Brian Epstein died.' This was not known by the Beatles who, Paul says now, 'might have asked what was going on' had they been alerted.

News of the change of hands of the golden Beatles songs re-verberated around the world. George Martin was among Dick's fiercest critics. For fifteen years his friend and producer, and the man responsible for sending Brian Epstein to his office to enable James to make his fortune, Martin fumed on the phone to James: *'This can't be true!'*

'Yes, it is,' Dick replied, adding: 'I have sold. I'm tired of being threatened by the Beatles, and being got at. So I decided to sell it.'

Martin: 'Why didn't you ask the Beatles first?'

James: 'If I'd done that it would have been all over the place and then I could never have done the deal with Lew Grade.'

'I told him he was a rat,' Martin remembers. 'I felt he'd betrayed everything we'd done together and I felt I was in a position where I could say that.'

'He was wrong not to consult his artists. *They wrote the stuff!*' insists music industry veteran Roger Greenaway, a prominent figure in the world of music publishing who was also signed as a songwriter to Dick James Music. He describes James's argument that Northern might have been eaten up on the Stock Exchange, had he not made a move, as 'rubbish. Dick ran the company. They had a piece of it but he had the major portion of it. Dick was making out a case to show that he was not the guy he was. He was trying to make the buck for himself. He may have *believed* that he was acting in their interests but that couldn't have possibly have been the case. If he was acting in their interests he would have waited until they had a chance to decide for themselves. After all, he was the one who fell into it. George Martin took the Beatles to Dick. He did not find the Beatles and make them.' This criticism comes from a warm admirer of Dick James. Adds Greenaway: 'This did not change my view of Dick James. I accepted him warts and all. He was very good to me. I still miss him. And he was very good for the Beatles in that no one would have worked harder than him for them in getting their songs covered.'

James told me at that time that he went to face Paul and John at the McCartney home in St John's Wood. 'Linda had made tea. Everything was very civilized. I explained why I had done what I had done, supported by the board. Paul sort of shrugged it off.

John, who always placed great emphasis on respect and integrity for each other, was very cynical.'

James continued: 'I said: "Your financial gain will at least give you, regardless of what your earnings are from records, a substantial income." Although they were established at that time as certain great catalogue sellers, no one could really visualize how they would continue to sell in ten, twelve, fifteen years' time. I tried to point out to John that his capital gain, which wasn't like earnings from records on which tax was astronomical because his royalties were subject to ordinary tax . . . the reward he would get from his shares was in fact a capital gain and that was at the lowest rate of tax you pay anywhere in the world. I endeavoured to give John that point of view and I said: "At least that means you can put some money by for your children." To which he retorted quite cynically: "I have no desire to create another fucking aristocracy." That'll be the only four-letter word that you'll get from me, but that is verbatim what he said.'

With the die cast by the purchase of such a hefty part of their work, could the Beatles prevent ATV from wresting total control? With lawyers and accountants, they did some analysis to see if they could mount resistance, even at this late hour.

The Beatles themselves controlled 29.7 per cent of Northern Songs, and could find another 0.6 per cent among their nest of companies. Paul had 751,000 (worth around £1.4m), John had 644,000 (£1.25m) plus another 50,000 as a trustee. Ringo Starr owned 40,000. George Harrison had sold his 40,000 shares when his songwriting contract expired in March 1968, but Pattie, his wife, owned 1,000.* Subafilms, a company owned by Apple Corps, had 30,000 shares. One surprise owner of a block of 237,000 Northern Songs shares (equivalent to 4.7 per cent of the company) was Triumph Investment Trust, which had acquired NEMS Enterprises from Clive and his mother, Queenie Epstein,

---

* These figures, revealed when ATV made its bid to take over Northern, gave Lennon his first knowledge that McCartney owned 107,000 more shares in the company than he did. This caused conflict between them. John suggested that he and Paul had made a verbal pact to keep their ownership of the company on an equal footing. Paul later explained that he was investing in both himself and John and that, in his memory, he had told John about it and they had often agreed that investing in their own work was a good principle.

only two months earlier, in February, in a battle which the Beatles' Apple Corps had also lost.

Although, financially, the Beatles were not (yet) in a position to
put in a cash counter-bid, a bitter power struggle ensued, quickly
joined by a third force: a consortium of brokers and investment
fund managers which, together, owned the key 14 per cent of
Northern shares. The battle was played out between Grade, Allen
Klein and others on the financial pages of the newspapers for
several weeks. The Beatles finally succeeded in putting together a
counter bid but, although it was in excess of ATV's, there was a
fear over the possibility that Allen Klein would be installed as
manager of Northern should the Beatles' bid win. Klein sought to
defuse this argument by hosting a press conference at Apple on
28 April in which he announced that the experienced music
publisher David Platz would be appointed manager should the
Beatles win the battle. John Lennon enlivened the conference by
making an appearance and describing the ongoing battle as "Like
Monopoly, man.'

And so it went on, and on, and on, until an announcement was
made the evening of 19 May 1969: ATV had acquired an *option* to
purchase the share block belonging to the consortium should it
ever sell; this would give ATV 51 per cent of Northern Songs and
thereby control of the company. On 19 September 1969, the consortium fell apart – and ATV bought up enough shares to prove
to the Beatles that the battle was over.

Further action ensued when Maclen Music filed a writ against
ATV claiming extra royalties from past public performances of
their songs. (This dragged on for years, being settled in two parts,
in February 1983 and October 1984. Some additional backdated
royalties were indeed won, but other elements of the lawsuit were
lost.) And, interestingly, ATV incurred the wrath of the City
Takeover Panel by attempting to keep Lennon and McCartney
locked into ATV as minority shareholders. ATV was forced to
buy John and Paul's shares at the same price it had paid to other
former shareholders, the company giving the two Beatles £3.5m
in ATV loan stock. By January 1970 ATV controlled more than
99 per cent of the company. (Amusingly, ATV had considerable
trouble locating the holders of the remaining 0.7 per cent of
shares in order to buy them out, because they remained in the
hands of around 500 Beatles fans worldwide who, in the pre-
ceding five years, had been keen to buy a few shares in the group's

publishing company. Although they held only 0.7 per cent, these 500 or so fans represented over 25 per cent of the shareholders, and the Companies Act insisted that ATV obtain the approval of 75 per cent of the shareholders before it could enforce compulsory purchase of the outstanding shares.)

Considering all that had happened, it is not entirely clear why Paul and John both individually renewed their songwriting agreements with ATV when the eight-year contract engineered in February 1965 expired. The deals were probably struck in order to maintain good relations with ATV in case it ever decided to dispose of Northern. Paul was the first to do so, signing a new seven-year agreement on 1 June 1972 (effective from 10 February 1973), ATV commenting that Paul and Lew Grade 'have amicably settled all differences between them. They look forward to a successful new association.' (This was a co-publishing deal between ATV and McCartney Music, the terms of which were such that, upon conclusion of a fixed term, full copyright would be transferred to McCartney Music, later MPL Communications.) John Lennon signed his new deal with ATV in July 1974, backdated to 10 February 1973. Demonstrating that they had no ill will towards Grade, John and Paul both went out of their way to please the legendary British showman. In 1973 Paul made a television special (*James Paul McCartney*) for the TV side of ATV, on which he sang 'Yesterday' exquisitely and poignantly. Paul also agreed to Grade's 1974 request to compose the theme tune for a new ATV adventure series called *The Zoo Gang*. And in 1975 John performed live on stage (it turned out to be his last ever stage appearance) at a New York benefit dinner thrown in Grade's honour.

Even by the early 1970s, 'Yesterday' occupied a unique position inside the song empire controlled by Lord Grade. An estimated 1,000-plus cover versions had been made by 1973.

In those early 1970s, Paul McCartney had many other things to concern him beyond the possible eventual retrieval, with John Lennon, of their song copyrights. Alone among the ex-Beatles upon the dissolution of the group in 1970, Paul hankered for intensive activity, a fruitful solo career and the strengthening of his happy family unit. And a new decade had arrived, with rock succeeding pop as the language of modern music, albums becoming more significant than singles. The Beatles were not exactly consigned to history but nor were they lauded as they are in the

1990s. Before 1976, when nostalgia for the Beatles returned as people realized what had been lost, many thought of them as merely a fine 1960s pop group. They had been succeeded in the affections of a new generation by fresh groundbreakers such as Led Zeppelin.

It would be at least ten years, with the perspective of history, before the full significance of the Beatles, and McCartney and Lennon's work, was recognized seriously. By then, Lennon would be dead, the songs would be merely 'products' to owners who viewed them dispassionately . . . and the public would never be able to comprehend how Paul McCartney could not be the owner of the treasure chest he built.

7

Enter Michael Jackson

'I'm going to buy your songs . . .'

Michael Jackson was not born when Paul McCartney travelled by bus from his home in Allerton, Liverpool, to meet John Lennon for the first time at a church garden fête on 6 July 1957.

Born on 29 August 1958, Jackson was aged six in the year when the Beatles gripped America. He was then beginning his career as lead singer in his brothers' group the Jackson Five. By the time Jackson began his solo career in 1971, John Lennon had emigrated to the US, never to return. And the Beatles had split.

The prospect of Paul McCartney eventually collaborating musically with Michael Jackson, if predicted in the early 1970s, would have been met with derision. Sixteen years older, Paul was even then a universally acclaimed elder statesman of music. Though he would later mature his talent, Jackson was essentially a teen idol.

The end of the Beatles, however, left Paul feeling bereft. For although he has an iron determination and decisiveness to contrast with his charm, the insecurity that sits inside every artist is more present in Paul than in many of his kindred spirits. Despite the reality that many of the Beatles' most celebrated songs were written by him alone, Paul was wounded by the group's break-up and the void left by Lennon's departure was to be felt for several years. 'There was always the competitive thing with John,' Paul says, 'which I know was very good for me and I think he appreciated it, too.'

Paul's need for a collaborator partly to succeed John always seemed totally unnecessary, reflecting an odd lack of self-esteem. The fact that McCartney had assumed the mantle of a modern Cole Porter, George Gershwin or Lorenz Hart seemed utterly lost on him. Aside from the truth that his alchemy with Lennon was and is irreplaceable, Paul had proved his solo genius in and out of the Beatles. Any man who could write 'Yesterday' and 'Here, There And Everywhere' alone, followed by such powerful ballads as 'Waterfalls' and 'My Love' when the Beatles ended, does not need a co-writer. McCartney's is a self-contained talent when he wants it to be. He is a musician, lyricist and singer. Thousands boast of their abilities in just one of those compartments. McCartney, however, never seemed entirely satisfied or confident in his songwriting when his magical union with Lennon ended.

Feeling exposed and bruised at the break-up of the Beatles and the bitter war of words that followed, Paul decided to look for a songwriting mate from time to time. Eventually he settled for a working relationship with people less accomplished than himself, but sufficiently established to give him a fresh credibility. He linked with people who, just as Lennon had done, could assist him both in songwriting and vocally. There were to be liaisons with Eric Stewart, Elvis Costello, Stevie Wonder . . . and Michael Jackson.

One of the uglier sights of the early 1970s was of two geniuses of popular music, whose contribution to the world's pleasure would remain immeasurable, sniping at each other in the world's media across the Atlantic. John, feeling detached about the Beatles, wanted to build a new world, mentally as well as geographically. He denigrated many of his former colleagues in and around the Beatles; later, he would admit apologetically to George Martin that he had been 'out of his head' when he gave such interviews. Paul dealt with the end of the Beatles resolutely. Always more of the traditional show-business trouper than Lennon, he knew there was but one solution. After two solo albums, *McCartney* and *Ram*, he formed a new band, Wings, controversially featuring his wife, Linda. And he did what he loves best and could not persuade the Beatles to do during their battling final years. He went back on the road.

Working and writing prolifically with Wings, Paul continued to blend tough rock 'n' roll songs like 'Jet' with romanticism in song. And on Wings' sixth album, recorded in 1978 in the Virgin Islands, he wrote and sang an attractive song called 'Girlfriend'.

This was to mark the start of his creative link with Michael Jackson, not surprisingly, since McCartney sang the song in a falsetto style.

Asked later if he had written 'Girlfriend' with the American singer in mind, Paul said no, but he wondered what Michael might make of it.* The following year, Paul was surprised when Jackson's album *Off the Wall* included a cover version of the song. Issued as a single in July 1980, it reached number forty-one in the British chart. Michael Jackson arranged for Paul to receive a presentation disc to mark the fact that one of his compositions was on the album. People speculated on whether two giant songwriters representing different eras might one day work together.

To millions of pop watchers, the partnership of Paul McCartney and Michael Jackson was an exciting 'dream ticket'. Two different generations with unique talents, combining for occasional works, seemed to offer real potential. Michael Jackson must have thought so, because on Christmas Day 1981 Paul remembers, 'Michael rang me and said he wanted to come over and make some hits.' Initially, Paul did not believe it really was Jackson on the phone. When identities were firmly established and Michael reiterated his wish to collaborate, Paul told him he would ponder the idea. Later, he decided: 'Why not? I really liked his singing, dancing and acting abilities.'

In May 1981 Michael Jackson travelled to Britain, meeting Paul for the first time at his London office. Paul began strumming a guitar and the pair quickly came up with the basis for a song called 'Say Say Say'. Michael then went back to his hotel room and wrote most of the words for it, returning next day to Paul with his efforts. They were on the way to completing their first joint composition. Michael was invited to Paul's home in Sussex, where Linda took photographs of the pair at the McCartney stables, Michael riding a horse.

---

* Michael Jackson relates the history of 'Girlfriend', and his first meeting with Paul, differently. He says they first met at a party on the *Queen Mary*, which is docked at Long Beach, California. 'We shook hands amid a huge crowd of people and he said: "You know, I've written a song for you,"' Jackson writes in his autobiography, *Moonwalk*. 'I was very surprised and thanked him. And he started singing 'Girlfriend' to me at this party.' Jackson says they exchanged phone numbers but 'didn't talk again for a couple of years. He [Paul] ended up putting the song on his own album *London Town*,' Jackson adds.

On that same visit, Paul played to Michael on the piano an introduction for a song he had yet to complete, suggesting how it could continue. Michael completed the lyric for what turned out to be a song called 'The Man'. It was, therefore, a true joint effort, Paul writing the music and Jackson supplying most, if not all, of the words.

Those two songs were then recorded during the remainder of Jackson's stay in London, with George Martin producing. Paul's new album, *Tug of War*, had already been completed (and was to be released in March 1982), so the two new songs were planned for Paul's follow-up, entitled *Pipes of Peace*. This became delayed until October 1983, allowing Paul and Michael time to refine the recordings in the intervening period. Horns were overdubbed on to 'Say Say Say' and 'The Man' at Cherokee Studios, Los Angeles, in April 1982. Their friendship was growing. During that visit, another Jackson solo composition, 'The Girl Is Mine', was recorded, Paul duetting with Michael on vocals.

With 'Say Say Say' and 'The Man' held in abeyance, 'in the can', the first McCartney-Jackson collaboration released was therefore 'The Girl Is Mine', which came out on Jackson's *Thriller* album in November 1982. Released as a single, this peaked at number two in the US and number eight in Britain. It was considered by many to be the oustanding track on Jackson's album. With sales topping 40 million, that was to become the biggest-selling album in history and Michael Jackson was, at the start of the 1980s, the hottest property in the music world since Elvis Presley and the Beatles.

Just as *Thriller* was starting to take off, Jackson returned to Britain in early February 1983. He worked with Paul on the completion of 'Say Say Say' and 'The Man' in sessions produced by George Martin. Jackson again stayed with the McCartneys at their home, and went with Paul, Linda, George Martin and long-time Beatles and McCartney studio engineer Geoff Emerick to the annual British Phonographic Industry (BPI) dinner at the Dorchester Hotel on 10 February 1983, where Paul was presented with two major awards as 'Best British Artist' (1982) and representing the Beatles who were acclaimed for their 'Outstanding Contribution to Music'.

At that time, Paul was shooting his feature film *Give My Regards to Broad Street*, in which one sequence found him playing 'Yesterday' as a busker outside Leicester Square underground station. Explaining the origin of the sequence, Paul said that when he and John Lennon were teenagers, 'if you had to go to somebody's house you always had your guitar with you because you were going to practise together'. When planning the movie he told film director Peter Webb that 'we would wander along singing songs and showing off to the girls on our way to John's house or mine'.

The busking scene in the film stemmed from that recollection by Paul. 'The crew took me to Leicester Square one night, grotted me up with mud from the car-park, ripped my jeans and stood me on a corner. So there I was, standing there, plunking chords, doing a lousy honky-tonk version of "Yesterday". No one wants to look a busker in the eye so no one noticed it was me.' He wore dark glasses and a battered guitar case at his feet collected the coins.

'So money was thrown at me by an unsuspecting public. I'd be going: "Yesterday/all my troubles/oh, thank you, Sir/seemed so far away.' The money I made went straight to the Seamen's Mission. An old Scottish drunk unloaded all his small change at my feet, put his arm around me and said: "Awright, son, yer doing greet!"' A few punks clad in studs and leather passed him by and started dancing, not realizing he was Paul McCartney.

To preserve Paul's anonymity, the film crew shot the scene from the inside of a darkened van parked across the street. Paul described the short busking experience enthusiastically as 'the ultimate theatre for a guitar player'. He was not to know that when the time came to negotiate with the publisher for the performance rights for the song, he would be dealing with . . . Michael Jackson.

'I always felt like an older brother to Michael, that was my relationship with him,' says Paul, remembering precisely how 'Yesterday' and his other songs began their journey into the ownership of the man he considered an artistic partner and friend. During Jackson's visit to London, Paul and Linda were invited for lunch to the home of British actor Adam Faith and his wife, Jackie. 'I said: "Can I bring a friend along?" Adam's jaw dropped as in walked Michael Jackson, but he's not easily thrown, Adam: "All right, mate?" he said. So we were sitting around chatting. We had a lovely lunch and afterwards Michael just pulled me aside in the corridor. He said: "Can I have a word with you? I'd like to talk to you for some personal advice you might give me." I said: "Sure."'

It seemed such an innocent aside in that atmosphere of bonhomie. But the 'fateful five minutes', as Paul described what ensued in the corridor at Adam Faith's house, were to cause the ex-Beatle great emotional anguish in the years ahead. Rich from *Thriller*, twenty-four-year-old Michael Jackson listened to business advice from a forty-year-old artist who had been round the track a few times and had emerged battle-scarred but shrewd.

Paul remembers: 'I said: "You are now earning a lot of money. You are really hot. First of all, get someone watching the money that you trust. Make sure of that first – because it can all go out of the window and you won't ever know about it. That's an old show-business story". Next, I said, make videos of your stuff now, and own them. You're so hot; in ten years time you will own the rights to these videos. And I said: think about getting into music publishing. Those were my three things: make sure who controls the money flow; make some videos; get into music publishing.'

Michael Jackson returned to America and changed his manager. 'He went and made the *Thriller* video. And then,' Paul says, 'when I saw him again, he started joking. He said: "I'm going to buy your songs." I went: Pfffffffff! Elder brother, get outta here! Good joke, though!'

Paul's album *Pipes of Peace*, including 'Say Say Say', finally came out on 31 October 1983. 'Say Say Say' was the lead single. Paul and Michael joined forces to shoot a highly acclaimed video from 4 to 6 October in Los Alamos, California. Two years after beginning their collaborations, this was the first time Paul and Michael had been seen together beyond still photographs.

'Say Say Say' entered the US chart on 15 October 1983 at number twenty-six in *Billboard*'s Hot Hundred. It was the highest new entry since John Lennon's 'Imagine' had débuted at number twenty on 23 October 1971. Eight weeks later, 'Say Say Say' romped to number one on 10 December, and it stayed there for six weeks. In Britain it reached number two.

At Christmas 1983, the harmony between the two men was palpable. In Paul's news magazine to his fans, *Club Sandwich*, in which all the material is endorsed by Paul, a gushing article by a staff writer declared:

> Michael's collaboration with Paul stems both from mutual professional admiration and a true friendship which has grown between them. Both are legends in popular music, both have felt the strengths and limitations this imposes. Beyond that, they share much in their lifestyles and attitudes. Neither lives the life of the successful superstar, preferring family life and close friendships. They share a passion for cartoons – both are avid collectors – and an interest in art and drawing . . . Observing them together in the brilliant 'Say Say Say' promotional film one can only describe the combination as pure dynamite!

All this should have presaged a warm and fruitful association between two creative artists who even had vegetarianism in common. But Paul's free advice to Michael Jackson to buy songs as assets was to have a cataclysmic effect on Paul's wish to re-possess 'Yesterday' and a couple of hundred other compositions which he had written with and without John Lennon.

'I thought no more about it,' Paul says of that first mention by Michael of buying the Beatles catalogue. 'but then he said it once or twice later and I thought the joke was now not quite so funny. But he was still joking: "I'm gonna buy your songs." I said [Paul laughs]: "Yeah, great, well, that's good . . ." ' because it *was* the third piece of advice I'd given him.' The mere notion that a fellow artist and friend might be serious in a statement about purchasing Beatle songs was too fanciful to be taken seriously.

In 1981, just as Paul's friendship with Michael began, ATV had been re-named ACC (Associated Communications Corporation). Meanwhile, in November of that year, in the midst of the takeover battle, it was revealed that Lord Grade was seeking a buyer for ATV Music, which contained Northern Songs. This was surely the news Paul McCartney was waiting for.

At the age of seventy-five, Lord Grade was head of one of the world's most successful entertainment organizations. As chairman and chief executive of ACC, he controlled a company which had a turnover in 1980 of £167 million and profits of £14 million. With nearly 6,000 employees, it had massive international interests including cinemas (a chain of eighty Classic cinemas), Ansafone telephone answering equipment, control of the London Palladium and seven other major London theatres, and even the theatrical costumiers Bermans and Nathans. (Bermans provided the Beatles with their uniforms for the *Sgt Pepper* project.) In the music area, ACC owned Pye Records and RCA Records as well as Northern Songs. Lew Grade had a penchant for activities in the cinema and in recent years had become the most significant movie maker in the world outside Hollywood, with *The Pink Panther* and *The Muppet Movie* among his successes.

A resourceful expansionist, Grade announced in 1981 an extraordinary film-making programme, investing $120 million. This included a controversial plan to make a film entitled *Raise the Titanic*, a subject which fascinated Grade. That project alone was expected to cost his company some $33 million. Experts forecast that with that conservative estimate of its level of investment, the Titanic project was aptly named and could only lose money. And it did.

'I went to see Lew that year, when he was in trouble,' Paul McCartney says, noting the *Titanic* cash-drain that faced Grade. 'Lew was very good in the end; I got to know him quite well and went to lunch with him a few times. I like Lew Grade. Linda and I went to see him; he liked Linda and he'd do his Charleston routine – he used to be a hoofer. He was great. He was a lovely guy and we got to like him. I said: "Hey, Lew, these are my babies, these songs. I wrote them for nothing! And the price of them now is scandalous!" I said: "If you ever do want to sell it, would you please ring me and let me know, because I'd love to do it. And if you'd ever consider separating off Northern Songs from it (ATV), that would be incredible.

'I don't think Lew was very hip to publishing. He actually, I think, wanted to have it because he has so many TV shows for which he was always having to pay music publishing fees. He thought: "If I have an in-house publishing organization, I can use all those songs in my incidental music in the films." He wasn't a music publisher so he didn't quite understand, perhaps, just quite how valuable they were.'

Paul remembers his delight and amazement when Grade phoned him in Sussex to offer to sell his songs back to him. 'It was very nice of him, in the end when he was selling it, to ring me. "Lew Grade on the phone." "Hey, Lew, how are you doing?" He said: "Look, Paul, finally I'm selling it and I want to give you first offer of it all." I said: "Wow, that's fantastic." Against everyone's advice, he was willing to extract them from ATV. He was willing to take Northern, the jewel in the crown, out. Everyone had told him: "*Don't!* You'll never sell ATV unless it's got that in it. That's what everyone wants!" Everyone was getting wise to it.

'Lew said: "I'll pull it out for you. I'll sell it separately. Only to you." And he said: "The price is going to be £20 million."

'I gulped, thinking: Oh my God, I wrote them for nothing! Your own children are going to be sold back to you for a price. It's like buying your postcards back from Sotheby's. A bit of an indignity.' McCartney says he understood the reality of the business scenario and asked Grade for time to consider his situation.

He remembers swallowing hard. 'I thought: "Well, that's the ball game and, having spent so much for them, he can't give them away. So I said: let me get back to you on that. That's very nice of you to ring me and let me know. How long have I got on this?" He said: "Well, I'll give you a week or so." He was really nice about it. He didn't need to ring me at all. He could have just gone, like everybody else, behind our backs.'

Paul phoned New York to discuss Grade's offer with his lawyers, his father-in-law Lee Eastman and Lee's son John. They said that maybe something could be put together to meet Grade's figure, but they added what Paul guessed, that 'It's an awful lot of cash to raise, even if you're doing fantastically well.'

'I thought immediately: well, I have two choices. I can either try to find £20 million and it is not easy to find. I thought: well, I can't buy it all. Because John is involved. And John had died by now. And I thought: even so, it would just look terrible if I suddenly buy the Lennon–McCartney songs and bypass Yoko, and Sean and Julian and all the other various interested parties. My morals wouldn't let me do that. There was no way I was going to be seen as the guy who had stolen John's songs.

'I had had enough of this flak with Northern Songs and the Beatles case and the Klein stuff. There had been a lot going on that had been separating the three against one. I had been the baddie who had taken them all to court.' (Paul is referring to his High Court action in 1971 which formally dissolved the Beatles

partnership.) Paul reflects: 'That was a very, very difficult situation to find yourself in, to be suing your best friends. I wanted to
sue Klein but he wasn't a party to the agreements. They said the
only people you can sue could be the guys. Phew. I spent a month
up in Scotland walking round in the clouds trying to work that
one out. In the end, they said: 'Well, it's a simple thing. You
either lose everything or you do this. It's the only chance. I got
grey hairs over that.'

Paul decided to take what he believed was the second choice
facing him. 'So (after Lew Grade's call) I said to myself: 'what I've
got to do is ring Yoko, and we should split it. That would be the
ideal coming home of the babies, the songs. You have John's half,
I have half and that will be fine. The two of us will own the company; and that's the way it should be.'

Paul's version of what happened next is, he says, disputed by
Yoko. A few years have passed, and memories differ, but Paul
contends: 'I rang her up and I said: "Lew Grade has just offered
me the company. He said it's £20 million. We should do it. You'll
have half of it, I'll have half of it. That will feel good to me. John
will have his half back. It's ten to me and ten to you. I don't know
how easy it's going to be to find it. But that's the deal."

'And she said: "No, no. Twenty is way too high a price."

'I said: "Well, you may be right. Certainly as I wrote 'Yesterday'
for nothing! It certainly seems a little expensive for me, but that's
the ball game and we can't ignore it."

'And she actually did say to me: "No, we can get it for five."
From twenty to five? I said: "*Well*, I'm not sure that's right. I've
spoken to the man who's selling them. He says £20 million. But
you'd better get back to me."

'She said: "No, let me talk to a few people. I can do something
here."

'And of course, it fell through, obviously. We couldn't get it for
five.'

Grade was reported to have received five different offers, from
giant entertainment corporations including Warner Communications, CBS Records and Paramount. But none reached the figure
he was apparently seeking. 'I would like Paul McCartney to have
his songs back but he must come up with the right offer,' Grade
was quoted as saying.

The warm relationship Paul enjoyed with Lew Grade would, sadly, have no bearing on the future ownership of 'Yesterday' and all those songs which Paul sought. In 1982, after a protracted takeover battle for Associated Communications Corporation, the Australian businessman Robert Holmes à Court won control of ACC's shares. Paul says he went to see Holmes à Court 'but the price had gone up', and part of the deal was that Paul would have had to visit Perth to appear on a telethon on Channel Nine, the television station owned by Holmes à Court. 'That was the final clincher for the deal if I was going to do it. But it was all too much money so I couldn't do it.'

Shortly afterwards, the ATV Music catalogue featuring 263 Beatles songs and other catalogue properties was withdrawn from sale. For three years, there was no activity and Paul assumed the situation was deadlocked. And then, on 10 August 1985, the bombshell news hit Paul; Michael Jackson had implemented the priceless advice he had been given. On that date, Jackson bought ATV Music for $53 million.

McCartney was especially hurt that an artist with whom he had a firm relationship had not phoned him to forewarn him of such a plan. Paul says: 'This is where our friendship suffered a bit of a blow. He didn't ring me. I was rung by someone who said: "Michael Jackson has just paid $53 million for Northern Songs." I've hardly spoken to Michael Jackson since then except to say, er Michael you're the man who could give me a deal now, then. Will you give me a deal? Talk about stonewalling! He's worse than all of them. At least Dick James said: "I'm sorry, lads, I can't do any-thing."

'Michael Jackson told me: "I let somebody else deal with that." Of course, he's made himself just the latest in a line of people who won't talk to me about it. Which is to his discredit.

'I went to see him once when he was doing 'Black and White', off his last album. He was doing the video with John Landis in Los Angeles and I made a special appointment to go and see him. He said: "Hi, it's so great to see you." I said: Michael, I hope you'll understand, I'm under a slave agreement. Really, you could be the historical person who could actually put things right. I said: it's not like you're aching for money. You're doing all right. I think you should do this, morally . . .

'He said: "You know, I've cried so much about this, Paul." I'm going: Well yeah, OK, Michael, but please, will you see your people? Give me a promise that you will talk to your people about this. He said: "I've cried. I have told them . . .' "

Paul also told Michael that he was unhappy about the commercialization of his compositions, the licensing of them for advertising purposes. 'I said: let me explain why. We were very smart not to let them be used for Coca-Cola ads, all the songs, because it kept the integrity of the songs. The songs will last longer, Michael, if they're not cheapened. ['All You Need Is Love', 'Revolution' and 'Good Day Sunshine' have been licensed for those purposes.] Michael said: "I've cried over this, Paul. I've cried." So I thought: I'm getting nowhere fast, here. And I've not heard from him since. I've written him three handwritten letters and he has not even answered me. I'm a thirty-year employee of this company, on a slave deal, and the guy won't even answer my letters.'

McCartney might be less vexed about the matter if he received a message saying: 'Dear Paul, got your letter, thanks. Sorry, I've handed it over to my business manager.'

'He's stonewalling the only living writer of that company. He will not deal. It was on my advice that he bought it, the fact that he stepped into publishing at all, and I've got only myself to blame really. But I'm not going to give up. They're my babies.'*

Ten years after his purchase, in 1995, Michael Jackson has proved to be the longest-serving owner of Northern Songs. He tenders its administration to an outside company. At the time of writing, it is EMI in Britain. Needing permission to reproduce the lyrics of 'Yesterday' in this book, I could not secure these from Paul McCartney, but did so from the administrator representing Michael Jackson's organization in London. Paul, of course, owns the copyright in his own handwriting and could approve the reproduction of that; but the actual song lyrics and music are not his to license.

Theoretically, 'Yesterday' could be licensed for any commercial

* Michael Jackson's office in California was asked by this author in May 1995 if he might consider negotiating with Paul McCartney in the future on the sale of Northern Songs. There was no reply to the question.

use at any time. And Paul McCartney would have no recourse legally. It should be stressed that, with the exception of the Northern catalogue's first fifty-six songs, which were sold by Lenmac into Northern, both McCartney and the Lennon estate do continue to receive songwriting royalties from Michael Jackson. They still profit from the songs' performances. They just don't *own* them, so that the complete exploitation of Beatles songs is outside the control of Paul and Yoko. When 'Yesterday' is performed by someone else, Paul receives half of the writer's 50 per cent royalty (i.e. 25 per cent) for the world outside the USA and half of the 33⅓ royalty (i.e. 16⅔ per cent) for the USA.

While Paul is upset with Michael Jackson's continued ownership of the catalogue, and the secret manner in which he did the deal, he remains disappointed with Brian Epstein for negotiating what he considers were weak contracts in the first instance, and livid over what he still describes as the 'betrayal' by Dick James of the Beatles, and his parsimony in not reviewing the writers' terms when their bandwagon was making so much money for them.

Hindsight is a wonderful science: the story of the Beatles, particularly this dramatic, exhausting, tantalizing saga of how Paul and John lost control of their material, and in particular 'Yesterday', is littered with hypotheses: 'perhaps...' and 'what if...' Perhaps Dick James felt he had been overly generous, in the first instance, by suggesting a shared company with 'the boys'. He may well have thought he could 'score brownie points' with the brilliant new writers and their manager by forming a company for them, rather than 'hiring' them. But he certainly did not need to break the publisher's mould in 1963 by launching a dedicated publishing company. He could undoubtedly have encouraged Paul and John to sign a deal with Dick James Music, although it is George Martin's view that had he done so, he would 'probably have lost them after a year'. However, if Paul and John were as naïve as Paul says, that might not have happened. They were so industrious as songwriters and performers that they might have left their songs to Dick James to run, and there might never have been a public flotation of shares.

But should they have asked James to go to Apple for that provocative confrontation, which he found embarrassing and degrading? Would he have sold his shares if they had not, in his view, rounded on him? Was James's lack of consultation truly prompted by the need for secrecy, his claimed responsibilities to Northern's shareholders? Or did he sell because of selfishness? Or in anger and frustration at their lambasting of his refusal to budge on their royalties? Had Paul and John simply struck a raw nerve?

Perhaps it was a mistake to commit the copyrights to Northern for ever. A fixed-term deal might have given Lennon and McCartney less money in the first place but the songs would have returned to their ownership long ago. What if Northern had not been floated into a public company in 1965? Then ATV's aggressive takeover could never have happened. Dick James could still have sold his 50 per cent, but the remaining half would have remained safe. The decision to put Northern on the Stock Exchange had the advantage of turning McCartney's, Lennon's, Epstein's and James's assets into cash. They obviously felt the need for it, but what was their motivation? The Beatles were fully aware of the plan to 'go public'. If this had not been their apparent priority decision, the flotation would not have occurred and the ship would have been easier to control.

Perhaps Paul, John and Epstein should have challenged the appointment of Charles Silver as chairman, and such a major shareholder, in Northern. Historically, he was Dick James's accountant and confidant and worked in tandem with James without any particular affinity with the Beatles or the music industry. Paul told me he could not recall ever having met Silver, an utterly fantastic piece of news, even in 1995. How could a chairman not ensure that he had at least an acquaintance with a songwriter who was responsible for making him and his company a fortune? Paul and John might have insisted on an independent chairman, or a non-shareholder, or an alternating chairman. This would have radically changed the power base. When James and Silver decided to sell off to Grade, they owned 35 per cent of Northern between them and this was a huge body blow to Paul and John. Operating alone, James could have mustered only about half this amount and an 18 per cent holding would have been of such little interest to ATV that they probably would not have bothered to buy.

What if Paul and John had never sold Lenmac Enterprises back to Northern Songs? Though they may have been badly advised, it was still their decision. They were foolish to grab the £365,000 (a pittance compared with the revenue since raised by those fifty-six songs) instead of hanging on to the rights, but Paul points out that they trusted the business sense of their advisers at that time, who included the highly respected lawyer Lord Goodman. Perhaps Paul should have made Lew Grade an offer for *all* of ATV Music, not just the Northern Songs element, when in 1981 it was known that Grade was seeking to sell. McCartney could simply have kept Northern and sold the unwanted parts later, or even kept them, for the catalogue included plenty of other valuable copyrights among its 5,000 titles.

Did Paul really need to consult Yoko? His ethics in doing so were magnanimous. But she did not write the songs and could never assert Paul's emotional attachment to them and to the entire Beatles story. Yoko did not meet John until 9 November 1966, by which time many of these songs had been written. Valuable time was lost when Paul quoted her the price of £20 million and she responded that the figure could be reduced to £5 million. Should Paul, who surely knew instinctively that such a counter-offer would scupper the deal, have waited at all? Should he not have moved immediately and independently, with Lennon dead, to buy back his babies?

What if the Beatles' internecine battles had not wrecked their chances of mounting forceful opposition to Lew Grade's takeover designs in the pivotal year of 1969? Paul and John, though united on this issue, were divided on most others at that time. They even had different representatives, Paul choosing Lee and John Eastman, John opting for Allen Klein. Better united, these elements might have forged a deal to hold on to Northern. Divided, they lost it. 'What happened,' in the view of song-writing expert Roger Greenaway, 'is that Paul let pride get in the way . . . and he probably regrets that more than ever now. It's a pity he let them out of his grasp, but that's so easy to say now.'

If Paul had written 'Yesterday' today, he would be infinitely richer from it, as would he and John from all their songs. And that has no bearing on the sale of Northern. From the start, their deal with a publisher would be far more in their favour. 'They were on 50-50, as I was,' says Roger Greenaway, 'but if only they'd lived in these times they would be on a 90-10 in their favour after that first hit record. Writers today don't understand how good they've got it by comparison with the 1960s. You never hear of an artist getting less than 70 or 75 per cent, or of them giving more than

25 per cent of their royalties away – at source, too.' His own
royalties with his co-writer were 50-50 on the publisher's *receipts*,
not at the source. 'That word 'source' never came into it. The
publisher knew about it, but he would never put it in a document.
It meant they sold your stuff abroad and they had to pay us 50
per cent. They wanted to keep their 50 per cent overseas, send 50
per cent back to Britain, and pay us half of it. So actually it became 25 per cent at source! That's all we got from abroad in those
years. They all did it. It was called business practice then. It was
not regarded as cheating. But as the judge said in the famous
Elton John case, accepted business practice does not make something right.'

It seems faintly ironic that Michael Jackson should dedicate his
autobiography, *Moonwalk* published in 1988, to Fred Astaire,
whose dancing clearly inspired him. Paul McCartney has carried a
lifelong torch for the charming singing of Astaire. Yet two artists
with that inspiration in common seem unable to unite on a wider
issue.

Writing that he considers himself a musician who is incidentally
a businessman, Michael Jackson states that both he and Paul
McCartney have learned the hard way, about business and the importance of publishing and royalties 'and the dignity of
songwriting . . . Songwriting should be treated as the lifeblood of
popular music.' The creative process, Jackson observes, does not
involve time clocks or quota systems, but inspiration. Many of his
ideas came in dreams, he says. Elsewhere, Michael states that he
believes in wishes and in a person's ability to make a wish come
true.

Since his old friend Paul McCartney wrote 'Yesterday' in his
dreams, perhaps Michael Jackson will one day lift the phone or
write a letter to England, to help a friend's wish to reach fruition.

8

Paul McCartney Today

'I don't want to be a living legend'

Linda McCartney was twenty-three and living in Arizona when 'Yesterday' was released in America in 1965. Separated from her first husband, and living with her daughter, Heather, nearly two years old, in a semi-detached house, Linda recalls visiting her friendly neighbours to watch the Beatles on *The Ed Sullivan Show* on 12 September 1965.

'I remember thinking "Yesterday" was so poignant and so meaningful. I loved it. Everybody was going: "Wow; it isn't *just* their looks any more." It was their music. I was never a fanatical Beatles fan. I was always more into it for the music. The song was meaningful to a lot of people because, while we always think we won't look back, we do.' Linda ordered her copy of the 'Yesterday' single by mail order from New York. 'Why I didn't get it in Arizona, I don't know.'

An artistic spirit, Linda had a family background steeped in music, like that of Paul. In a parallel with Paul's musical inspiration from his dad, Linda's introduction to the entertainment world came from her father in the pre-rock 'n' roll years.

Linda's father, Lee Eastman, was the son of Russian-Jewish immigrants to the US who had met on Ellis Island. He had married Louise Linder, whose Cleveland family was independently wealthy, owning department stores. Linda has an older brother, John (who is now Paul's lawyer) and two younger sisters, Laura and Louise.* Graduating from Harvard, to which he had won a scholarship at age sixteen, Lee Eastman had first joined a New

---

* When Linda was eighteen her mother died in a plane crash. Her father died of a stroke in New York Hospital on 30 July 1991, aged eighty-one.

York law firm and specialized in divorce. He hated that and, with a love of music, headed for the world of entertainment, striking out with his own firm. At the start of the 1950s he began his meteoric rise to success as one of the world's top show-business lawyers. His early clients were bandleader Sammy Kaye, a bandleader/clarinettist who had a 1964 hit with 'Charade'; Tommy Dorsey, in whose band a singer named Frank Sinatra would serve a crucial apprenticeship; leading jazz pianist Joe Bushkin, a star soloist who also starred with Benny Goodman and Bing Crosby; songsmith Jerry Herman, and a host of influential songwriters and musicians who made their mark on the music map in the 1940s and beyond.

The songwriters and musicians who would visit the Eastman house socially were legends. Linda grew up hearing the family piano being played by such friends of her father as Harold Arlen, composer of a huge list of evergreens including 'Stormy Weather', 'I've Got the World on a String', 'It's Only a Paper Moon', 'Over the Rainbow', 'Let's Fall in Love', 'Come Rain or Come Shine', 'Blues in the Night', 'That Old Black Magic' and 'The Man That Got Away'.

Another family friend was Hoagy Carmichael, the writer and singer of classics including 'Stardust', 'Skylark', 'Rockin' Chair', 'Georgia on My Mind', 'Lazy River', 'Lazy Bones', 'How Little We Know', 'Baltimore Oriole' and 'The Nearness of You'. Yet another was Jule Styne, the British-born lyricist who worked with Sammy Cahn on such perennially popular songs as 'Three Coins in the Fountain', 'The Party's Over', 'Just in Time', 'People', 'Don't Rain on My Parade' and 'Diamonds Are a Girl's Best Friend'.

The songwriter Jack Lawrence was also an Eastman client. When Linda was two, Lee suggested he wrote a song as a dedication to his daughter. That song, 'Linda', co-written with Ann Rohell, was included in the Robert Mitchum-Burgess Meredith movie *The Story of GI Joe* in 1945. Recordings of the ballad were made by Buddy Clark (a highly rated former singer with the Benny Goodman band) who had great success with the single in 1947; Perry Como; Charlie Spivak and his Orchestra, and Jan and Dean, who had success with the song in 1961 before adapting it to the surf sounds that made them popular. In Britain, 'Linda' was recorded by two popular 1950s crooners: Jimmy Young, now a Radio 2 broadcaster. And . . . Dick James.

Against this family background of a passion for songs and the people who made them, Linda remembers: 'I used to go to all the Broadway shows. My father put together the E.H. Morris publishing company for Buddy Morris; everybody in the music business who was friendly with my father would come by our home.' Though she was raised as a child in suburban Scarsdale, the Eastmans later had an apartment on Park Avenue in Manhattan, and a house in the Hamptons.

Linda's home must have been alive with beautiful music. Lee Eastman, astute and respected though he was as a music publisher, also loved great art and amassed a priceless collection of works by Picasso, Rothko and De Kooning (whom he represented). That was the foundation on which her future union with Paul would flourish, for while Jim McCartney's financial status was very different, he adored the kind of melodies, and the non-materialistic characteristics, which were among the characteristics of his daughter-in-law.

Contrary to myth, Linda is not related to the Eastman-Kodak name, and her successful career as a photographer was established before she met Paul. Her early love of standard popular music merged with the arrival of rock 'n' roll. Linda was attracted by the energy of rhythm-and-blues as well as by the melody of the Everly Brothers and Buddy Holly and the Crickets. This was a precise parallel with her future husband, who was similarly stimulated by youthful rock and straight pop, enabling him to come through with beautiful ballads like 'Yesterday'.

Linda's first rock photograph was of the Rolling Stones at a press reception aboard a ship cruising the Hudson River in 1966. As she became an *habitué* of the New York clubs, she empathized with the lifestyle of the musicians she photographed. She hung out with them and knew their music in exhaustive detail. An upwardly mobile photographer throughout 1966, she caught the spirit of the era skilfully with seminal photographs of such Sixties icons as the Doors, the Who, Cream, Simon and Garfunkel, Bob Dylan, Buffalo Springfield, Jimi Hendrix, Janis Joplin and Otis Redding. She was an accepted part of the music crowd and her career was in orbit. The artists, in turn, had found a kindred spirit in the press, someone who understood their muse.

At the New York home of a friend of Linda's, Brian Epstein would join the throng for parties. Visiting London, Linda impressed Epstein with her photographs of him and Brian Jones of the Rolling Stones. He bought them. Now she was 'in' with a tsar of Swinging London, and Epstein invited her to the party on 19 May 1967 at his Belgravia home to launch the Beatles' epochal album *Sgt Pepper's Lonely Hearts Club Band*. Her pictures from that night, particularly of a smiling Paul shaking hands with John, were among her brilliant evocations of the decade.*

Visiting a London club with some musicians, she met Paul again. Their eyes connected. A year later, when he was at a New York press conference with Lennon to launch Apple, they met again and their romance blossomed in California before she came at his invitation to London. Witnessing the slow disintegration of the Beatles, in and out of the recording studio, she continually took photographs, demonstrating what Lennon called her 'eye for an eye'.

Her first attraction to Paul was cerebral when they discovered mutual interests in the arts. 'He was into Magritte,' Linda remembers. 'She knew all those Broadway songs; you could never catch her out on that,' Paul smiles. Linda believes their mutual love for the older music helped to pull them together: 'We used to sing a lot driving around.'

Paul's breadth of knowledge of music impressed Lee Eastman. 'When I was going out with Paul,' Linda says, 'I remember we were sitting on my father's porch with John Barry [the film composer who scored the music for the James Bond films *Dr No, From Russia With Love, Goldfinger* and *Thunderball*]. And my father said: "Oh, my daughter's going out with one of the Beatles."' John Barry was able to assure Lee Eastman that Paul was not a raucous rock 'n' roller. 'John Barry really respected Paul so that made my father feel quite good,' Linda says.

Lee's knowledge of music and its people, shrewdness in entertainment law and properties, came to be a prime influence on the future of Paul McCartney as a businessman. 'My father believed that artists should own themselves,' says Linda. When Eastman became Paul's lawyer as well as his father-in-law, he asked how Paul wished to invest his money. In music, Paul answered. Lee Eastman agreed, pointing out that it was wise to deal with a subject Paul understood, rather than putting money into, say, oil or

---

* Her book *Linda McCartney: Sixties/Portrait of an Era* was published by Reed in 1991.

industry. And so he set about acquiring for Paul what stands today as one of the most glittering catalogues in music publishing.

Paul was thrilled that he was able to become the copyright holder of many of the songs he had always admired. The current list of copyrights and productions held by Paul's company MPL includes the work of his beloved Buddy Holly, Jerry Allison, Harold Arlen, Sammy Cahn, Hoagy Carmichael, Ira Gershwin, Marvin Hamlisch, E.Y. 'Yip' Harburg, Jerry Herman and Jack Lawrence, Frank Loesser, Johnny Mercer, Norman Petty (co-writer of some of Buddy Holly's smashes), jazz giants Jelly Roll Morton and Bessie Smith – which would have delighted Paul's jazz-conscious father – Jule Styne and Meredith Willson.

Totalling about 1,000 songs and including the acquisition of the E.H. Morris publishing company, which Lee Eastman had originally helped to set up, this makes Paul the proud copyright owner of such classics as 'Peggy Sue', 'That'll Be the Day', 'True Love Ways'; Hoagy Carmichael's compositions 'Skylark', 'My Resistance Is Low' and 'Hong Kong Blues'; Ira Gershwin's 'The Man That Got Away'; Jack Lawrence's compositions 'All or Nothing at All' (Sinatra's first hit), 'Tenderly', the classic recorded by Nat King Cole and many others,'The Poor People of Paris' . . . and that song 'Linda'; and Frank Loesser's big list of songs, including 'Luck Be a Lady', 'Spring will Be a Little Late This Year', and 'The Most Happy Fella'.

There is a substantial collection of soundtracks from shows, including those from *Annie, A Chorus Line, Grease, Guys and Dolls, How to Succeed in Business Without Really Trying, La Cage Aux Folles, The Most Happy Fella,* and *The Music Man.* Paul is especially touched that publishing the music to this last-named show brings under his roof 'Till There Was You', which he sang on so many Beatles concerts. He clearly revels in being a music publisher. Since he had lost the copyrights to his 'babies', he said, the precious catalogues which he bought, and which did phenomenally well for him, were effectively his 'adopted children', bringing some consolation for the loss of his and John's songs.

The Beatle who wrote 'Yesterday' so intuitively yet painstakingly thirty years ago has changed remarkably little. Some who have known him since the 1960s talk of a growing benignity with his realization that the enjoyable job of Chief Beatle is his for life. He has added layer upon layer of activity to that role, vigorously assuming a solo career and other projects.

The twin spirits of the Gemini, which he recognizes, are transparently evident. He has retained the core of his 1960s hippie philosophy but is diamond-hard in business. From the ruggedness of 'Long Tall Sally' to the gentility of 'Yesterday' is quite a leap but he validates both songs, and the differing facets of his tastes, as fine creative works. He respects both effort and success in every genre of the arts and espouses primitivism, debunking rules for artistry: 'I've been painting a lot for the last ten years. I have never had a lesson but I love that fact, because I'm working it all out myself. I identify very closely with the caveman who painted on the walls. I'm sure he didn't go to art school, but he had a passion, and he did it.' He sails a small boat, too. 'I'm out there with just a piece of cloth and me against the wind. I have a huge love of that. The primitive aspect appeals to me.'

His father's suggestion that he should get proper piano tuition, an idea Paul rejected, has found an amusing repetition with his own son, James. 'I'm telling him he should get piano lessons, but he doesn't want them, just as I didn't. It must be in the genes.'*

Like many artists, Paul is able to tap into at least three separate aspects of his consciousness, creatively working on his art, dealing with his business interests, while alternately enjoying the role of father and family man. Though he relishes his history and knows that his hits of yesteryear, when he and John Lennon were, as he says, 'mining gold', cannot be surpassed, he will probably never stop songwriting. These days, he carries a notebook with him regularly so that inspirational thoughts are not forgotten. When he accompanies his wife to business meetings for her food enterprise, or when she goes to take photographs for her cookbooks, he takes his guitar. 'I say: "How long are you going to be?" She'll say: "Two or three hours." I'll go into the back room and see if I can come up with a song in that time. Childish, really, but people need goals, deadlines. It's a little game I play with myself: "How long have I got here to come up with something?"'

* The McCartney children are Heather, born on 31 December 1963 in Linda's first marriage; Mary, born on 28 August 1969; Stella, born on 13 September 1971; and James, born on 12 September 1977.

George Martin, the Beatles producer who helped to shape the McCartney classic 'Yesterday' in the studio (*Linda McCartney*)

Paul hugs Yoko Ono at the Rock 'n' Roll Hall Of Fame Awards in New York in January, 1994, after he had inducted John Lennon posthumously (*Bob Gruen/Star File*)

The Beatles vote for the week's new records on BBC TV's 'Juke Box Jury', transmitted from the Liverpool Empire on 7 December 1963 (*Star File*)

Paul on a Beatles concert tour of Britain, 1964 (*Star File*)

During their first US tour in 1964, John and Paul are about to listen to Bob Dylan's new album, held by Paul (*Star File*)

At the piano in his London home in 1970 during the preparation of his debut solo album, entitled *McCartney* (*Linda McCartney*)

In the Arizona desert in 1975, Paul is photographed for a poster used with his *Venus And Mars* album (*Linda McCartney*)

The artist at work, in the garden of his home (*Linda McCartney*)

During his record-breaking world tour, Paul is photographed on stage at Madison Square Garden, New York, on 11 December 1989 (*Phyllis Lattner*)

Paul with Jane Asher at the world première of the film *How I Won The War*, featuring John Lennon, at the London Pavilion on 18 October 1967 (*Star File*)

Two men who have been instrumental in the destiny of 'Yesterday' and the Beatles song catalogue: Lord Grade and Michael Jackson (*Pictorial Press/Vinnie Zuffante-Star File*)

Feeding the lambs at his farm in Scotland in 1990 (*Linda McCartney*)

Because he defies categorization, and especially does not wish to be merely a rock 'n' roll person, he confuses critics who, since the 1970s when the word rock became generic, classify the Beatles as a rock group. As Paul insists, they were something wider than that. He straddles rock, pop and vaudeville quite comfortably, but some see that as a debit or a problem for him. In May 1976, for example, Robert Palmer, reviewing a Wings concert at Madison Square Garden, wrote in the *New York Times* that rock singing was 'only one of Mr McCartney's many disguises. He is just as convincing as a crooner on "You Gave Me an Answer" or as a straight pop balladeer on "Yesterday".' The problem, insisted Robert Palmer, was precisely the ease with which Paul changed roles. His facility had 'also prevented him from ascending to the most hallowed heights of rock greatness'. Twice Robert Palmer absurdly invoked the Rolling Stones as a comparison. Wings aspired to the Stones' brand of hard rock, he asserted, adding that 'his rock fails to generate the sort of communal ecstasy the Rolling Stones and a handful of other bands create'. Paul's ballads, the writer added, which would be affecting in a more intimate environment, sounded frail and disembodied in the cavernous stadium.

Unusually for such a wise owl, Robert Palmer missed the elusive truth of Paul McCartney's appeal. Writing his own textbook as neither a rocker nor a pop singer, McCartney discovered something more tricky: how to touch people as an entertainer, a weaver of dreams. After absorbing every influence from Fred Astaire and Gene Kelly to Little Richard and Elvis Presley, he came forward as Paul McCartney . . . neither a rocker nor a balladeer, but an extraordinary hybrid from whom sprang 'Yesterday' and 'Lady Madonna'. Analysing him will always be an inexact science, and pigeon-holing him is impossible. Linda describes him as an unpredictable mixture of sentimental romantic and 'very obscure . . . because he was known as the cute one [in the Beatles] people don't realize how artistic he was and is, what a spiritually weird mind he has. He's not just totally sentimental; he could be harder than John; yet John could be much more sentimental than Paul.'

Yes, he was tearful, she said: 'Like most people who allow themselves to be. He gets sad if he thinks about someone he loves who's not living. Or when he's watching a movie. I love that. I think the most macho thing a man can be is kind.'

The activities of Paul McCartney reflect his wide interests. He and Linda, evangelical vegetarians for nearly twenty-five years since they committed themselves to animal rights and helping to improve the environment, bought land in Exmoor, Devon, purely to stop stag-hunting taking place on it. Linda is more visibly active in her battle for vegetarianism, and while she is introspective by nature, she becomes feisty and combative as she ignites her attacks on butcher's shops with their 'slabs of fear' and on abattoirs which she insists are called slaughterhouses. 'We are doing to animals what Hitler did to humans,' she says sombrely, and it's clear that the freewheeling spirit of the 1960s can be spiky on behalf of her *cause célèbre*. 'We soil our own nest, we humans,' she says.

Her book *Linda McCartney's Home Cooking*, a collection of recipes, became a best-seller. 'To my husband and children who, like me, love animals and enjoy cooking . . . you won't miss meat,' she promised readers.

Selling more than 200,000 copies, the book was such a hit that Ross Young's, the frozen food company, asked her if they might adapt some of her recipes for Britain's supermarkets. This aspect of her campaign to convert meat-eaters has been enormously successful: in her first year of marketing veggie meals, sales topped £10 million. To Beatles fans of yesteryear, the sight of the McCartney name staring from the supermarket freezer cabinet on items like meatless sausages, hamburgers, pasties and deep country pies may seem bizarre. But Paul approves, declaring: 'If it was not for saving the lives of so many animals we wouldn't be doing it.'

The work ethic has remained steadfastly with him. When I went to interview him for this book, he appeared unchanged in his habits from the Beatle I had travelled with thirty years earlier. Punctual, precise, totally involved in what was under discussion, he is without any of the posturing that afflicts lesser artists. He knows precisely where he stands in the pantheon of popular music. As the key surviving Beatle, he is conscious of the group's heritage and determined to preserve it.

He is particularly soft on the subject of children, and quite content to be viewed as such. He aided the Nordoff Robbins Music Therapy charity, which helps severely autistic children by using live music to reach their psyches, where nothing else seems to communicate. Visiting the therapy centre to play guitar to the children, in a performance that was televized, Paul was visibly moved.

'Yesterday' always comes into play in his life, both as a song and as his personal retrospective to his formative past. In 1995, after six years of planning, the Liverpool Institute for the Performing Arts was to be established in his old school building, the Liverpool Institute. Paul has been largely instrumental in establishing the *'Fame'*-type school, teaching people of all ages from all over the world the intricacies of the music industry, as well as constructively helping to channel their artistry and energy. Paul's personal involvement in LIPA was triggered by a Liverpool friend shortly after the city's Toxteth riots in 1981. The suggestion was that local youth might be diverted from trouble if something more tangible were on offer in which to focus their abilities. Seven years later, in 1988, Paul revisited the Liverpool Institute and was saddened to see the closed building needing restoration. This, he felt, should be the centre for the school. Paul has said he may host composing or guitar workshops when LIPA is running; and he helped the £12 million fund-raising campaign in 1991 with a large personal donation, and vigorously helped the fund-raising campaign. He also appeared in a short video presented by Liverpool City Council.

That same year, Paul's roots in his native city were strengthened even further by the performance of one of his most formidable musical challenges, Paul McCartney's *Liverpool Oratorio*. With his collaborator on the project, the conductor-composer Carl Davis, Paul found himself pitched into working with the Royal Liverpool Philharmonic Orchestra and Chorus, along with the choir to which, as an eleven-year-old, Paul was declined admission. At the city's Anglican Cathedral, the soprano Dame Kiri te Kanawa, one of the 2,500 artists to have recorded 'Yesterday', was a star performer of the McCartney *Oratorio*.

To prepare himself for the composition phase, Paul went to several concerts by the Philharmonic Orchestra and also to operas. 'I think Carl was surprised to find out that I did have a bit of musical knowledge,' Paul recalled to the US magazine *Musician*. 'I don't look like I do, but obviously I've been around for quite a while now. Carl would occasionally say: "Let me give you a little lesson," and, depending on what mood I was in, sometimes I would say: "No, Carl, we won't do that," because I felt too much like a student. But occasionally if I was in a receptive mood I'd say: "Go on." And he'd say: "This movement is based on the rondo form." So I'd say: "What's a rondo?" And Carl would explain. If I was interested in it and thought it would be a good idea for us to use, then we would use it, which we did in the last movement; "Peace" is roughly based on the rondo form. But he tried to sit me down one day with Benjamin Britten's *Young Person's Guide to the Orchestra* and I wouldn't do it. I refused and said: "No, Carl, it's too late for all that, luv."'

Jerry Hadley, the American tenor whom Paul chose to take the key role of Shanty in the *Oratorio*, was singing in a memorial service for Leonard Bernstein at Carnegie Hall, New York, when the call came requesting his visit to Liverpool. 'Lenny was not afraid of sentiment in the best sense of the word and neither is Paul,' he decided after their first meetings. 'I'm not talking about heart on the sleeve, overly saccharine kind of sentiment; I mean real honest human sentiment.'

Declaring that Paul had one of the keenest musical minds he had encountered, Hadley told *Musician*: 'He has one of the most profoundly clear visions of what he is creating of anybody I've ever met, on a level equal to Lenny's . . . perhaps it's clarity that all the greats have had. *West Side Story* did not happen by accident. The *Liverpool Oratorio* and the great McCartney pop songs did not happen by accident. These people don't flail in the dark.'

The *Liverpool Oratorio* was a watershed experience for McCartney, dealing largely with his pre-Beatle life: although it was not said to be entirely autobiographical, it could only have been so in parts: his wartime birth; the loss of parents; his first experience of fatherhood. In a spiritual-like song which he wrote, Paul had used the words spoken to John Lennon as he lay dying from gunshot wounds in the back of a Manhattan police car: "Do you know who you are?" asked a policeman.

'John would have loved the spirit of doing this after thirty years of rock 'n' roll,' Paul said after the *Oratorio*. 'He would have loved the idea of risking such a huge gamble. Not many days go by when I don't think of John.'

Paul received considerable praise from the media for his enterprise. 'The *Liverpool Oratorio* doesn't sound like anything else . . . McCartney has pulled off something viable and memorable,' said the *Daily Telegraph*. The *Daily Express* went further: 'In a city desperate for an evangelical pick-me-up, St Macca has come charging to the rescue. The Mersey Beat will never be the same.' The *Liverpool Echo* stated: 'It does for the age-old oratorio format what the American composer Stephen Sondheim does for the stage musical. It updates it, combining clever lyrics with sometimes daring musical expression.'

Liverpool had already embraced Paul in a cultural and civic sense; on 28 November 1984 he had been awarded the Freedom of the City. On the same day, his film *Give My Regards to Broad Street* had its première in the city that had belatedly realized what it had reason to be proud of. 'To the City of Liverpool . . . and a son,' said the city formally as Paul received his key in a ceremony at the Picton Library. Linda McCartney commented: 'I have rarely seen him so nervous. He was like he was on his wedding day.'

With the dawn of a new decade, Paul McCartney seemed more comfortable than he had been in previous years to deal with his illustrious past. Embarking in late 1989 on his first international tour for thirteen years, he enjoyed also the most successful world tour of his career. Public demand took him to America four times and he played to nearly three million people in more than 100 shows. In Rio de Janeiro, on 21 April 1990, at the Maracana Stadium, Paul set a new world record, performing to the biggest stadium crowd ever gathered in the history of rock 'n' roll: 184,368.

The filmed backdrop that preceded his appearance was a sharp evocation of the 1960s that had shaped Paul McCartney, spiritually as well as musically. In the midst of such major Beatles events as the film *A Hard Day's Night*, their Shea Stadium experience and the *All You Need Is Love* TV film, there were reminders of dark moments in history, such as the Vietnam War and Prague Spring.

'People tend to dismiss me as the married ex-Beatle who loves sheep and wrote "Yesterday",' Paul McCartney told *USA Today* in 1989. 'They think I can write only slushy love songs. My image is more goody-goody than I actually am.'

A feeling of *déjà vu* inevitably punctuates his life, but he is quite happy about that. 'I don't think I have improved as a songwriter. I haven't written better songs than "Yesterday" or "Here, There and Everywhere",' he said.

Ultimately it has been his openness in his work, his biological need to push on, making fresh music and launching new projects, and an ability to confront his peccadilloes that confounds his critics. From his teenage years onwards, he moved in an un-yielding straight line, from that romantic dream of songwriting to the master plan of being a Rodgers and Hammerstein or a Lerner and Loewe. The strategy of the aftermath of that finds him, in his fifties, dealing quite logically with yesterday and today.

Difficult though it is for a person of his means, he tries to maintain the attitude and lifestyle of Ordinary Man. With the Beatles such hard currency in 1995, we have his accessibility to thank substantially for our knowledge of what went on during that period. His 1989 world tour programme, entertaining and informative, was the nearest he has yet come to autobiography, shedding new light on his life in the 1960s and his relationship with John. About life in the fast lane, Paul wrote:

> People ask me: Why d'you do it? Why bother with the distractions? You're rich. Cos I think everyone's little dream, certainly mine when I was at school, was, what you'll do is get a lot of money and then you'll go off on holiday for ever. Just go off on a boat. But when you grow up you realize it doesn't work.

He went on to say that a year of holidays might be 'a great groove', but after a year he might think: what next? 'For me, I'd start to wonder . . . I'd pick up a guitar.'

If that was the Northern ethic of hard work becoming visible in McCartney's psyche, there were other pieces of self-psychoanalysis in which he laid himself bare.

> I came into this to get out of having a job, and to pull the birds. And I pulled quite a few birds and got out of having a job so that's where I am still. It's turned out to be very much a job, a bloody hard job the way I do it,

running a company and stuff, but I like it. I don't actually want to be a living legend.

Facing the reality that he is exactly that, Paul revealed much of himself, his random thoughts and his music in a series of question-and-answer items put forward by readers of his fan club magazine, *Club Sandwich*, at the end of 1994.

If he could return to 1962, one asked, would he still choose to become famous or would he opt for an ordinary life?

Paul said: 'No, thank you. I had an "ordinary life" for twenty years and this one's been better.'

He confessed to now being 'wary of collaborations', having enjoyed the chemistry of 'one of the best collaborations of the century, I think, with John'. He spoke of a wide range of music that moved him and made him cry. Asked, provocatively and interestingly, whether there was one song by someone else he wished he had written, he replied: 'I don't really want to have written anyone else's song, but, as a fantasy question, I love 'Stardust' by Hoagy Carmichael and Mitchell Parish. It's a beautiful song. And I remember thinking that Billy Joel's first hit, 'Just the Way You Are', was a nice song.* I'd like to have written that one, too. "Stardust" first, though. But when it comes down to it, the truth is that I feel so lucky at what I've done . . . if I ever start listing them: "The Long and Winding Road", "The Fool on the Hill" . . . it's difficult to take it all in.'

Paul revealed that Linda's father was a great fan of an appealing song of his which bears a contrasting title with 'Yesterday'. Called 'Tomorrow', it appeared on the Wings *Wild Life* album; Lee Eastman believed it should be re-recorded, slowed down for better effect. Asked what he considered was the stronger, his sense of melody or his ability as a wordsmith, Paul answered: 'Probably my sense of melody because it comes easiest to me. But I hate to be classed as a melodist because I would consider "Maybe I'm

* Ironically, 'Stardust' is among 'Yesterday's' nearest competitors for the title of most recorded song in history. See 'Miscellany', on page 158.

  Billy Joel names Paul McCartney's work as among his strongest musical inspirations. One of his songs, 'Scandinavian Skies' on his album *The Nylon Curtain*, was written as a tribute to Paul's romanticism in composing.

Amazed", "Blackbird", "Lady Madonna", "Paperback Writer" and a whole bunch of other songs as being quite good, lyrically.'

In dealing with his personal yesterdays, the unashamed sentimentalist is ever apparent. Rarely has he been so openly emotional about his relationship with Lennon as on the night of 19 January 1994, when he inducted John posthumously into the Rock 'n' Roll Hall of Fame. At the ceremony at the Waldorf Astoria Hotel in New York, Paul's induction speech took the form of an open letter to his old friend.

In an address of nearly 1,200 words, Paul encapsulated their relationship from their earliest years together, the period he had immortalized in touching songs, from 'The Two of Us' through to 'Here Today'. He exhibited his truly phenomenal memory for detail: the smoking of the Ty-Phoo tea in his dad's pipe as he and John 'sagged off' school to write songs. The visits to the house of John's mother, Julia, to play her ukulele. The visit to Paris where they met the photographer Jurgen Vollmer, who steered them towards a 'Beatle haircut'. The Cavern, where they pioneered pop music against the club policy of jazz and blues. Hamburg, and meeting Little Richard. New York and Los Angeles, where they met heroes like Phil Spector, the Supremes and Elvis Presley. *Abbey Road* and 'Love Me Do'. Yoko Ono and the *Two Virgins* album.

Paul did not back away from dealing with the rift with John. 'The joy for me, after all our business shit that we'd gone through, was that we were actually getting back together and communicating once again. And the joy as you told me about how you were baking bread now. And how you were playing with your little baby Sean. That was great for me, because it gave me something to hold on to.

'So now, years on, here we are . . . all these pople, assembled to thank you for everything that you mean to all of us. This letter comes with love from your friend Paul. John Lennon, you've made it. Tonight you are in the Rock 'n' Roll Hall of Fame. God bless you.'

The picture of Paul embracing Yoko after the ceremony beamed around the world, signifying a healing of one of the most publicized battles between 'brothers' in the history of the entertainment industry.

On his 1989 tour, Paul made perhaps his most significant musical statement about all his yesteryears. A dozen Beatles songs were performed with tremendous verve. Sitting watching the show on 28 November at Los Angeles Forum with Alistair Taylor, a former member of the Beatles' executive team, I saw the un-ashamed tears of joy in many of the crowd as, three songs from the end, Paul cruised into 'Yesterday'. Alone on stage, with his acoustic guitar, he delivered a short, spine-chilling version of the song that says it all – about him, about his era, and, for many, about a better time.

'Yesterday' might not be Paul's best composition. It has many competitors, and most students of McCartney's career would find it hard to agree on his top ten most significant works from his Beatles years and beyond. But 'Yesterday' seems destined to be his most *important* song. Its impact and influence, as a vehicle for others, its stretching of the Beatles' acceptance, and its effect on Paul's personal evolution, has completely transcended the normal expectations of any one piece of music.

Today, wary of revisionism and aware of the fallibility of his memory, Paul is able to divide pride from conceit but talks openly of having achieved his 'romantic dream, which was my strong feeling from teenage years onwards'. Watching a film on Mozart, he felt proud to be in that same league generically, as a composer of a record-breaker like 'Yesterday': 'As kids from the sticks there was no guarantee that we were going to make it. So suddenly to be looking at this huge song – fantastic! It's not bad for a scruff from Speke. I love all the versions, whether it's some Dutch organ grinder or Frank Sinatra!

'I walk into a restaurant and a pianist starts playing [hums 'Yes-terday']. I buy him a drink. The other side of it is that John went into restaurants and they started playing it, he hated it. I used to have a good laugh with him. I'd say: "Well, you would have your name first, wouldn't you?"'

Postscript

Paul McCartney's frustration over the ownership of the copyrights in Beatles' songs continues. Chapter 7 of this book documents the purchase by Michael Jackson of ATV Music, a strong catalogue of songs that contains the 251 compositions by the Beatles (including 'Yesterday').

In November 1995 those songs made yet another major move. Michael Jackson placed them under the wing of the giant Sony Corporation who announced the establishment of a 'worldwide music publishing joint venture', namely Sony-ATV Music. It is in that company that the Beatles' songs now reside.

Reasons for Michael Jackson's sale to Sony were debatable. He was reported to have been hit by money problems. His album HIStory was not so well received as had been hoped and he spent millions of dollars on videos to boost it. Additionally, his personal expenditures were reportedly in the millions following the investigations into alleged child molestation, though no charges were ever formally filed against him.

While no price was officially given for the merger, Jackson was said to have made about $95 million. Negotiations had been going on for about a year with Sony. The actual value of the 251 Beatles' songs was estimated by some music industry professionals to be $500 million, but such skyscraper figures are plucked from the air when it is obvious that the Lennon-McCartney songs will go on earning money until the end of time.

Jackson's merger of ATV into Sony created the world's third largest music publishing company. EMI Music Publishing and Warner-Chappell have been competing for years for the title of the world's dominant music publishing force.

The ATV Music portfolio included songs popularized by such artists as Elvis Presley and Little Richard. Sony has been the world's leading country and western music publisher for two decades, while also owning or administering songs by many top writers including Neil Diamond, Bob Dylan, Bruce Springsteen, Oasis, Pearl Jam, Sade, Barry Mann and Cynthia Weil, Mariah Carey . . . and the work of John Lennon and Yoko Ono.

Michael Jackson records for Sony's Epic Records imprint but, interestingly, publishing rights to Jackson's own compositions were not part of his deal. Warner-Chappell, which is part of the Time-Warner conglomerate, administers Jackson's MIJAC catalogue. And EMI Music, a division of Britain's Thorn EMI, will continue to administer the Beatles' compositions and other songs within the ATV catalogue, until 1998. 'Revenues from that catalogue will be paid to Sony-ATV Music Publishing', said a statement from Sony. That includes, of course, 'Yesterday', the subject of this book.

'It is very doubtful indeed', a music industry insider told me, 'if Paul will be able to get his hands on these songs now. Sony have got hold of a goldmine. The Beatles' songs are among the jewels in the crown of the music business'.

There remain two bizarre ironies about the destiny of Beatles' songs copyrights, including of course this gem called 'Yesterday'.

The first, as documented earlier, is that it was Paul McCartney who recommended to Michael Jackson that he invested his newly-earned fortune (from performing) in song publishing. Michael grasped quickly from Paul the crucial value of owning songs. He was able to convert that free advice from Paul into millions of dollars. So he has Paul to thank, both for writing such winners and for steering him towards investing in them.

The second huge irony is linked to a slice of Beatles' history. On 1 January 1962, the young Beatles travelled from Liverpool to London to attend an audition for Decca Records. The head of artists and repertoire was the late Dick Rowe. He rejected them. Across four decades, Dick Rowe became a disparaged name in the annals of the Beatles. Many felt this was unfair, since he had no evidence of their musical genius that would unfurl under the supervision of George Martin within a year of Rowe's dismissal of them.

The wheel turns. The president of Sony Music Publishing who was a key figure in the negotiations to bring Beatles' songs into his company, is none other than Richard Rowe . . . son of Dick Rowe. Richard Rowe described the combination of ATV with Sony as 'a tremendous coup . . . the best possible combination for growing our music publishing companies worldwide'.

Quanti est sapere! (How valuable is wisdom!)

'Yesterday': A Miscellany

'Yesterday' by the Beatles finally reached the British singles chart eleven years after it had been recorded. In February 1976 the Beatles' contract with EMI Records expired and the label reissued twenty-three Beatles singles, unleashing a wave of nostalgia. 'Yesterday' was among these. In March 1976 it peaked at number four in the Top 30 chart compiled by *Melody Maker*, five in the *New Musical Express* list, and eight in the Top Fifty of the trade paper *Music Week*. In that year, Paul's new band Wings triumphed in the USA, playing in twenty-one cities. He included 'Yesterday' in his repertoire and it was on the live triple-album that came from that tour in December 1976, *Wings Over America*.

'Yesterday' became, in 1988, the most performed song on American radio in fifty years, with five million airplays registered by that year. The citation was made by Broadcast Music Incorporated, one of the two major song royalty collection organizations in the USA. The first song in the repertoire of the performing rights organization to reach the 5 million figure, the achievement of 'Yesterday' represented more than 250,000 hours of airplay. If broadcast continuously, the 5 million performances until 1988 would account for more than twenty-eight years of airplay, until the year 2016.

By 1993 the figure had risen to 6 million broadcasts of the song, and Paul was honoured with a presentation at the annual awards dinner in London hosted by Broadcast Music Incorporated and Britain's Performing Right Society. Paul is a member of the latter organization. By 1994, the figure for US broadcasts was

6,480,000. The song is averaging 50,000 plays on American radio every three months.

'Yesterday' is not the only Beatles song to achieve a landmark statistic in American airplay. Paul's song 'Michelle' and George Harrison's 'Something' have each been played 4 million times. Three-million-airplay awards have been made to Paul's compositions 'Let It Be' and 'Hey Jude', with 2 million to 'Here, There and Everywhere', 'Eleanor Rigby', 'Penny Lane' and 'The Long and Winding Road'. John Lennon's 'Imagine', and George Harrison's 'Here Comes the Sun', have passed the 2 million mark.

These figures are provided by Broadcast Music Incorporated, a performing rights organization which represents songwriters and publishers around the world. Since 1940, BMI has accumulated more than 1½ million songs in its repertoire. Performance figures are determined from logged reports of approximately 500,000 hours annually submitted by US radio networks plus local outlets, and a census of 6 million hours of television annually in the US.

There are six verses, comprising eighty-four words and twenty-five lines, in the song, including the final 'humming' of the main theme to the tune of 'I believe in yesterday'. In all his post-Beatles recordings and performances of the song, Paul has omitted the last two verses, whose words repeat the second and third verses. 'I use it as a highspot but try not to milk it dry,' he says of his live shows. 'I realize I only do half of it. I'm so inexact, it's unbelievable! I suddenly realized during one tour that I hadn't been doing it right. I'd cut it short, which is a weird, inexact attitude. But I quite like that. I'm not too fussed, not too precious with it.'

'Yesterday''s nearest competitors for the title of the world's most recorded song are both American: 'Tie a Yellow Ribbon Round the Old Oak Tree' (1973) and 'Stardust' (1929). Both have been recorded more than 1,000 times.

Sung by Dawn, featuring Tony Orlando, 'Tie a Yellow Ribbon' topped the British and US charts in the spring of 1973. It was written by Larry Russell Brown and Irwin Levine, and the storyline of the song was based on truth: a man who had served three years in prison was returning home on a bus in Georgia. He had written a letter to his wife saying that he would understand if she had not waited for him, but if she still loved him, her message of confirmation could be a yellow ribbon tied around the old oak tree in the city square of their home town. She did this, and the man saw it as his bus arrived.

Yellow ribbons became symbolic of peace in the US as a result of the song. In 1981 they were displayed nationally to celebrate the release from Iran of hostages after 444 days in captivity; and ribbons reappeared during the 1991 Gulf war.

'Stardust' is, ironically, one of Paul McCartney's favourite compositions. It was written by the legendary Hoagy Carmichael, with lyrics by Mitchell Parish. The song was featured in *The Eddy Duchin Story*, a biographical movie about the 1930s and 1940s pianist-bandleader. 'Stardust' was first recorded in 1930 by Irving Mills and his Hotsy Totsy Band, with Hoagy Carmichael playing piano, ragtime-style.

'Stardust' has for decades been considered by ballad singers and musicians to be one of the most beautiful songs in its genre. Frank Sinatra has described it as also one of the most difficult to sing. Hoagy Carmichael, a pianist who had a unique, hesitant and charming baritone delivery, sang a definitive version. Born in Bloomington, Indiana, on 22 November 1899, he died in Palm Springs, California, on 28 December 1981.

'White Christmas', often thought of as a possible contender for the title, falls far short of either 'Yesterday', 'Stardust' or 'Tie A Yellow Ribbon', with approximately 300 cover versions on record. However, the Bing Crosby record alone of 'White Christmas' has sold more than 25 million copies. Sheet music sales averaged 300,000 annually during the 1950s.

The song was featured in the movies *Holiday Inn, Blue Skies* and *White Christmas*. The music and the lyrics were written in 1942 by Irving Berlin, born Israel Baline in Russia on 11 May 1888. He died in New York on September 1989.

Six years after 'Yesterday', Paul wrote and recorded a song called 'Tomorrow' for the Wings début album, *Wild Life*. Continuing the theme of time, he wrote 'Backwards Traveller' (on his 1978 album *London Town*) and 'Here Today', his tribute song to John Lennon (on his 1982 album *Tug of War*). This latter session was the only time since 'Yesterday' that he again used a string quartet, although he has featured strings on his work many times. *Tug of War* marked a reunion by Paul with George Martin.

'Yesterday' has not won a Grammy Award. It was expected to figure in the 1966 presentations but the Record of the Year title went to 'A Taste of Honey' by Herb Alpert and the Tijuana Brass. Song of the Year went to 'The Shadow of Your Smile' written by Paul Webster and Johnny Mandel. Best Male Solo Vocal was won by Frank Sinatra for 'It Was a Very Good Year'; and Best Contemporary Single went to 'King of the Road' by Roger Miller. However, in 1967 Paul's 'Michelle' won a Grammy for Best Song, and in the same year he won another Grammy for the Best Contemporary Solo Vocal performance (with 'Eleanor Rigby'). Paul won a Grammy Lifetime Achievement award in 1990.

As a single, 'Yesterday' sold more than 3 million copies internationally. It was number one single in Canada, New Zealand, Finland, Norway, Denmark, the Netherlands, Belgium, Spain and Hong Kong. It reached number two in Australia. It was also a hit in Italy, France and Malaysia.

Apart from Paul McCartney's theatrically-released films, 'Yesterday' is thought to have been included in only one feature film, *All This and World War Two*, released in 1976, which married cover versions of Beatles songs ('Yesterday' was sung here by David Essex) with powerful war images.

'Yesterday' was not performed in concert by the Beatles until the tour which took them to West Germany, Japan, the Philippines and the USA/Canada from 24 June to 29 August 1966. They did not perform the song in concert in 1965.

Since the Beatles, Paul has chosen to perform 'Yesterday' in concert from 1975.

The first tour, 1975/6, visited Britain, Australia, Europe, the USA/Canada, Europe again and Britain again.

The second tour, 1979, was of Britain only.

The third tour (called the World Tour) was 1989/90.

The fourth tour (called the New World Tour) was 1993.

Paul did not perform 'Yesterday' during the Wings 1972 and 1973 concert tours.

In 1966 'Yesterday' was named Outstanding Song of the Year in the prestigious Ivor Novello Awards in Britain. Completing their hat-trick of wins, Lennon and McCartney's 'We Can Work It Out' won an award for the highest certified record sales by a British composition, while 'Help!' was the runner-up in the same category.

'Yesterday' was among the songs sung by Paul in jail, where he spent nine days after marijuana was found in his possession at Tokyo airport on 16 January 1980. With other inmates he had occasional sing-songs, and the tunes they knew were the Al Jolson standards 'Baby Face' and 'When the Red, Red, Robin Comes Bob, Bob, Bobbin' Along' . . . and 'Yesterday'. Paul sang while they clapped along to the tune.

On 24 October 1979 a tribute to Paul McCartney as 'the most honoured composer and performer in music' was presented by Guinness Superlatives, publishers of the *Guinness Book of Records*, at a reception at Les Ambassadeurs, London. His awards were:
1. Most successful composer of all time (forty-three songs written between 1962 and 1978 which had each sold more than a million copies).
2. Record number of Gold Discs (forty-two with the Beatles, seventeen with Wings and one with Billy Preston. Total: sixty).
3. World's most successful recording artist. (Estimated record sales by that year of 1979 were 100 million albums and 100 million singles).

McCartney was presented with a unique disc cast of rhodium, one of the world's rarest and most precious metals, twice as valuable as platinum. Norris McWhirter, editor of the *Guinness Book of Records*, explained: 'Since, in the field of recorded music, gold and platinum discs are standard presentations by recording companies, we felt we should make a fittingly superlative presentation of the first ever rhodium disc with a special label listing Paul McCartney's three achievements.'

Paul told me at the ceremony: 'I'm surprised because I never count how many songs I've written or what they've sold. I'm always on to the next thing when a record's in the charts. This takes a bit of sinking in, what they've set out today.

'I always write what I hope will be commercial stuff. I try to write hits. If you ask me about Gerry Rafferty, I'll talk about 'Baker Street'. That's his big song. That's what I see a songwriter as trying to do: reach the public. But that doesn't make me the best. These awards don't say that. I can't pitch myself against the great classical composers. I'm just representing a different era. The best, not necessarily. The most successful, well, yeah!'

In a BBC television programme broadcast on 26 May 1986 based on the *Guinness Book of Records* Hall Of Fame, Paul told host David Frost and Norris McWhirter about 'Yesterday': 'I didn't believe I'd written it! I sat at the piano next to my bed . . . after two weeks I realized that I *had* written it . . . you feel as though you haven't really written it, as if this really came through you.'

'Yesterday' was a highlight of the show called *An Evening with Paul McCartney and Friends*, a charity concert to help London's Royal College of Music, held at St James's Palace on 23 March 1995. An audience of 300 specially invited guests who had paid a minimum ticket price of £250, with the musicians playing for free, raised £75,000 for the college.

After a solo set from Elvis Costello, Paul went on stage with him to mark their stage début together, both playing acoustic guitars to perform their collaborative song 'Mistress and the Maid'. Paul then performed three of his best-loved ballads, 'For No One', 'Eleanor Rigby' and 'Yesterday', each with new arrangements, to the accompaniment of the string ensemble the Brodsky Quartet. 'Yesterday' was scheduled to be the show's finale, but Paul added an impromptu 'Lady Madonna' at the piano.

The concert was held in the presence of the Royal College's patron, Prince Charles. At the end of the concert before the pre-show vegetarian dinner, he declared: 'I'm enormously grateful to Paul McCartney for having given up so much time and putting so much into this evening. I hope this evening will enable a great deal more to take place at the Royal College of Music than might otherwise have been the case. This evening reminds one that the music Paul McCartney wrote with John Lennon never fades. That's the test of real music, I think.'

Recognizing 'the remarkable talents of Paul McCartney and all that he has done for music this century, and in particular the Royal College of Music', Prince Charles bestowed on Paul an honorary Fellowship of the Royal College of Music, Britain's highest honorary award for a musician.

Appendix A:

The Songs Sony-ATV Music Bought

Published here for the first time, this list of 263 songs (including 'Yesterday') identifies all the Beatles' compositions in the golden Northern Songs copyrights which were bought by Michael Jackson in 1985 and then by Sony-ATV Music in 1995.

'Across the Universe'   (John Lennon–Paul McCartney)
'All I've Got to Do'   (John Lennon–Paul McCartney)
'All My Loving'   (John Lennon–Paul McCartney)
'All Together Now'   (John Lennon–Paul McCartney)
'All You Need Is Love'   (John Lennon–Paul McCartney)
'And I Love Her'   (John Lennon–Paul McCartney)
'And Your Bird Can Sing'   (John Lennon–Paul McCartney)
'Another Girl'   (John Lennon–Paul McCartney)
'Any Time At All'   (John Lennon–Paul McCartney)
'Baby, You're a Rich Man'   (John Lennon–Paul McCartney)
'Baby's in Black'   (John Lennon–Paul McCartney)
'Back in the USSR'   (John Lennon–Paul McCartney)
'The Back Seat of My Car'   (Paul McCartney)
'Bad to Me'   (John Lennon-Paul McCartney)
'The Ballad of John and Yoko'   (John Lennon–Paul McCartney)
'Because'   (John Lennon–Paul McCartney)
'Being for the Benefit of Mr Kite!'   (John Lennon–Paul
                                                        McCartney)
'Birthday'   (John Lennon–Paul McCartney)
'Blackbird'   (John Lennon–Paul McCartney)
'Blue Jay Way'   (George Harrison)
'Can't Buy Me Love'   (John Lennon–Paul McCartney)
'Carry That Weight'   (John Lennon–Paul McCartney)

'Catcall'	(John Lennon–Paul McCartney)
'Christmas Time (Is Here Again)'	(John Lennon–Paul McCartney–George Harrison–Richard Starkey)
'Cold Turkey'	(John Lennon)
'Come and Get It'	(Paul McCartney)
'Come Together'	(John Lennon–Paul McCartney)
'The Continuing Story of Bungalow Bill'	(John Lennon–Paul McCartney)
'Cowboy Music'	(George Harrison)
'Crippled Inside'	(John Lennon)
'Cry Baby Cry'	(John Lennon–Paul McCartney)
'Crying'	(George Harrison)
'A Day in the Life'	(John Lennon–Paul McCartney)
'Day Tripper'	(John Lennon–Paul McCartney)
'Dear Prudence'	(John Lennon–Paul McCartney)
'Dig a Pony'	(John Lennon–Paul McCartney)
'Dig It'*	(John Lennon–Paul McCartney–George Harrison–Richard Starkey)
'Do You Want to Know a Secret'	(John Lennon–Paul McCartney)
'Doctor Robert'	(John Lennon–Paul McCartney)
'Don't Let Me Down'	(John Lennon–Paul McCartney)
'Dream Scene'	(George Harrison)
'Drilling a Home'	(George Harrison)
'Drive My Car'	(John Lennon–Paul McCartney)
'Eight Days a Week'	(John Lennon–Paul McCartney)
'Eleanor Rigby'	(John Lennon–Paul McCartney)
'The End'	(John Lennon–Paul McCartney)
'Every Little Thing'	(John Lennon–Paul McCartney)
'Every Night'	(Paul McCartney)
'Everybody's Got Something to Hide Except Me and My Monkey'	(John Lennon–Paul McCartney)
'Everywhere It's Christmas'	(John Lennon–Paul McCartney)
'The Family Way'	(Paul McCartney)
'Fantasy Sequins'	(George Harrison)
'Fixing a Hole'	(John Lennon–Paul McCartney)
'Flying'	(John Lennon–Paul McCartney–George Harrison–Richard Starkey)
'The Fool on the Hill'	(John Lennon–Paul McCartney)
'For No One'	(John Lennon–Paul McCartney)

'From a Window'   (John Lennon–Paul McCartney)
'From Me to You'   (John Lennon–Paul McCartney)
'Gat Kirwani'   (George Harrison)
'Get Back'   (John Lennon–Paul McCartney)
'Getting Better'   (John Lennon–Paul McCartney)
'Girl'   (John Lennon–Paul McCartney)
'Give Me Some Truth'   (John Lennon)
'Give Peace a Chance'   (John Lennon–Paul McCartney)
'Glass Box'   (George Harrison)
'Glass Onion'   (John Lennon–Paul McCartney)
'Glasses'   (Paul McCartney)
'God'   (John Lennon)
'Golden Slumbers/Carry That Weight'   (John Lennon–
                                                     Paul McCartney)
'Good Day Sunshine'   (John Lennon–Paul Mccartney)
'Good Morning Good Morning'   (John Lennon–
                                                     Paul McCartney)
'Good Night'   (John Lennon–Paul McCartney)
'Goodbye'   (John Lennon–Paul McCartney)
'Got to Get You into My Life'   (John Lennon–Paul McCartney)
'Greasy Legs'   (George Harrison)
'Guru Vandana'   (George Harrison)
'Happiness is a Warm Gun'   (John Lennon–Paul McCartney)
'A Hard Day's Night'   (John Lennon–Paul McCartney)
'Hello, Goodbye'   (John Lennon–Paul McCartney)
'Hello Little Girl'   (John Lennon–Paul McCartney)
'Help!'   (John Lennon–Paul McCartney)
'Helter Skelter'   (John Lennon–Paul McCartney)
'Her Majesty'   (John Lennon–Paul McCartney)
'Here, There and Everywhere'   (John Lennon–Paul McCartney)
'Hey Bulldog'   (John Lennon–Paul McCartney)
'Hey Jude'   (John Lennon–Paul McCartney)
'Hold Me Tight'   (John Lennon–Paul McCartney)
'Hold On'   (John Lennon)
'Honey Pie'   (John Lennon–Paul McCartney)
'Hot as Sun'   (Paul McCartney)
'How'   (John Lennon)
'How Do You Sleep'   (John Lennon)
'I Am the Walrus'   (John Lennon–Paul McCartney)
'I Call Your Name'   (John Lennon–Paul McCartney)

'I Don't Want to Be a Soldier' (John Lennon)
'I Don't Want to See You Again' (John Lennon–Paul McCartney)
'I Don't Want to Spoil the Party' (John Lennon–Paul McCartney)
'I Feel Fine' (John Lennon–Paul McCartney)
'I Found Out' (John Lennon)
'I Need You' (George Harrison)
'I Saw Her Standing There' (John Lennon–Paul McCartney)
'I Should Have Known Better' (John Lennon–Paul McCartney)
'I Wanna Be Your Man' (John Lennon–Paul McCartney)
'I Want to Hold Your Hand' (John Lennon–Paul McCartney)
'I Want to Tell You' (George Harrison)
'I Want You (She's So Heavy)' (John Lennon–Paul McCartney)
'I Will' (John Lennon–Paul McCartney)
'I'll Be Back' (John Lennon–Paul McCartney)
'I'll Be on My Way' (John Lennon–Paul McCartney)
'I'll Cry Instead' (John Lennon–Paul McCartney)
'I'll Follow the Sun' (John Lennon–Paul McCartney)
'I'll Get You' (John Lennon–Paul McCartney)
'I'll Keep You Satisfied' (John Lennon–Paul McCartney)
'I'm a Loser' (John Lennon–Paul McCartney)
'I'm Down' (John Lennon–Paul McCartney)
'I'm Happy Just to Dance with You' (John Lennon–Paul McCartney)
'I'm in Love' (John Lennon–Paul McCartney)
'I'm Looking through You' (John Lennon–Paul McCartney)
'I'm Only Sleeping' (John Lennon–Paul McCartney)
'I'm so Tired' (John Lennon–Paul McCartney)
'I've Got a Feeling' (John Lennon–Paul McCartney)
'I've Just Seen a Face' (John Lennon–Paul McCartney)
'If I Fell' (John Lennon–Paul McCartney)
'If I Needed Someone' (George Harrison)
'If You've Got Troubles' (John Lennon–Paul McCartney)
'In My Life' (John Lennon–Paul McCartney)
'In the Park' (George Harrison)
'The Inner Light' (George Harrison)
'Isolation' (John Lennon)
'It Won't Be Long' (John Lennon–Paul McCartney)
'It's All Too Much' (George Harrison)

'It's for You'   (John Lennon–Paul McCartney)
'It's Only Love'   (John Lennon–Paul McCartney)
'It's So Hard'   (John Lennon)
Jazz Piano Song*   (Paul McCartney–Richard Starkey)
'Jessie's Dream'   (John Lennon–Paul McCartney–
                              George Harrison–Richard Starkey)
'John Sinclair'   (John Lennon)
'Julia'   (John Lennon–Paul McCartney)
'Junk'   (Paul McCartney)
'Kreen-Akrore'   (Paul McCartney)
'Lady Madonna'   (John Lennon–Paul McCartney)
'Let It Be'   (John Lennon–Paul McCartney)
'Like Dreamers Do'   (John Lennon–Paul McCartney)
'Little Child'   (John Lennon–Paul McCartney)
'The Long and Winding Road' (John Lennon–Paul McCartney)
'Look at Me'   (John Lennon)
'Love in the Open Air'   (Paul McCartney)
'Love of the Loved'   (John Lennon–Paul McCartney)
'Love Scene'   (George Harrison)
'Love You To'   (George Harrison)
'The Lovely Linda'   (Paul McCartney)
'Lovely Rita'   (John Lennon–Paul McCartney)
'Lucy in the Sky with Diamonds'   (John Lennon–
                                              Paul McCartney)
'Maggie Mae'*   (Trad. arr John Lennon–Paul McCartney–
                              George Harrison–Richard Starkey)
'Magical Mystery Tour'   (John Lennon–Paul McCartney)
'Man We Was Lonely'   (Paul McCartney)
'Martha My Dear'   (John Lennon–Paul McCartney)
'Maxwell's Silver Hammer'   (John Lennon–Paul McCartney)
'Maybe I'm Amazed'   (Paul McCartney)
'Mean Mr Mustard'   (John Lennon–Paul McCartney)
'Michelle'   (John Lennon–Paul McCartney)
'Microbes'   (George Harrison)
'Misery'   (John Lennon–Paul McCartney)
'Momma Miss America'   (Paul McCartney)
'Mother'   (John Lennon)
'Mother Nature's Son'   (John Lennon–Paul McCartney)
'My Mummy's Dead'   (John Lennon)
'New York City'   (John Lennon)

'The Night Before' (John Lennon–Paul McCartney)
'No Reply' (John Lennon–Paul McCartney)
'Nobody I Know' (John Lennon–Paul McCartney)
'Norwegian Wood (This Bird Has Flown)' (John Lennon–Paul McCartney)
'Not a Second Time' (John Lennon–Paul McCartney)
'Nowhere Man' (John Lennon–Paul McCartney)
'Ob-La-Di, Ob-La-Da' (John Lennon–Paul McCartney)
'Oh! Darling' (John Lennon–Paul McCartney)
'Oh Woman, Oh Why' (Paul McCartney)
'On the Bed' (George Harrison)
'The One After 909' (John Lennon–Paul McCartney)
'One and One Is Two' (John Lennon–Paul McCartney)
'Only a Northern Song' (George Harrison)
'Oo You' (Paul McCartney)
'Paperback Writer' (John Lennon–Paul McCartney)
'Party Seacombe' (George Harrison)
'Paul Piano Intro' (John Lennon–Paul McCartney)
'Penina' (Paul McCartney)
'Penny Lane' (John Lennon–Paul McCartney)
'Please Don't Bring Your Banjo Back' (John Lennon–Paul McCartney)
'Polythene Pam' (John Lennon–Paul McCartney)
'Rain' (John Lennon–Paul McCartney)
'Ram On' (Paul McCartney)
'Red Lady Too' (George Harrison)
'Remember' (John Lennon)
'Revolution' (John Lennon–Paul McCartney)
'Revolution 9' (John Lennon–Paul McCartney)
'Rocky Raccoon' (John Lennon–Paul McCartney)
'Run for Your Life' (John Lennon–Paul McCartney)
'Sexy Sadie' (John Lennon–Paul McCartney)
'Sgt Pepper's Lonely Hearts Club Band' (John Lennon–Paul McCartney)
'She Came in through The Bathroom Window' (John Lennon–Paul McCartney)
'She Loves You' (John Lennon–Paul McCartney)
'She Said She Said' (John Lennon–Paul McCartney)
'She's a Woman' (John Lennon–Paul McCartney)
'She's Leaving Home' (John Lennon–Paul McCartney)

'Shirley's Wild Accordion'	(John Lennon–Paul McCartney)
'Singalong Junk'	(Paul McCartney)
'Singing Om'	(George Harrison)
'Ski-ing'	(George Harrison)
'Smile Away'	(Paul McCartney)
'Step Inside Love'	(John Lennon–Paul McCartney)
'Strawberry Fields Forever'	(John Lennon–Paul McCartney)
'Suicide'	(Paul McCartney)
'Sun King'	(John Lennon–Paul McCartney)
'Suzy Parker'*	(John Lennon–Paul McCartney–George Harrison–Richard Starkey)
'Tabla and Pakavaj'	(George Harrison)
'Taxman'	(George Harrison)
'Teddy Boy'	(Paul McCartney)
'Tell Me What You See'	(John Lennon–Paul McCartney)
'Tell Me Why'	(John Lennon–Paul McCartney)
'Thank You Girl'	(John Lennon–Paul McCartney)
'That Means a Lot'	(John Lennon–Paul McCartney)
'That Would Be Something'	(Paul McCartney)
'There's a Place'	(John Lennon–Paul McCartney)
'Things We Said Today'	(John Lennon–Paul McCartney)
'Thingumybob'	(John Lennon–Paul McCartney)
'Think for Yourself'	(George Harrison)
'This Boy'	(John Lennon–Paul McCartney)
'3 Legs'	(Paul McCartney)
'Ticket to Ride'	(John Lennon–Paul McCartney)
'Tip of My Tongue'	(John Lennon–Paul McCartney)
'Tomorrow Never Knows'	(John Lennon–Paul McCartney)
'Too Many People'	(Paul McCartney)
'Two of Us'	(John Lennon–Paul McCartney)
'Valentine Day'	(Paul McCartney)
'Wait'	(John Lennon–Paul McCartney)
'We Can Work It Out'	(John Lennon–Paul McCartney)
'Well Well Well'	(John Lennon)
'What Goes On'	(John Lennon–Paul McCartney–Richard Starkey)
'What You're Doing'	(John Lennon–Paul McCartney)
'What's the New Mary Jane'	(John Lennon–Paul McCartney)
'When I Get Home'	(John Lennon–Paul McCartney)
'When I'm Sixty-Four'	(John Lennon–Paul McCartney)

'Why Don't We Do It in The Road'   (John Lennon–
                                                Paul McCartney)
'Wild Honey Pie'   (John Lennon–Paul McCartney)
'With a Little Help From My Friends'   (John Lennon–
                                                Paul McCartney)
'Within You Without You'   (George Harrison)
'Woman'   (John Lennon–Paul McCartney,
                under joint pseudonym 'Bernard Webb')
'Wonderwall to Be Here'   (George Harrison)
'The Word'   (John Lennon-Paul McCartney)
'Working Class Hero'   (John Lennon)
'A World Without Love'   (John Lennon–Paul McCartney)
'Yellow Submarine'   (John Lennon–Paul McCartney)
'Yer Blues'   (John Lennon–Paul McCartney)
'Yes It Is'   (John Lennon–Paul McCartney)
'YESTERDAY'   (John Lennon–Paul McCartney)
'You Can't Do That'   (John Lennon–Paul McCartney)
'You Know My Name (Look Up the Number)'
                                (John Lennon–Paul McCartney)
'You Like Me Too Much'   (George Harrison)
'You Never Give Me Your Money'   (John Lennon–
                                                Paul McCartney)
'You Won't See Me'   (John Lennon–Paul McCartney)
'You're Going to Lose That Girl'   (John Lennon–
                                                Paul McCartney)
'You've Got to Hide Your Love Away'   (John Lennon–
                                                Paul McCartney)
'Your Mother Should Know'   (John Lennon–Paul McCartney)

* copyright shared with other publisher(s)

Important notes: The above list is current at 1995. Northern Songs no longer publishes a number of copyrights which, although formerly vested in the company, now rest elsewhere as a consequence of business negotiations. These include compositions recorded by Paul McCartney ('Another Day', 'Bip Bop', 'C Moon', 'Dear Boy', 'Eat At Home', 'The Great Cock and Seagull Race', 'Dear Friend', 'Give Ireland Back to the Irish', 'Heart of the Country', 'Hi Hi Hi', 'I Am Your Singer', 'Little Woman Love', 'Long Haired Lady', 'Mary Had a Little Lamb', 'Monkberry

Moon Delight', 'Mumbo', 'Some People Never Know', 'Tomorrow', 'Uncle Albert'/'Admiral Halsey', 'Wild Life') and by John Lennon ('Angela', 'Attica State', 'Au', 'Cambridge 1969', 'Do the Oz', 'God Save Us', 'Imagine', 'Instant Karma!', 'Jamrag', 'Jealous Guy', 'Love', 'The Luck of the Irish', 'Oh My Love', 'Oh Yoko!', 'Power to the People', 'Scumbag', 'Sunday Bloody Sunday', *Two Virgins* (LP), 'Woman is the Nigger of the World').

Other Beatles-related copyrights remain vested in Northern, such as George Martin's orchestral soundtrack cuts for the *Yellow Submarine* film and album, his orchestral versions (which carried different names) of Beatles songs – 'Auntie Gin's Theme' (originally 'I've Just Seen a Face'), 'Ringo's Theme' ('This Boy'), 'Scrambled Eggs' ('Yesterday') and 'That's a Nice Hat (Cap)' ('It's Only Love') – and other oddities such as pieces of music which incorporated original Northern Songs copyrighted material.

Appendix B:

'Yesterday' on Record

BRITAIN

By the Beatles
On the album *Help!*, released on 6 August 1965.

As the title track on the EP *Yesterday*, released on 4 March 1966.

On the 'best of' compilation album *A Collection of Beatles Oldies*, released on 10 December 1966.

On the 'best of' compilation double-album *1962-1966*, released on 19 April 1973.

As a single (b/w 'I Should Have Known Better') (also as part of *The Singles Collection* boxed set of 23 seven-inch singles, the original 22 plus this new one), released on 8 March 1976.

On the compilation album *Love Songs*, released on 19 November 1977

On the compilation album *The Beatles Ballads*, released on 13 October 1980

The above releases all feature the same recording, the only variations being of the mono/stereo kind.

By Paul McCartney
On the live-in-concert triple-album *Wings Over America*, released on 10 December 1976.

A new studio recording on the soundtrack album for *Give My Regards to Broad Street*, released on 22 October 1984.

On the live-in-concert triple-album *Tripping the Live Fantastic*, released on 5 November 1990.

The above three releases all feature different recordings.

The USA

By the Beatles

As a single (b/w 'Act Naturally'), released on 13 September 1965

On the album *Yesterday . . . And Today*, released (with the so-called 'butcher' sleeve) on 15 June 1966; reissued (with a new sleeve) on 20 June 1966.

On the 'best of' compilation double-album *1962-1966*, released on 2 April 1973

On the compilation album *Love Songs*, released on 21 October 1977.

On the compilation album *20 Greatest Hits*, released on 15 October 1982.

The above releases all feature the same recording, the only variations being of the mono/stereo kind.

By Paul McCartney

On the live-in-concert triple-album *Wings Over America*, released on 10 December 1976.

A new studio recording on the soundtrack album for *Give My Regards to Broad Street*, released on 22 October 1984.

On the live-in-concert triple-album *Tripping the Live Fantastic*, released on 5 November 1990.

The above three releases all feature different recordings.

Appendix C:

'Yesterday' on the Charts

Britain: Singles

By Matt Monro
Entered the *Record Retailer* Top 50 on 21 October 1965 and
peaked at number 8, leaving the chart after twelve weeks. It
peaked at 6 on the *NME* chart.

By Marianne Faithfull
Entered the *Record Retailer* Top 50 on 4 November 1965 and
peaked at number 36, leaving the chart after four weeks.

By Ray Charles
Entered the *Record Retailer* Top 50 on 20 December 1967 and
peaked at number 44, leaving the chart after four weeks.

By the Beatles
Entered the *Music Week* Top 50 on 13 March 1976 and peaked
at number 8, leaving the chart after seven weeks. Positions
were 41, 17, 10, 8, 9, 13, 18. It peaked at 5 on the *NME* chart
and 4 on the *Melody Maker* chart.

Britain: EPs

By the Beatles
Entered the *Record Retailer* Top 20 on 10 March 1966 and
peaked at number 1, staying at number 1 for eight weeks and

leaving the chart after thirteen weeks (by which point the chart had been reduced in size to a Top 10).

The USA: Singles

By the Beatles
Entered the *Billboard* Hot 100 on 25 September 1965 and peaked at number 1, staying at number 1 for four weeks and leaving the chart after eleven weeks. Positions were 45, 3, 1 (it displaced 'Hang On Sloopy' by the McCoys), 1, 1, 1, 3 (it was displaced by 'Get off of My Cloud' by the Rolling Stones), 11, 13, 26, 45, and then out. It also peaked at 1 on the *Cashbox* (for 3 weeks), *Variety* (for 3 weeks) and *Record World* (for 2 weeks) charts.

By Ray Charles
Entered the *Billboard* Hot 100 on 11 November 1967 and peaked at number 25, leaving the chart after seven weeks. Positions were 62, 51, 41, 25, 25, 25, 54, and then out.

As an Album Track: 'Yesterday' on the Charts

Britain

By the Beatles
The album *Help!* entered the *Record Retailer* Top 20 on 14 August 1965 and peaked at number 1, staying at number 1 for nine weeks (it was displaced by the soundtrack for *The Sound of Music*, enjoying its second spell at the top; this, in turn, was displaced by the Beatles' next album, *Rubber Soul*) and leaving the chart after thirty-seven weeks. It subsequently re-entered the by-now-renamed *Music Week* chart for two weeks in 1971, and two more in 1987, making forty-one weeks in total. It also peaked at 1 on the *Melody Maker* and *NME* charts.

The album *A Collection of Beatles Oldies* entered the *Record*

Retailer Top 40 on 10 December 1966 and peaked at number 7, leaving the chart after thirty-four weeks. It peaked at 4 on the *Melody Maker* chart and 6 on the *NME* chart.

The album *1962-1966* entered the *Music Week* Top 50 on 5 May 1973 and peaked at 3, leaving the chart after 148 weeks (by which time the chart had become a Top 75). It re-entered when the title was reissued on CD in 1993 and peaked at 3. The original issue peaked at 1 on the *Melody Maker* and *NME* charts.

The album *Love Songs* entered the *Music Week* Top 60 on 17 December 1977 and peaked at number 7, leaving the chart after seventeen weeks. It peaked at 12 on the *NME* chart.

The album *The Beatles Ballads* entered the *Music Week* Top 75 on 15 November 1980 and peaked at 17, leaving the chart after sixteen weeks. It peaked at 21 on the *NME* chart.

By Paul McCartney
The album *Wings Over America* entered the *Music Week* Top 60 on 15 January 1977 and peaked at 8, leaving the chart after twenty-two weeks. It also peaked at 8 on the *Melody Maker* and *NME* charts.

The album *Give My Regards to Broad Street* entered the *Music Week* Top 100 on 3 November 1984 and peaked at number 1, staying at number 1 for one week (it was displaced by *Welcome to the Pleasure Dome* by Frankie Goes to Hollywood) and leaving the chart after twenty-one weeks. It peaked at 3 on the *NME* chart.

The album *Tripping the Live Fantastic* entered the *Music Week* Top 75 on 17 November 1990 and peaked at number 17, leaving the chart after eleven weeks. It peaked at 10 on the *NME* chart.

The USA
The album *Yesterday ... And Today* entered the *Billboard* Top

200 on 9 July 1966 and peaked at number 1, staying at number 1 for five weeks and leaving the chart after thirty-one weeks. Positions were 120, 18, 2, 1 (it displaced *Strangers in the Night* by Frank Sinatra), 1, 1, 1, 1, 2 (it was displaced by the Beatles' next album, *Revolver*), 7, 8, 15, 19, 30, 39, 39, 42, 48, 45, 49, 51, 56, 63, 72, 108, 118, 130, 132, 134, 138, 136 and then out. It also peaked at 1 on the *Cashbox* and *Record World* charts.

The album *1962-1966* entered the *Billboard* Top 200 on 14 April 1973 and peaked at number 3, leaving the chart after seventy-seven weeks. Positions were 94, 23, 9, 6, 4, 3, 3, 5, 5, 5, 11, 13, 17, 17, 20, 21, 24, 29, 39, 49, 47, 49, 52, 57, 60, 64, 68, 72, 84, 86, 88, 111, 111, 110, 124, 123, 120, 115, 113, 109, 108, 119, 122, 124, 126, 129, 129, 134, 137, 131, 125, 119, 111, 116, 123, 120, 128, 144, 140, 132, 134, 130, 126, 128, 124, 118, 123, 132, 136, 129, 126, 137, 147, 154, 181, 193, 200 then out. It peaked at 1 on the *Cashbox* chart and 4 on the *Record World* chart.

The album *Love Songs* peaked at number 24 on the *Billboard* Top 200 chart. It peaked at 28 on the *Cashbox* and 36 on the *Record World* charts.

By Paul McCartney

The album *Wings Over America* peaked at number 1 on the *Billboard* Top 200 (it displaced *Hotel California* by the Eagles and was displaced by the Barbra Streisand soundtrack for *A Star Is Born*), staying at number 1 for just 1 week. It peaked at 2 on the *Cashbox* and 3 on the *Record World* charts.

The album *Give My Regards to Broad Street* peaked at number 21 on the *Billboard* Top 200 chart.

The album *Tripping the Live Fantastic* peaked at number 26 on the *Billboard* Top 200 chart.

Reports compiled by Mark Lewisohn.

Index

Note: Abbreviations used in the index are: Bs for the Beatles; MJ for Michael Jackson; JL for John Lennon; Liv. for Liverpool; PM for Paul McCartney; NS for Northern Songs; 'Y' for the song, 'Yesterday'. Songs are listed under their titles. Illustrations are indicated by il.

YESTERDAY

Yesterday, all my troubles seemed so far aw
now it looks as though they're here to sta
    oh I believe in yesterda

Suddenly, I'm not half the man I used to b
There's a shadow hanging over me
Yesterday came suddenly.

middle ♪
   Why she had to go, I don't know
     she wouldn't say,
I said something wrong. now I long
     for yesterda .....

Yesterday, love was such an easy ga
         F
Now I need a place to hide awa
  oh I believe in yesterda

Paul McCartney's handwritten words for 'Yesterday', the world's
most recorded song.

YESTERDAY.

Words and music by John Lennon and Paul McCartney